The Diary and Memoirs of an Incarcerated Granny

Angela Lister

The Diary and Memoirs of an Incarcerated Granny

Published by The Conrad Press in the United Kingdom 2021

Tel: +44(0)1227 472 874
www.theconradpress.com
info@theconradpress.com

ISBN 978-1-914913-24-2

Typesetting and Cover Design by: Charlotte Mouncey, www.bookstyle.co.uk
The Conrad Press logo was designed by Maria Priestley.

Printed and bound in Great Britain by Clays Ltd, Elcograf S.p.A.

To my family and friends,
both two legged and four legged.
Without whom, none of this would have been possible.

Also a special mention to my right index finger,
which typed every single word of this book on my iPhone.

Preface

Welcome to *The Diary and Memoirs of an Incarcerated Granny.*

This was written starting on 23rd March 2020 when Boris Johnson announced that all UK citizens must stay at home to reduce the spread of coronavirus. I started this daily diary initially on my Facebook page as a way of keeping myself entertained, sane, and in touch with the outside world. What began as a daily diary of what was going on at home ended up becoming much more. It was shared with friends and from there it was suggested that a group page should be formed. This soon attracted over 800 members from all over the world. We covered many topics, ranging from the state of Boris's health, to what really pisses you off, to what you put on your toast in the morning. The diary was something to cheer people up and bring people together in what has been one of the strangest times in all of our lives.

From the diary, there then came interest from the media world in the form of a TV production company inviting me to take part in a new breakfast show via Zoom video link, this venture into the world of TV fame and fortune proved banal, boring and long-winded. Having decided that TV fame and fortune wasn't beckoning after all. I delivered my resignation and had a well-deserved granny nap.

After the first 100 days the diary reformed and became a weekly update of events.

Key people and places mentioned in my diary

'Me' - Angie Lister

'James' - My husband who died five years ago.

'The Tall Man' and family - My stepson, his wife and my granddaughter and grandson.

'No. 1' and family - My stepdaughter, her husband and my two granddaughters.

'No. 2' and family - My eldest daughter, her husband, her stepson and my granddaughter.

'No. 3' and family - My youngest daughter, her husband , her stepdaughter and my youngest granddaughter.

'My BF' - My best friend who lives in France.

'The Baskervilles' - My dogs, Violet and Poppy.

'The Hobbit House' - My cottage in Tickhill.

The Diary of an Incarcerated Granny. Day 1

Well, Day 1 is drawing to a close. I haven't fallen out with myself, I haven't climbed the walls, and I haven't even had a granny nap!

Slightly formulating an ongoing plan, to keep me busy and amused. I admit to spending a rather long time on social media, lots of FaceTimeing, messaging and telephone calls. I've cleaned out the cutlery drawer, washed the dogs blankets and sorted out some paperwork.

I am bidding on some silver teaspoons and sugar tongs on eBay, that in itself is fairly exciting! Had two parcels delivered which was the cherry on the cake as far as excitement is concerned, as I can never remember what I've ordered. The industrial-sized toenail clippers were a teeny bit of a disappointment! The embroidered linen napkins, less so.

I have decided to buy a new address book. I have ordered one on Amazon Prime so it should be here tomorrow! My current one is falling to bits and most of the people in it have snuffed it! I used to think when I hung around with a slightly older crowd, that I was quite cool! That came back to bite me on the bum as I am now about the youngest person I know! I mentioned my new address book to Fordie during our telephone conversation earlier. He requested that I only pencil him in as he is 'in talks' with Dignitas. I thought that was a really kind and caring thing to suggest. I hate having to cross things out!

I've washed my hands quite a lot, and to be honest I'm getting a bit bored with belting out two verses of 'Happy Birthday'. So, I'm having a go at 'The Pearl Fishers Duet'.

Not easy as there is only one of me, but I expect I'll improve with practice. I cannot recommend Pears soap more highly. It's certainly in it for the long haul, I'm struggling to wear it out.

Tomorrow I shall have a hummus and beetroot sandwich for lunch, the anticipation is already paramount. I have weeded one of my tubs today, I think they were weeds anyway! All sorts of things coming up and out in the garden, maybe I should make a concerted effort to find out what they all are? Or shall I just rely on being surprised?

Just had a message from eBay, I have won the teaspoon auction!

So looking forward to my afternoon tea set up, when all this is over. My burr walnut tea table and cake stand have brought me a lot of pleasure over the last few weeks. It's the little things that keep you going. I always used to be a great letter-writer. (meaning I wrote a lot of letters, not that they were necessarily great). I did request from Pip for Christmas some writing paper and envelopes, so I might write to somebody, it should be comforting to receive something through the post that isn't a bill or a flyer from the local pizza emporium.

I had beans on toast for my supper... how many of you knew that Heinz spell Beanz with a Z? You learn something new every day.

Signing off now, I have a date with Netflix!

The Diary of an Incarcerated Granny. Day 2

Hmmm today wasn't quite as much fun as yesterday! (and yesterday was no fun at all, if you get my drift!)

Got up just before eight am, I had to wake up my dog Poppy as she was tucked up under the duvet... and very cosy, thank you! I looked out of the window to observe the next generation to run the country, skulking around the bus stop, grudgingly awaiting the arrival of the school bus. Same kids every morning, all totally ignore one another and stare into their phones. I sometimes wonder if they are secretly messaging one another... Is actually having a conversation not considered to be cool? Usual phone calls to the usual suspects.

FaceTime with West Sussex branch of the fam..., little chat with Scarlett (No. 2 junior) who had worn her new swimming costume to bed, she liked it so much! She did ask if I thought Daddy would look ridiculous if he dressed up as a frog? I then said he would look far more ridiculous if he didn't! Not 100% sure she got that!

Watched a bit of doom and gloom TV just to catch up with the depressing statistics. Some woman was demonstrating how to sanitise your door handles, and the pros and cons of wearing rubber gloves. I'm a teeny bit unclear about the fact that as there is only me here, is an unknown force going to swoop down and sprinkle germs on my handles and hard surfaces? Hard surfaces had a whole chapter to itself, much spraying and rinsing and hand-washing involved. Also double-bagging your rubbish... is that because the tissues you have used and immediately disposed of, are climbing over one another to fight their way out of the bin? Obviously wanting to waft themselves over your hard surfaces to facilitate yet another round of de-sanitising.

Whilst waiting for my toast to pop up, I wielded the little gadget that my West Sussex branch bought me for Christmas. This was, I hasten to add, at my request, having seen it advertised on the TV. Such a dear little gizmo the size of a XXXL lipstick and battery-operated to boot, nothing dodgy! It lives on the shelf next to the mugs and is a joy to behold. This is specifically designed to whisk away those annoying little hairs that spring up overnight on your top lip... it apparently combats 'peach fuzz' as well, whatever that is!

It did occur to me that if I let nature take its course, I might have a moustache to rival the man from Go Compare when they finally authorise my release.

Did you know, toast with Marmite is sooooo good for you, lots of B-vitamins buzzing about in secret!

Toast crumbs removed, hard-surfaces sprayed, I ventured into the garden. What a joy, so many things, including a magnolia (previously hidden behind the rhubarb) coming into flower.

I went and had a chat with the ducks and reviewed the situation with the stream. The water is still very cloudy and the levels are higher than normal even though the sluice gates are open on the mill pond.

Poppy was doing her usual racing around and then stopped and started to look a bit shifty. On further inspection and a thorough examination, it became apparent that she was suffering from what is known in the Lister family as a 'Bum Crumb'. Not for the faint-hearted. So, positioned on the very recently sanitised hard surface next to the sink, the Bum Crumb was dispatched into a double-bagged rubbish-bag to join forces with the marauding tissues! All hard surfaces tackled yet again.

Top tip, before cleansing the kitchen check the dog's rear end is fit for purpose!

Another parcel from eBay, Spode Blue Italian sugar bowl, a cheeky bargain for a fiver! Oh, and my new address book has arrived so I shall make a start on that tomorrow. I shall ration myself as I think I may be here for quite a while.

So another day done, bit of TV and a book tonight.

The Diary of an Incarcerated Granny. Day 3

Still haven't seen a soul, other than the post lady, who passed me a small parcel over the front gate. Another eBay find, Blue Italian jug to match the sugar bowl that came yesterday.

Got up around 8ish, the sun was shining and it was hard to believe that beyond my own little bubble, the world is in crisis. Eating my toast and Marmite in the garden things didn't seem that bad.

The person who lives across the road is rubbish at drawing her bedroom curtains! I have started giving her marks out of ten... very poor score this morning I'm afraid.

Usual FaceTime to family and quite a few phone calls and messages.

I am really struggling to understand how people can't grasp the meaning of isolation. Two phone calls this morning confirmed this. I had better not be too explicit, but a couple of octogenarians, that most certainly should be under lock and key... think it's all a bit of a fuss about nothing and anyway this virus is most unlikely to get as far as Hampshire!

Another pair who are under lockdown couldn't understand why it was unwise if somebody 'just popped round' for a coffee!

It would be laughable if it wasn't so serious.

I do wonder what my late husband's take would have been on all this? He was a firm believer in the fact that rules applied to everyone... apart from him! I can imagine him up there on his cloud, munching his way through a very rare roast beef sandwich and swigging a very large glass of Chateau Margaux... and shaking his head in disbelief. They would have had to literally demolish the pub to stop him going!

This is the man, who on the occasion of his demise, requested that his ashes were mixed with cement and turned into garden gnomes. As a family, we struggled with this as you can imagine. Eventually we decided to have him decanted into five little urns each in a velvet box. One for me and one for each of the kids. Good move, we all have a little bit of him. As I speak, he is in a very pretty Wedgwood cheese dish on the shelf under the TV.

The year after he died, I took the whole family on holiday to a chateau in France, not far from where we had our cottage and the big house where we lived permanently for nearly five years. We numbered nineteen and we had an amazing week. There were a small amount of ashes left over so we decided we would take the remainder to France and scatter them in the River Dordogne. Once there, we decided we didn't want to go ahead with that, as he would probably end up in the sea. So for the whole week we had him in a box on the dining table with a large glass of red wine balanced on the top and raised a glass to him at dinner every evening. He would have loved that! Once a year we try very hard to have a whole family meet-up weekend, and he is always included, he would love that too!

Mother's Day on Sunday, that should be a bit of a non-event under the circumstances. Three cards arrived so far, anyone guess who the latecomer will be? Answers on a postcard please.

I know this is only day three in Paradise, but so far I'm doing ok. I've been on my own now for four years so I'm used to my own company. I get on fairly well with myself, no arguments, no foot-stamping and no disagreements. Marvellous!

Tickhill, as a community, are pulling out all the stops. Shops delivering free of charge if you ring in your orders. I am actually well provided for on the loo roll front. I have more concerns over a national shortage of TENA Lady! They are a very versatile commodity and can be used for many things other than the obvious. When I lived in Bawtry, the bedhead in my spare room constantly clunked against the wall. The application of a couple of TENA Lady's to the back of the headboard solved the problem. When I was marooned in Venice a couple of years ago, they were amazingly useful to hold all the plugs in place when charging up my phone and laptop. Never make fun of Tena Lady... one day they may surprise you!

Tonight's delight is catching up on the earlier episodes of *Last Tango in Halifax* and my weekly catch up on the phone with my friend in Norfolk, which lasts for two hours! Sometimes we watch *Naked Attraction* with the sound off. The conversation is usually peppered with comments such as, 'OMG have you seen that one?' and 'Yuk' how gross is that?' Great fun!

It's getting increasingly difficult to dredge up amusing anecdotes. I shall have to rely on 'funny things that happened in the past'. You will all end up knowing me better than I know myself.

Onwards and upwards, at least the nights are becoming lighter and a little bit of spring is in the air! Keep safe and follow the rules!

The Diary of an Incarcerated Granny. Day 4

According to the news I might have another 361 days to go! That is just a little bit daunting. I actually slept quite well, which is unusual. I'm delighted to report that the 'worst curtain drawer' in the world has exceeded all expectations and was awarded a 6.5 this morning!

I am missing my cleaner very much, she always empties the crumb tray on the toaster and makes little pointy shapes on the ends of the loo rolls, and she changes the bedding on my comfy super-king (with room for a pony!)

Would she be allowed to come if I hid in the summer house for a couple of hours? I'll ring Boris and accept guidance on that one.

You will be pleased to know that I now have a full house of Mother's Day cards lined up on the dining table. I shall open them in the morning after *The Archers* omnibus. The last card was pushed round the door with a carrier bag full of goodies. Thanks Rach, and big thanks to her friend Katie who sent me a very tasty-looking dinner, which I shall eat later. Isn't it funny how you get into a bit of a routine, I listen to *The Archers* every Sunday morning, and most people know not to contact me between ten am and eleven-fifteen. If the phone rings I usually yell down it 'I don't know who you are, but it had better be good'!

It is becoming obvious that over the next few months we need to pace ourselves. No point whirling around getting everything ship-shape in a fortnight... I think we have a long way to go. Send for those books you've always wanted to read, watch the early series of *The Crown* and *Downton Abbey*, ring the person you keep meaning to contact. You now have the time to reconnect.

I have been in my little Hobbit House for nearly a year and still loving it. There are things over the last couple of days that I have noticed that I hadn't noticed before. This morning whilst waiting for the toast and paying homage to the hairs on my top lip, I looked down and discovered that my waste disposal unit is called an 'Insinkerator', how cool is that! There are so many things out there that we don't really pay much attention to. A few years ago we had a Rover 75 Estate car. Described by Jeremy Clarkson as an armchair in Eastbourne! It was an absolute gem, came and lived with us in France for nearly five years and then brought us back to England when the going got tough. 100,000 miles later when it went to the big scrap-heap in the sky, I was clearing out some bits and bobs and noticed a button near the gear stick with a snowflake on it. 10 years and that was the first time I had seen it. I just hope nobody ever calls me as an expert witness... I'm about as observant as a jar of marmalade!

Henry Davies (1871-1946) wrote a poem. The first lines being, 'what is this life if, full of care. We have no time to stand and stare'.

I think that was an amazing observation, we are so programmed to the pace of life, that we never get off the merry-go-round and really look at things. Well guys, I think we now have the time to open our eyes and take it all in.

A few things on my 'to do' list.

Start and delete some of the 62,000 unread emails that I seem to have acquired over the last few years. Work out what all those light switches are for on the landing. Start redoing my address book, I'm still waiting for my pal Fordelicious to finalise his talks with Dignitas... it will be a while before I get as far as the 'F's!

I'm pleased that the decision was taken to close the pubs and clubs, it has taken away the temptation from those who still 'don't get it'!

I think today's post has been a little bit less amusing than usual, I'll try harder tomorrow.

On a lighter note, I have treated myself to a bracelet that spells 'F...k it' in Morse code!

I think we may all need one of those soon.

The Diary of an Incarcerated Granny: Day 5

Only 360 days to go now... goodness me the time is flying by! Happy Mother's Day everyone. I have just awoken from a chocolate-induced coma, scrunched up on the sofa with a crick in my neck! Have you ever wondered what a 'crick' might look like in the flesh? Just wandering about in the garden when there is a rustling noise in your rhubarb patch. Everything on high alert... is it a hedgehog, is it a duck (very possible in my case) is it a very large worm? No... it's a 'crick'. Oh well, that's ok then, it must be the one that was in my neck yesterday!

I was woken just before six am, Poppy was on an 'I need a wee' mission, and I need it now! The curtain queen opposite was still slumbering, probably dreaming about vertical blinds and swags and tassels. No scoring possible at that time in the morning, she's a very late riser at the best of times!

Just getting light, the sky was a bit pink and my other dog, Violet-Elizabeth was still snoring loudly in her basket. I once had someone staying with me when I lived in Bawtryland, who was convinced that the weird noise was someone using a drill next door! They were a bit taken aback when I said it was the dog. I have had fifteen years to get used to it, I liken it to living in close proximity to an airport, you don't notice the planes after a while!

I made a coffee (hot drinks better for you than cold as far as the virus is concerned) and stood and looked down the garden. So much bird life going about its business, ducks and Canada geese flying over (a bit of honking going off there). A host of fat pigeons truffling about on the lawn, (give us another month or three of this and they may well be encased in a sheet of Jus-roll and liberally moistened with a drop of gravy), blackbirds (all boys) having a bit of a scuffle and the little Robin (which I always think is my late husband James) skipping about with gay abandon.

A bit later on I noticed quite a few bees on the flowers that have come out near my French windows. As I said yesterday, it's all happening out there.. you just need to take a look.

The Archers was a bit depressing, Linda Snell's life appears to be hanging in the balance, and Ben from Brookfield is having the p... s extracted from him about the colour of the car his granny has bought him for his birthday...usual nail-biting stuff!

I then got into a conversation with my friend in Norfolk, do the Archers include current events in their story lines? So far, no mention of Covid-19, no Brexit or election chat, and certainly no reference made to the fact that the queen is having a shit year! I think life in Ambridge just rolls along regardless of what the rest of the planet are experiencing.

Sat in the sunshine for a while, and pretended I was in France with a couple of croissants and some strawberry jam.

Reminded me of the time I was making James some breakfast and inadvertently spread Branston Pickle on his toast! (no specs). He took a bite and said, 'Goodness me this is interesting, is it Coopers Thick Cut Oxford Marmalade? Or have you changed brands?'

There was an occasion quite a few Christmases ago when I was writing Christmas cards at the kitchen table. James was making coffee and I said, 'Is Sweden in the EU?' No reply, then he came over and handed me a pack of Canderels. 'Why have you brought me these?' I said.

'Well,' he said, 'you just said to me are the sweeteners near you?'

You might have to think about that one!

I have decided that *The Pearl Fishers Duet* is far too difficult for one person to perform alone. After great deliberation, I am now washing my hands to two verses of 'Land of Hope and Glory', it seems more fitting somehow!

I have just lowered my shutters for the evening and discovered that 'her opposite' has either self-isolated for the whole day, or buggered off out and left the curtains fully drawn. Seriously, this is Tickhill, standards must be observed! When I lived in Bawtry we all ate petit pois, just so much more refined than the humble garden pea!

I have lived here for nearly a year now, and I have never seen one single cat! One of my outbuildings has a cat flap in the door... so there was evidence of them inhabiting Tickhill before they apparently became extinct.

When the kids were growing up we always had dogs, cats, ponies and even inherited a parrot when my mother-in-law fled the mortal coil. When we lived in Old Ravenfield we had a very miserable cat called Jeffery, who thought nothing of taking a swipe at you when you walked past. At that time there was a stray in the village that kept sneaking through the cat flap and feasting on Jeff's lunch. When we came across the cat in the kitchen we would all shout, 'Oi you, F...k off outside!'

As you have probably realised, she didn't and had made up her mind she was moving in whether we liked it or not. We called her FOO, an acronym of what we used to shout at her! She came along with Jeffery to France when we went to live out there. She was then called Madam Foo and was the nicest cat in the world. They came back to England when we moved back and lived until they were both seventeen... I miss them still.

I was once drying my hair in our bedroom in Bawtry and chatting away to Foo. I then looked out of the window and saw her sitting in the garden! I had been rabbiting away for ten minutes to my black leather jacket that had fallen off the back of the chair! Weird or what? Mother's Day has been ok, I have communicated with everyone, the West Sussex branch were even having a BBQ of sorts! All observing the rules, unlike some absolute pillocks... but don't get me started on that. Until tomorrow…

The Diary of an Incarcerated Granny. Day 6

Evening all, another day in Paradise! A whole week tomorrow... do you think we should get a badge for good behaviour? Bit like Weight Watchers when you've lost a stone? I've had several of those over the years.

Maybe this is the time to go on a secret diet and hopefully emerge twelve months down the line looking windswept and interesting. I'll bear that in mind once I've chomped my way through all the pies in the freezer.

Right, first things first, the curtain queen played an absolute blinder this morning. I have given her an 8.5 on the Granny scale. What an improvement, I wonder if she has twigged who I am and the embarrassment has set in? If she continues improving on the curtain debacle, and stops parking right outside my bloody gate, I feel that one day we may become friends and some good will have come out of all this.

I have had lots of lovely chats on the phone, bit of FaceTimeing from abroad and loads of messaging on FB. I am still unsure how much people are actually understanding this dreadful situation. I gather Boris is giving a statement this evening and maybe after that, the idiots will start to comprehend. Who knows?

I know that some members of my family are very frightened, and it's getting quite hard to try and keep things on a positive note. I am a bit Scarlett O'Hara in times of desperation, I lock it in a box and deal with it tomorrow.

I do think that all this is bringing people closer together (obviously not in the physical sense, although a baby boom is predicted if we ever emerge from all this!) and friends are keeping in touch and contacting people that they really haven't connected with for a while. One of my daughters has had messages from some of her old clients asking how she is and how are things with the baby? The baby was four last Christmas! She was so pleased to hear all the news and I'm pretty sure they will now keep in contact.

Two parcels today, left on the wall outside the front door. I have started keeping them in isolation in the porch for a few hours, before I take a peek. The big box is some lawn-edge trimmers, on the off chance that Titchmarsh and Sons are unable to come and tend my rolling acres! I do love a nice neat edge! The other parcel was a bit of a mystery, some things you order take several weeks to turn up, by which time you have forgotten all about them. Pity I didn't forget to order this in the first place, what in the lords name was I thinking? It's some sort of squashy, soft toy-thing that looks like a seal with constipation, the size of a football and really quite unpleasant. I've decided to call her Vera!

I keep getting messages from eBay to see if I'm still in the market for some vintage, EPNS teaspoons with matching sugar tongs. No way... I'm totally up to speed on the teaspoon front, and nobody I know takes sugar!

I still haven't got around to redoing my address book, tomorrow I will tackle the task head-on. I have of course sanitised my hard surfaces within an inch of their lives, bleached the loos and acted like a very responsible Granny. I am still formulating the action plan of 'things to do'. According to my notes I am down to mop the kitchen floor a week next Wednesday! I keep telling you, there is no rush!

I have had coffee outside a couple of times today, weeded a couple of planters and sauntered down to stream at the bottom of my garden. Five ducks dabbling around. I think it's 'that time of year' again, they really are quite brutal, no foreplay, just straight in there with no consideration! I certainly won't be coming back as a duck!

I was gutted to hear that filming of *Emmerdale* and *Coronation Street* has been halted, also the episodes of *The Archers* have been reduced! Most people's secret passions, and if you tell me you've never watched an episode of *Jeremy Kyle*, I won't believe you!

As I said the other day, as a result of being confined to barracks 24/7 you do become a little more observant. I wondered idly why I have three, car number plates propped up in my kitchen. No particular reason, other than in they almost spell my name, and if I'm here indefinitely they will be a reminder of who I used to be!

Let's see what Bojo has to say this evening at 8.30, can't say I'm looking forward to it!

The Diary of an Incarcerated Granny. Day 7

An actual whole week, to be honest it has flown by. Whether I will be saying the same thing a few weeks down the line remains to be seen!

First things first the curtain queen has surpassed herself this morning, I am delighted to report a 9.0 on the Granny scale! I could have only done it slightly better myself. This girl is getting good, if this continues I shall have to find another focus for my displeasure.

Nothing hugely exciting happening at the Hobbit House today. I have calculated if I walk up and down the length of my garden about twenty-eight times I will have walked a mile... and so will Poppy, because wherever I go, she goes!

I find it amusing that the bicycle shops are thronged with customers. All these folk that haven't been within fifty yards of a bike since they passed their cycling proficiency test when they were eight... are suddenly engulfed with a desire to hit the tarmac! What's all that about? They are obviously related to the hordes of people that never walk anywhere other than their local pub, who are, as we speak, lumbering up Mount Snowden in their flip-flops, armed with nothing more than a can of Red Bull and a packet of Walkers salt and vinegar crisps. How lucky you bought the sharing pack... plenty of folk up there to share them with!

Who are these people? Don't they listen to the news, or read the newspapers? We are in crisis you numpties, wake up and smell the Bovril!

I rest my case!

Managed to hang out some washing, as it really is a lovely day. I have one of these Brabantia folding washing lines. It folds back against the wall into a case when not in use, so doesn't come under the heading of 'eyesore'.

This is where it gets complicated... I can open it up no problem, but I can never work out how to fold it back up again!

This involves me having to go indoors and follow instructions on a YouTube video! How pathetic is that?

As most of my friends know, I am a great reader, and I mean REAL books. I have hundreds. When I moved house recently I had to get rid of so many, sad times! I could no more contemplate heading for bed without something to read than I could contemplate chewing a wasp! I hope to goodness Amazon are still in business, I order at least two books a week from them. I have always been a book fiend, my children had presents on birthdays and Christmas, but they could have books anytime. Even now, I would far rather buy the littlest ones a good hardback version of a classic than a load of plastic crap!

When I was about seven, my mother had a friend over to stay from Cornwall. She was called Mary Harris and she took me into town and bought me the full set of Katy books by Susan Coolidge. I remember them costing 7/6d. Seriously, I was in heaven!

Trying to think of positives today.

1) The big bottle of Jo Malone, Lime Basil and Mandarin that I had for my birthday will last twice as long, no need to have a daily squirt!... My youngest daughter is a total perfume addict, she has loads and loads, if Selfridges ever run out of stock, all they need to do is give her a call.

When they were both away at school in York my eldest would say, 'I can tell when she's been down a corridor before me... I can smell her!'

The phrase 'like a tart's hanky' springs to mind.

2) The twelve tins of Kenco coffee I bought when they were on sale in SPAR four months ago are still going strong. I wasn't stockpiling... I just like Kenco coffee.

3) Can't think of a third!

Does anybody realise how hard it is to try and think of something to write every day? I have a notebook in the kitchen and I jot down everything that may be of vague interest, and I mean vague!

Do you ever try and think of things you think you are quite good at?

My stepson, when he was about five, said that I made the best mashed potatoes ever. He will be forty-eight in July, and I sincerely hope he still feels the same way.

I am good at keeping in touch with people. I still have lots of friends (good ones) from school, college, work, etc and I do make an effort to keep them all on their toes.

I have a very dear friend, that we met on holiday in Ibiza when the children were small. I think Rachel was two, she's forty in September! We met up a few times after the holiday and as usual with holiday 'romances' they rarely stand the test of time. Probably eighteen months down the line she rang me one Boxing Day morning... From that day forward they have been the most wonderful friends anyone could wish for. I shudder at the thought of having missed all the wonderful times we have spent together. So, Linda Hopkins, thank the Lord you made that call!

Maybe, now that you have more time on your hands... get in touch with that person to whom you send a Christmas card every year, but haven't spoken to in three decades. You may be pleasantly surprised!

I know, having been widowed for over four years, just how valuable friends are. There are so many people that live in the 'couple bubble', do everything together, never join anything, and usually in the case of the wife, stop driving! Unless you both get run over by the same bus at the same time, one of you is going to be left. Grim but true! While you are lucky enough to have an 'other half', make sure you know how to put petrol in the car, draw money from the ATM, sort out all those household things, change your utility suppliers and learn how to work all those buttons on the TV remote, and whilst I'm issuing instructions, make sure your Will is up to date.

Crikey, I'm depressing myself... but you know it makes sense.

So that's all for today, all government guidelines adhered to and hard surfaces dealt with!

The Diary of an Incarcerated Granny. Day 8

Well, day 8. I'm still getting on terribly well with myself. No snarky comments or anything. Long may 'me' continue. It's a glorious morning today. The curtain queen has yet again made another fantastic effort, achieving a 9.25 on the Granny scale. I love her now!

I have pottered around a fair bit outside, quite a few bumble-bees and loads of. butterflies. Kept popping out and drinking my coffee in the sunshine, absorbing all the vitamin D that was on offer. The Baskervilles were snoozing in sunny patches and a good time was had by all. I am lucky that the back of my house is south facing, so always sunny if there is any on offer.

Emptied the dishwasher and decided to poke around in the filter. Hmmmm, note to self, must attend to this more often!

I would like to talk to you about sandwiches... a much

neglected subject in my opinion. I like a good sandwich for lunch. Today's choice was corned beef and piccalilli. Delicious. That then reminded me that many moons ago, the main culprit causing an upturn in badly gashed fingers rolling up at A&E, was the humble corned beef tin! Was it 'the man from Fray Bentos' who decided that the most interesting shape for a lump of corned beef should be based on an obelisk without the pointy bit? Apparently so, he then decided to encase it in a tin, which could only be entered with a key, that usually snapped off? I think he also had another company manufacturing bandages and sticking plasters. Smart chap. After obviously taking all this into account it was little wonder that 'the man from Delmonte' said YES!

Back to the sandwich and other delicacies debate. I am oldish, so look back fondly at the grub on offer at birthday parties back in the day. Even now I could sometimes kill for an egg sandwich. I think in those days the eggy bits were probably prevented from falling out of the bread with a good glug of salad cream to stick everything together. Mr Hellman eventually jumped on the bandwagon and you all know what he came up with!

At parties there were always potted-meat sandwiches as well, and sometimes a dish of ready-salted crisps. If somebody's mum was a bit of a Fanny Craddock then there may well be the odd cornflakes or rice crispy bun. If you had a granny that rivalled Mrs Bridges, then there was a fair chance of butterfly buns and of course there was the 'The Cake'.

Virtually always a Victoria Sponge, bit of raspberry jam, buttercream made with Stork margarine and a slightly off-centred pattern on the top where someone had sprinkled some icing sugar through a doily. Those were the days eh. Jelly and ice cream to follow and the job was done!

A few rounds of pass the parcel, the game where you had to remember how many items were on a tea tray. Then came the finale… everybody sat in a circle, the curtains were closed, and in came the cake, candles flickering and everyone sang 'Happy Birthday' very loudly. The cake bit was timed perfectly with the doorbell starting to ring, and along came the mummies or the odd daddy to collect their offspring. Having said, 'Thank you for having me' you were off down the path clutching your lump of cake in a napkin and that was the end of it!

How times have changed!

Christmas 2019. My granddaughter (West Sussex branch) was four on 28th December.

I headed down there on the 27th by train. Lots of excitement in the air. The birthday girl had requested dinner at a Thai restaurant called Thai Street Food, because they do the best sticky rice ever, and besides Granny, 'Yamin has known me for ever, even when I was in Mummy's tummy!' Yamin is the lovely lady who runs the restaurant.

Fast-forward to New Year's Eve… the party! A large gathering of forty-plus people at one stage. Lots of mummies and daddies and siblings and cousins and probably people who were just passing, saw the door open and wandered in. Much Prosecco splashing around. Lots of grown-ups and kids in fancy dress and two little boys dressed as Elsa from *Frozen*. The smalls were put on lockdown in the sitting room with a magician and his lovely assistant (not quite Debbie McGee, but she was trying) the door was firmly shut and exactly what went on in there was anyone's guess, but there was a rabbit involved! Meanwhile in Prosecco-land, the party tea was being assembled in the kitchen along with about thirty people who hadn't seen one another for ages.

Vast amounts of hummus, carrot batons, cucumber sticks, radishes, tiny organic ham sandwiches, dishes of olives and gherkins, platters of strawberries, blueberries and grapes all provided a feast to behold. Paul Daniels and Debbie we're finally allowed to exit the sitting room, looking slightly worse for wear. There is always one child who spotted how you did the trick and won't let the matter drop. On this occasion it was Bertie! The cake lovingly baked by Mummy went down well. Although it was noticed that the birthday girl was far more interested in the pile of olives on her plate.

This is the child who wouldn't thank you for a fish finger, but who would happily chomp down on a prawn dansak or a lamb passanda.

How times have changed, eh? Very few people went home. There were kids leaping about everywhere. The playroom looked as though it had been burgled and the Prosecco was still flowing freely. A huge chilli con carne was dragged out eventually and an enormous cheese board graced the table. Quite a lot of folk made it until after midnight, including a few little people. We think we all had a lovely time, nobody can quite remember! Oh, and Paul Daniels didn't want the left over carrot batons for the rabbit, he says it had a sensitive stomach!

The news will be filtering in soon, let's all hope it isn't too upsetting. I'm still finding it hard to imagine all that is going on out there. To all of those out there in the front line, God bless you, and thank you from all of us safely tucked up at home.

The Diary of an Incarcerated Granny. Day 9

Jeepers, the ninth day already. Have you considered, if the days turn into months there might be an enormous baby boom? Or, on a more sombre note, a huge rise in divorce petitions! Neither of which, fortunately should affect me!

Back to the nitty-gritty, progress on the curtain-front has slipped considerably today. Struggling to afford a 5.5. Looking to the positive, there is a big rainbow in the window, so an extra couple of points for spirit-lifting!

Another lovely sunny day, a lot of it spent outside. Some washing done, including the oven glove and of course the usual sanitising of anything that stands still for longer than three minutes.

Anyone who knew my husband was aware that he was a great collector. Of what? you may ask. My reply was always anything that stood still longer than five minutes!

I moved from Bawtry to Tickhill a year ago. We had moved back from France in 2007, from a very big house. The double garage in Bawtry was full of unpacked boxes that had been there for over twelve years.

I was slightly wrong-footed when I sold my house to the first person that viewed it, and for the asking price! The buyer had already sold and wanted a quick turnaround. Panic set in. I became a slave to the skip. I had valuers and auctioneers turning up to catalogue and remove the good stuff. There were swords, pistols, paintings, furniture, military memorabilia and anything else you could think of. There was even a propeller from a Sopwith Camel (you may have to Google that one).

The big declutter can be cathartic once you have a deadline to work towards. So much family furniture and paintings that would no way even fit through the door of the Hobbit House. All the offspring were offered anything they wanted providing they used or displayed it. The West Sussex branch were coerced into finding house room for some quite large oil paintings, the family rocking horse and a few other things that were a surprise! These were all sent down by courier with a very visible 'No returns' label. One has to admit, the painting of Captain Pearson (who spent over forty years of his life in the dining room at The Brentwood Hotel) has found his niche in the lovely high-ceilinged dining room in Worthing, where he looks pretty splendid in my opinion! My son-in-law may well disagree, but marriage is a compromise, is it not? Quite a lot of other good stuff was destined for a Fine Art sale in Lincoln. One particular painting was due for the auction house. Not a favourite of mine particularly, but one that had always been over the fireplace of numerous family houses. I kept waking up during the night and thinking how cross James would be if I let it go. Eventually, I bit the bullet, rang the sales office in Lincoln and withdrew it from the sale. The relief was palpable! Safe to say I was not very popular, the catalogues had already gone out and apparently there was a lot of interest. Tough cookie, I'm looking at it now, resplendent over the fireplace in the little Hobbit House and thanking my lucky stars I have it back where it belongs.

I've spent quite a lot of time on the phone today and I've come to the conclusion that most people in lockdown wish that a) they weren't, and b) that circumstances were different. I wonder if all the people that knocked down every internal wall in their house, to provide a huge, open-plan living space, wish they hadn't bothered? Lockdown 24/7 with husband and children, there is suddenly nowhere to hide! The fabulous bifold doors leading into the garden are marvellous whilst ever the weather is good. Try it when it's raining continuously for three weeks and see how much you like it then?

As most of you might have guessed by now, I have downsized in a big way (to a really small way). You can see from my sofa of choice in the sitting room, straight through the dining room, through the kitchen and into the garden. I decided that I needed a big statement clock to go on the wall in the kitchen that I could see from the sofa.

Fast-track to my southern visit in June. Wandering around in Arundel - a very nice place to wander! - I came across a fabulous wall clock in a very trendy shop, and as an added bonus it was in the sale!

It looks amazing, it has a huge clock face and three smaller faces which tell you the time in Sydney, Paris and New York. I realise now why it was in the sale, the big bit won't work! In view of this I have left it as it is, safe in the knowledge that it is right twice a day.

I have come to the conclusion that if this diary continues, you will know me better than I know myself.

Please follow the guidelines, this will get worse before it gets better.

The James Webb painting rescued from the auction house in
Lincoln in the living room of the Hobbit House

The Diary of an Incarcerated Granny. Day 10

Not much fun is it? As time marches on it all seems to be getting a little bit worse!

I'm gutted that Boris has succumbed, just hoping he's well enough to steer the boat in isolation.

Total curtain fail this morning, struggling to scrape up a 3.5, but I guess depression is setting in a bit. Nice rainbow in the window though.

Have tried a dozen times to contact Juicy Fruits... I think they must be run off their feet.

Trying to replenish my stocks of five a day. Had some Beanz

for lunch (they count towards it, says so on the tin) I'm trying not to waste anything, so my supper last night consisted of two crusts, toasted with strawberry jam and a Birds Eye Chicken Kiev out of the freezer. Haven't had one of those for years. I remember why now! I have only three apples left, Poppy gets very excited at 'apple time' as she always gets given the core. A few weeks ago she was getting herself into a proper tiz, running around the kitchen and crying. I couldn't work out what she wanted… after opening every cupboard and drawer, all which drew a blank, I eventually found the culprit. An exceedingly small plum tomato on the top of the microwave. She could smell it and couldn't settle until it was hers! She then trotted off to eat it at the bottom of the garden in private. A vegetarian in the making!

I have in my freezer, a crispy duck with pancakes and hoisin sauce. As you will have gathered I live in harmony with quite a few ducks. However, after watching the brutal sexual exploits on my riverbank the other day, I thought, sod you Donald… I know what I'm having for my supper tonight.

I would like to draw your attention to house plants and deliveries of flowers. In a word, I don't do them… if I get an Interflora delivery, I can hear the flowers shrieking 'for God's sake don't leave me in there with her!'

I can't arrange flowers, I either over water or under water, they actually fill me with dread! After the recent move, the great and the good cottoned on to my lack of green fingers and gifted me plants for the garden. Once planted they tend to make their own arrangements and harmony is restored. A perfect solution and very well-received.

I ordered a new car just before Christmas, I said to the sales guy, who was lovely. 'Can I just say, when I pick it up, I don't want any ribbons, balloons and absolutely no bouquets of flowers!' Bless him, he gave me a cactus plant, even that should have come with a government health warning. It fell over in the back of the car on the way home and I spent far too long picking the spikes out of my hands with a pair of tweezers. I suppose he thought I was a prickly customer? You will be delighted to know it lives on the shelf next to the toaster, we have no eye contact and ignore one another absolutely. Result!

I am lucky in the fact that I can FaceTime my two smallest grandchildren every day. Most of the time they ignore me, but at least you catch a glimpse of them creating havoc in the comfort of their own home, and it acts as a sort of payback time, watching their Mothers climbing the walls! Fabulous to see them though. As a friend described something the other day, it's just like 'chicken soup for the soul'! I love that!

I wonder as this disaster continues if we will be reduced to bartering? Little boxes fastened on the gate-posts with a note saying. 'One loo roll (unused)! Two Tena Lady, (medium absorbency!) a 'Write your own Will' form, and three spring onions. Would like to exchange for... one large tin of Heinz Beanz and sausages, a pencil, two paracetamol and a dishwasher tablet! Keep an eye out, you saw it here first!

Children say the funniest things sometimes, and have a knack of knowing the words they shouldn't be saying at all! Many, many moons ago I was in Scarborough for the weekend with some friends. We decided to go to The Royal for afternoon tea accompanied by the crumb-snatchers, including the smallest member of the tribe. We were well into the scones and jam and on the second pot of tea, when the smallest Lister, who was trussed up in a high chair (to protect the general public) started shouting 'bollocks' in a very loud voice. The more we tried to shut her up, the more she continued to shout, getting louder and louder by the minute! Sooo embarrassing, she was removed by her ears and dispatched outside where she continued for quite a while! I blame her father!

Don't forget the clocks go forward this weekend (apart from my kitchen clock, which may as well stay as it is!) so at least we all have a bit more daylight to look forward to. Positive thoughts must abound! Stay in control... this too will pass. I'm not sure when, but it will.

The Diary of an Incarcerated Granny. Day 11

Day 11... where did the time go? I have to keep googling to check what day it is.

Just brewed an enormous vat of freezer-bottom soup. Go for it girls, kick out all those scratty bits of frozen veg and conjure up something that will contribute to your five a day.

I have just sent a shopping list to my lovely son-in-law, who is braving the masses and trying to fill the cupboards for another week.

It's a bit concerning that various outlets that were trying to stay open are now having to close their doors... I'm unsure how long the takeaway culture is viable. Tomorrow I'm having afternoon tea delivered from the Tea Rooms in Bawtryland. Long may it continue.

As some of my friends will tell you I can be a bit of an

impulse buyer, and when I get a bee in my bonnet, then watch out!

A few months after James and I were first married, I went to a farm auction with a friend - I think she's still cringing! To cut an extremely long story short... I bought a horse! A 15hh Fell Mare, who gave me a 'for God's sake get me out of here' look! As luck would have it, we did live next door to a farm, there was an apology for a stable at the bottom of the garden, and some grazing was found pretty quickly. Imagine having to explain that one? My next super purchase was a 'pram dinghy' advertised for sale in the local rag. Everybody that lives at least fifty miles from the coast needs a small rowing boat. Every home should have one obviously! However, as luck would have it, we did have an above-ground swimming pool in the back garden. What better opportunity for the little Listers to learn to row? When we moved from that house, we gave the pool to some friends in Tickhill and I'm pretty sure it's still there and still going strong! Upstairs, hidden away, is a very weird Kate Spade camel handbag. When I heard she had died I went on the internet and bought what I hope will be a collector's item! I could go on for ever!

I am an absolute property enthusiast. Some of my happiest hours have been spent gazing into estate agents' windows. Dress shops and jewellers have never had a look-in!

When the kids were quite young we went on a 3 centre Eurocamp holiday in France. Week one was just outside Sarlat in the Dordogne. Week two was on the west coast in Biarritz and week three was in Argeles in the south. The Dordogne was the instant hit, twelve months later we were the proud owners of a very run-down little cottage in SW France. That was the beginning of a very long love affair, which encompassed over thirty wonderful years. The Little Cottage, that was its name, was the best thing ever. Over the years we turned a pig-sty into a bunk-bedroom, sorted out all the grotty bits and ended up with a very rustic little number that we managed to rent out whenever we weren't there ourselves Looking back they were amazing days. We always went for two weeks at Easter and for a month in the summer. The brood became quite handy at the language and we had quite a few grade A, French GCSE's. Numerous friends came over to stay, and quite a few ended up buying somewhere nearby. Where else could you eat out every night for a fiver a head, including wine? As ever, when the children got that bit older they began to hanker for the bright lights. One summer, when we were waiting for A level and GCSE results, the youngest two were being particularly evil! We dropped them off in Brive at the bus station, gave them some money and they arrived home about three days later, exhausted, but having gained some useful navigation skills. Fast-forward nearly twenty years and we decided we would move over to France and live there full-time. We found an amazing house about ten miles away from the cottage and headed out for a new life in the sun. Be careful what you wish for! The first couple of years were magical, loads of people coming to stay and a good social life as well.

Then, James had his first stroke, we soldiered on with things starting to deteriorate rapidly Our first granddaughter was born when were out there, she will be fifteen in October, and shortly afterwards, I made the decision that we were heading home! We put the Big House and The Little Cottage on the market, and again we were in luck as they both sold quickly. I left James with friends and flew back to try and find somewhere to live back in the UK. We ended up in Bawtry, in a house that ticked all the boxes for the situation we found ourselves in.

If I have any regrets I think selling The Little Cottage would be one of them... so many happy times!

Now then, here's an opportunity. I'm fairly sure that somewhere hidden away you are bound to have a container full of toiletries that never quite made the grade. All those iffy Christmas and birthday presents that weren't quite what you would have chosen for yourself. Well folks, get 'em out, get 'em used and save the good stuff for when they let us out! Let's face it, you ain't going nowhere!

I am currently slathering my post-shower self with a huge tub containing something called Lemon Meringue Butter! I smell like a lemon tart, and nobody cares!

My dear departed mother once went into a bakers and asked for four 'lemon turd carts'! The shame and humiliation stayed with her, and she never ever bought another one for the rest of her life. Some things are never forgotten, are they?

My shopping has just been manhandled over the gate, and I am now the proud owner of a bunch of bananas (and a few other things!) and some blueberries. Such joy!

Today's offering has been a bit of a mixed bag, so I hope it wasn't a disappointment. Keep safe!

The Diary of an Incarcerated Granny. Day 12

Day 12, just like spending the twelve days of Christmas all on your own. A few more months of lockdown and the partridge and the three French hens will have been eaten! Closely followed by the turtle doves and the colly birds. I think the swans are a no, they belong to the queen, so she gets to decide whether she should eat them or not! If the geese are still laying, it might be a plan to hang on to them for a while? Due to social distancing the ladies won't be dancing, the pipers will all be holed up individually in their high-rise blocks playing 'Little Donkey' from their Juliet balconies! The lord's will be doing no leaping whatsoever, all the chauffeurs are on lockdown, so they couldn't get into Westminster, even if they wanted to.

The maids will have given milking a miss because they are all self-isolating at home and watching 'A Calf is Born' on Netflix. The five gold rings are frankly no bloody use at all. The pawn shops are shut, so there is no ability to raise funds for a Chinese takeaway!

That leaves us with the drummers, personally, I think they should all isolate together. It stands to reason, that at some stage they will be making so much bloody noise that they will be arrested by the mask-wearing vigilantes and jailed for life on a breach of the peace offence!

So, thank your lucky stars it's only March, you now know how Christmas could turn out!

Moving swiftly on... I remembered to put the clocks forward so I was up and running all ready for *The Archers* at 10am precisely. I had a 'big shop' delivered yesterday by a masked, gloved, anti-bacterial wipe waving chap. My son-in-law, bless him. We passed the time of day observing the required distance and off home he went. I'm pretty sure that when he got home he was immersed in an extremely hot bath, laced with Domestos, and all his clothes were microwaved until they started smoking.

My big treat this morning, after a Marmite overload, was going to be a big bowl of Greek yoghurt with granola and some blueberries and strawberries. Not so... the only thing I missed off the shopping list was the yoghurt, seriously I could have wept!

Yesterday, via Amazon, my new Black and Decker Dustbuster arrived. As I only have hard floors downstairs, it seemed ideal for crumbs and stuff. Having lived in France, I know that most French houses are knee-deep in breadcrumbs... all those baguettes and croissants to wrestle with on a daily basis. You certainly don't get the volume of crumbs from a Warburton's toastie or a packet of crumpets. I think the Dustbuster and I will rub along very well together!

Next subject... Money! Glanced at my bank details online this morning. I seem to have spent far more since I've been incarcerated than I did when I was free to roam! There is a payment that went out on the 27th March for £154.01p? I honestly have no idea what it could be for. Quite worrying really, I do sometimes write cheques for the odd thing but I've looked at my cheque stubs and nothing there. It's the 1p that seems ridiculous. I suppose if I ring the bank they should know?

My afternoon tea was delivered at one pm, and very nice it looks too, the little finger sandwiches are wrapped in cling film, so not sure what sort they are yet. I know traditionally tea should be served at four o'clock, but we are living in very strange times.

Keep safe and keep washing your hands. Just to keep you up to speed on the hand washing… I have moved on from 'Land of Hope and Glory' and I'm now considering a couple of verses of Hubert Parry's 'I was glad…' very rousing. Watch it on YouTube.

The Diary of an Incarcerated Granny. Day 13

Oooh, just the number sounds ominous! It's a bit chilly, realised I had slept on my specs and one of the lenses has dropped out. Only got to eight-fifteen and the gilt had started wearing off the gingerbread. I think the curtain queen has disappeared into the sunset. No window activity in evidence whatsoever!

Something wonderful happened yesterday. I was bemoaning the lack of Greek yoghurt and someone out there was obviously reading my diary. I received a message saying that there was a spare tub up for grabs if I would like it. As the proud owner of a bucketful of granola this was music to my ears. Within an hour there was a tap on the door, and a big pot of Greek yoghurt was sitting on my gatepost! The donor was continuing his walk and all was good with the world! You know who you are, and thank you. Breakfast this morning was delicious.

Now, nicknames… most of us have them, and most of us give them to others. Some are affectionate, some are amusing and some are just a teeny bit insulting. I have friends that I was at school with that still go by the names we gave them well over fifty years ago.

A very long time ago I lived in a hamlet where nicknames were the norm. The guy with no teeth was called 'Gummy', his wife was known as 'Mrs Gummy', and their son was known as 'young Gummy'. How simple was that! The ex-army guy who lived at the end of the lane was known as 'Captain Peacock'. The idiot that stole a horse and got arrested when he was drunk was always referred to as 'Pillock Paul'. My husband had a shooting friend whose initials were GBH, he was and still is known as 'Grievous Bodily'.

I remember a neighbour telling me a story about somebody he went to school with. The boy sneaked into a shop and stole a tin of shoe polish He got caught and there was all hell to pay. He sorted himself out eventually, ended up doing very well for himself and made a big success of his life... unfortunately all the people he knew when growing up still insisted on calling him 'Cherry Blossom'! I could go on... but maybe I better stop now.

Family stories. I had a cousin who was a bit of a monkey in her teens. She had an almighty row with her parents and took off upstairs with much door-banging taking place. Her father stood at the bottom of the stairs and shouted up, 'Get yourself downstairs now, behave yourself and do as you're told... I'm not your mother you know!' The reply that was fired back down the stairs was 'No, and you're not forced to be my bloody father either!'

Another from the Lister side, a particularly annoying little cousin was desperate to get into the workshop at the back of the hotel. Nobody was taking him seriously and he was getting more and more frustrated. Eventually his big brother said 'what do you want to go in there for?' The younger brother said, 'I want to go in there because I want to make something...' 'What can you make?' asked big bro. 'I can make anything,' said the little chap. 'ok,' said big bro, 'In that case, go and make yourself a key for the workshop!'

I'm struggling a bit today aren't I?

I'm starting to feel as though I'm living in a parallel universe. Other than being confined to quarters, life is not hugely different. Watching everything on the news is almost like watching a very frightening film. It's all happening out there and quite easy to feel quite detached.

Stop press! Sorted the query with the banking. My fault, I had moved some money from a business account into my current account and forgotten!

I've been looking at the disappointingly unattractive, constipated-looking seal I bought, The one that I affectionately named 'Vera' and I have come to the conclusion that I don't think the world is bursting with famous Vera's, do you? Vera Lynn, obviously, just celebrated her 102nd birthday. Then there's Vera Brittain, the mother of politician Shirley Williams and author of *A Testament of Youth*. That's my complete Vera list. Anyone else know any?

I'm always being asked how Violet-Elizabeth came by her name. We bought her when we lived in France and we were going to call her Poppy. A couple of weeks after we got her, a fairly heavy book slipped off the back of the sofa and landed on her head. She screamed and screamed, just like Violet- Elizabeth Bott in the Just William books. Instant name change... and it's served her well for fifteen years. Nowadays, you can call her anything, as she's as deaf as a post, but still an absolute star!

I have been living in the Hobbit House for a whole year on 12th April. That has gone pretty quickly. A couple of weeks after I moved in, there was a hammering on the door at midnight. Outside were four uniformed police officers with a warrant to search the Hobbit House for drugs. Really? One stayed with me, one searched upstairs, one searched downstairs and one stood outside the front door. Apparently, they had someone in custody who had links to this address and had in their possession several sets of keys. I think they realised pretty quickly that I wasn't an international dope pusher, and I have to admit that I played the 'Actually, I'm a retired magistrate' card. That is reserved for very special occasions!

All's well that ends well, but it was a bit unnerving at the time.

I have quarry tiles in the porch, dining room and kitchen, inset with little medieval type blue and white tiles. Earlier I was searching for something to store my granola mountain in, and I came across a big container of quarry tile sealant. I must have bought that in a flush of enthusiasm! So, as my ongoing project I am going to scrub and seal two tiles every night before I go to bed. No rush, it sounds as though we may have another five or six months to while away the hours. Sad, but probably true!

I'm afraid today's effort has been a bit of a mish-mash. Till tomorrow, take care!

The Diary of an Incarcerated Granny. Day 14

Day 14 and counting! Bit of an odd day so far. Lots of the usual FB messenger, phone calls and FaceTimeing.

Answer me this one! How can you lose a bagful of dust-buster attachments, if you haven't been out of the house for two weeks? I have searched high and low, including the fridge and the freezer. I've even rooted in the bins to no avail! When you live in a cottage the size of a medium-sized box of Tena Lady... there should be nowhere to hide. Totally flummoxed.

The post is a bit thin on the ground, not too interested in a conservatory, or the *Chums Catalogue*. That seems to be an outlet for bulk purchases of XXXL men's Y-fronts with a double cotton gusset! As if?

I am so looking forward to my letter from Boris, I think it may take a while having to sign them all, and I hope he isn't licking all the stamps personally. I may just send off a quick email to Number Ten on the off chance they may not have 'stamp licking' on their list of things not to do!

Being on lockdown, you certainly start to appreciate the little things that you always took for granted. All the new growth in the garden is amazing, every day there is something new that has popped up overnight. Believe you me, I'm no gardener, but whoever lived here before me obviously was... and I'm very grateful.

It appears that the ducks have been right up as far as the kitchen doors this morning. Don't ask me how I know... I just do... ok!

As I'm sure you can imagine, finding something to write

about when you aren't going anywhere is a bit difficult. I have resorted to giving you all an insight into me, and what makes me tick.

Horses... always a part of my early life. My grandfather farmed, back in the day, before the tractors made an appearance. My father grew up with horses and was determined that I should. Fast-track, a section of ponies, pony club, cross-country, shows, visits to Hoys and weeks spent at Olympia for the Christmas show.

I remember being ten and keeping my pony at a farm in Whiston. On Sunday mornings at the crack of dawn we used to get ready (no parents involved) and my friend and I would hack all the way to Wentworth to a Pony Club rally. I remember there was a dentist that lived in Greasbrough and we used to call in there for a glass of water on the way to Wentworth. Full day at the rally and then ride all the way back in the evening to Whiston.

Can you imagine anyone letting a couple of ten-year-olds do that today. Social services would have been knocking on the door and we would all have been put in foster care!

As today is day fourteen of lockdown, I was thinking back to when I was fourteen, and what a lovely time we had. It was the first time I ever went to Pony Club camp, my friends from then are still my friends now, and we still fall about at the tricks we got up to!

Manton Forest Farm, bang in the middle of Clumber Park, and with a permit to ride virtually wherever we wanted.

Much shopping before the event, I remember my dad taking me to Thomas and Taylor in Sheffield to buy some new jods and boots! The horsey bit was down in the basement, and the smell of the hoof oil was just amazing... I can smell it now!

My mother took me to the Army stores and bought me my first pair of jeans a sleeping bag - we're talking 1965 here folks - and a big, sloppy, blue jumper. Bliss! The horses went via a Pawsons wagon and I can't for the life of me remember how we all got there.

We were in big, old army tents, that smelled of big, old army tents... a very evocative smell. We slept in a row of five and argued over who was going to sleep on the ends. Wendy opted for one of the ends as she could almost guarantee she would be able to locate her specs in the morning. We all had a torch and did a lot of sabotaging by moonlight. As always in the summer of your childhood, it never ever rained, the sun always shone and the sky was always blue. We all took a packet of cigarettes and a bottle of vodka, and someone furnished us with a copy of *The Kama Sutra*, you can imagine the hilarity that caused! At the end of the week, we wrapped it in a plastic bag and hid it under some logs. Some people used to leave their wellingtons outside their tents when they went to bed (big mistake! and we used to go and wee in them in the middle of the night. Whether we ever got washed is anyone's guess, there were certainly no showers or wash basins in the mix. The loos were a hole in the ground surrounded by some sacking nailed to tall posts. Environmental health and health and safety would have had a field day!

There was some structure, with riding lessons and cross-country courses and all that sort of thing. We couldn't wait until the formal stuff was over and then we would make a hasty exit and go galloping down Lime Tree Avenue bareback with much whooping and yelling. The horses were all in outdoor scaffolding loose boxes, and were very well looked after. A few mothers (certainly not ours) were drafted in to provide some sort of sustenance. They were up in a caravan somewhere as far away from us as possible and ventured out only to bring in the food. I think we frightened them to death. There were a few spinsters of this parish, who were PE teachers and such like. We raided their tent and fastened their bras to the top of the tent poles. I had never been spanked before... nor since I hasten to add! Dodgy or what? We were there for a whole week, and I can honestly say it was one of the best weeks of my life! I know my camping companions will be reading this, and I'm fairly sure they will point out any errors!

Enough of reminiscing…

Me and Pony Club camp

The Diary of an Incarcerated Granny. Day 15

As you can imagine, it's not that easy to keep thinking up things to talk about. I had scrambled eggs for breakfast, and very good they were too. Eggs are, well, eggs really! I quite like them, I try not to overthink where they come from, but they seem to be a fairly versatile commodity.

Poultry-keeping for beginners… Once upon a time, the man of the house decided to build an aviary and very impressive it was too. It was fairly enormous; in fact, Chester Zoo (where I spent a couple of days last year) would have been seriously impressed! The boss man had a hankering for several pairs of ornamental pheasants. Many hours were spent looking through the small ads in the *Shooting Times* and decisions were finally made. This involved many phone calls and eventually we were informed by the breeders that our order would be dispatched and would arrive at Sheffield Railway station at midnight. Excitement all round, a fitting culmination to all those months of preparation and research. Or so we thought, all the birds were bedded down by torchlight and that was that. We were also the proud owners of two Gordon Setters and a Labrador. When we went down to view the new recruits later that morning, we discovered that one or all of the dogs had dug their way into the aviary and killed the whole bloody lot! Oooh tempers were a bit frayed that day.

Parrots, we inherited one! I hated it and it hated me. It said bugger all, other than 'Hello Ben' and 'Who's a good boy, Mummy?' Sometimes it would repeat the word 'good' for up to twenty times. It had a very big cage which it used to sit in outside in the summer. I had the brilliant idea of opening the cage door so it could sit in the Fig tree next to the cage and it wandered back in at dusk. This was a marvellous plan, until one day it took off into the skies above Old Ravenfield and was never seen again! Result! For a few days the strains of 'who's a good boy, Mummy?' could be heard filtering down from the trees in various parts of the village... and then nothing. We left the cage outside and somebody stole it! Just goes to show, a bird in the hand...!

We had chickens for a while. Baby Lister once considered herself the juvenile version of Bernard Matthews. Daddy duly built her a chicken hut and away we went.

The first three were bantams called Faith, Hope and Charity. I think Charity was the 'runt of the clutch' if such a description exists. She had one functioning leg and one less so. A rather unequal pair of eyes and a totally mystified look on her face. Sadly, Charity was soon summoned to the big hen house in the sky, and life was never quite the same! Faith and Hope tanked along for a few months, never laid a single egg, and we assume were taken by a fox when 'she who shall not be named 'forgot to lock them up for the night. Poultry farming was put on the back burner for quite a while, and then we decided to have another bash.

Rescued battery hens were the next venture to be explored. Our neighbour ordered six and persuaded us to have two. Sharon and Tracy, what a joy they were, they laid more eggs than we could eat, and spent some naughty times digging up our neighbours flower beds. They used to spend a fair bit of time in the paddock next door with the other six, all identical. Come lock up time we used to yell 'come on ladies' over the fence and they would split from the group and come legging up the paddock for their supper. They were fab.

Back to eggs... one of my friends had a budgie that laid an egg. She fried it and shared it with a pal! I once went on a school trip with a packed lunch lovingly prepared by my mother. Unfortunately, she had apparently forgotten to boil the eggs. Say no more! Do any of you watch *Four in a Bed*? I've come to the conclusion that a business can prosper or fail depending on the ability of the hosts to poach an egg properly! Chatting to a friend the other day she was bemoaning the fact that there seemed to be a shortage of large eggs. Her other half always has two eggs for breakfast and he only likes big ones! The world is in crisis darling, get over it!

Everybody has a talent for something; it sometimes takes a while to discover it. Some people make excellent yorkshire puddings, I do not, well I probably could if I could be faffed. My friend, who shall remain nameless, makes marvellous yorkshire puddings. She would rather allow the grim reaper into the house than a packet of Aunt Bessie's!

Would just like to say a big congratulations to my BF who became a granny for the fourth time yesterday. More expense, eh?

I promise, that for the sake of my sanity, and probably yours, I shall never ever mention birds again. RSPB, the ball is in your court!

However I am still unsure of which came first... the chicken or the egg? Answers on a postcard please.

I was in conversation with the 'very tall one' last night. He suggested that one of my topics should be about 'our family', and how marvellous we all are! When I eventually stopped laughing, I think maybe he has a point! Plenty of ammo there! Please stay at home... you know it makes sense! X

The Diary of an Incarcerated Granny. Day 16

Parcels, two yesterday (are they considered essential?). One was a book I had ordered weeks ago and the other was a hard-skin remover for my feet. I personally count the latter as an essential item. It's DIY or a visit to the blacksmiths when all this is over!

Feet are a bit of a Marmite subject. I don't know anyone that actually loves them, but I do know plenty of people that are singularly unimpressed by them.

So, today's random topic is feet...

Most people have them and as a whole, they are pretty useful. Without them, we would be unable to balance and actually fall over. That would probably cause numerous injuries and end up adding more strain on the already overburdened NHS... so, feet are good!

As a family, we are not blessed with spectacular feet. Some of us are bordering on being pretty fabulous from the ankles upwards, but below the ankle we have had some serious crosses to bear.

When I was at school I was diagnosed with flat feet. The remedy for this involved Wednesday lunchtimes spent sitting in a circle in the gym, passing pencils with your toes to the next person, who was suffering from the same affliction. It made no bloody difference whatsoever, although in retrospect, I could probably write my name using my foot?

On a 'girls only' trip to Florence many moons ago, we walked and walked for miles and miles. I remember sitting on the pavement outside the gallery that housed Michelangelo's *David* (his hands are far too big in my respectful submission... Google him and have a look), and saying to my best friend that I was in agony, there was a definitive moment when I realised that my arches had fallen, and would she please take me back to the hotel by taxi.

I remember Lister Sister No. 2, squirming with embarrassment at the end-of-term picnic, when her housemistress bellowed across the lawn, 'No. 2, all the medication for your verrucas is on the shelf at the side of the Aga. Don't forget to take them home with you'. The shame!

Lister Sister No. 1 was in a hall of residence at University. The girl in the next room was studying to be a chiropodist. Why No. 1 would think it fitting to Sellotape a detached, big toenail to her neighbours door was anyone's guess! When questioned she said, 'I thought she'd like it.'

Lister Sister 3 has pretty evil feet! Over the years she has had a goodly selection of chaps. I always wondered if the reason that they couldn't fully commit, was the thought of living 24/7 with those trotters?

I am delighted to report that the one who finally asked for her foot in marriage, loves her just the way she is. He just avoids looking at her feet!

As far as I am aware the 'tall man' has managed to avoid the foot perils that have blighted the lives of his three sisters. At almost 6 feet 7inches, he can barely see his feet anyway! And certainly nowadays, not without wearing his specs.

All I can say is, anyone who goes down the 'foot route' as a career commands my total respect!

Enough of feet, thank goodness!

Good things that have happened today:

1) When I came downstairs this morning it appears that Titchmarsh and Sons have been and mowed the lawn? Never heard or saw a thing!

2) I have taken the scissors to Poppy's fringe and she now looks like a Jack Russell.

3) I have finished my bar of Pears soap, and have opened a new one. Always reminds me of home when I was small!

4) I have found a 'fun-sized' Mars bar in a jug on the plate rack. (Are we all to assume that a normal-sized Mars bar is at the miserable end of the market?)

5) That's it!

As you are all getting to know me a bit better, I thought I would devise a list of things that annoy me, so that you will know what to avoid if we ever meet up! Are you ready?

1) People that write 'would of' instead of 'would have'. You can almost get away with it in the spoken word, but not when you write it down.

2) The word 'like' used five times in every sentence

3) Artichokes, both 'Globe' and 'Jerusalem'.

4) People who don't have any manners.

5) Miserable sods.

6) Old women who write idiotic blogs and expect people to read them.

I could go on, but frankly I've had enough for today.

I expect to get a bit of a rollicking from certain family members after today's effort... but heigh-ho, every word is true!

Please keep safe everyone and don't go out if you don't have to...

The Diary of an Incarcerated Granny. Day 17

I think it's day 17, and I understand that it's Friday? Who knows! I love it when you start a post on Facebook and it says 'what's on your mind'. I'm not convinced I have a mind anymore.

This morning not a lot happened, not likely to is it? I seem to have gone off granola a bit, and I have enough in stock to fill a wheelbarrow. If I put a little bagful on the gatepost, would anybody like to swap for some of those cinnamon shreddie type things?

I actually cried this morning! Somebody sent me a quote-thingy, and underneath it said, 'even if you do have fallen arches!'

It's the little things that bring a tear to my eye. When I was abandoned in Italy for four nights, I never shed a tear... I was too bloody cross!

Sit me down, and make me watch *The Incredible Journey* (you know the bit where the old Labrador comes limping over the hill?) And you might as well put me to bed with a hot water bottle and a lorry-load of tissues.

Yesterday, one of my feet (yeah, feet again) was a bit itchy and red-looking. Last night my tongue was quite sore. Within thirty seconds I had convinced myself I had foot-and-mouth disease. Google has a lot to answer for... I bet there is a lot of self-diagnosis going on at the moment. I spoke to Lister Sister Three, who has a medical background and always knows the answer to everything. She dismissed me very quickly and said I was eating too much fruit and to drink more water.

No. 3 is one of those people that always notices where things are. When she was about eight, I had to ring the school secretary to ask if she would take her out of class and bring her to the phone. We were having some work done on the house and I had searched high and low and couldn't find the architect's plans anywhere. How they had found their way into the playroom, and were on top of the radio is anyone's guess! She knew exactly where they were, of course.

Now I think about it, I might feature quite heavily on No. 3 today. There is very little else to write about. She won't see this until I send it to her later. Whereas, the other three will be busy organising gagging orders and injunctions to stop me in my tracks.

Four crumbsnatchers is plenty for anyone, unless you live in Morecambe, run a pie shop and are going for the world record. James had read somewhere that every fifth child born in the world was Chinese, he wasn't sure how that would apply to him, but to be on the safe side he booked himself in for a vasectomy!

No. 3 was born the day after we all came back from a Round Table camping weekend in Appletreewick. Bit of a surprise really, as she wasn't expected for another five weeks! But life is full of surprises, is it not?

We were totally renovating a very big house at the time and almost every floor was up and every ceiling was down... she is used to dust! I had decided that Cow and Gate was the nutrition of choice, and how lovely it would be to share night feeds! One week in I had pleurisy and was quite unwell. The father of my child was instructed by our doctor to take charge overnight. Two am, No. 3 starts crying, father of the year, who had to be woken up, starts assembling the bottle and remarks after ten seconds, 'Crikey, she got down that quickly'. He hadn't screwed the top on properly, she was soaked through, so was he, and so was the bed! That was the end of all paternal participation.

Surprisingly, she thrived rather well. She was always determined to make herself heard and sort of grew up by remote control!

She wasn't into dolls, she had (and still has) a wooden Buddha that she used to throw out of the bedroom window and occasionally wheel round in a pushchair. She had a Fisher Price tool kit and loved taking things to pieces and putting them back together.

When Daddy was building himself an AC Cobra she spent hours covered in grease and engine oil in the barn.

She hated dresses and all things frilly and could be an annoying little sod. No. 2 was once heard saying, 'I don't know why you ever had her, she's ruined my life.'

Playschool was negotiated without anyone being seriously harmed... then real school happened. She loved it, managed to get herself into a few scrapes but thankfully avoided expulsion. Certain comments in her school reports spring to mind! No. 3 does not suffer fools gladly. No. 3 has the ability to bring people round to her way of thinking.

She was very into running, and won the sports cup on an annual basis. All in all, she did pretty well. When she was eleven, she was down to join No. 2 at boarding school in York.

She demanded a family meeting and said, 'why did you bother having me, if you want to pay someone else to look after me? 'Not many answers to that one are there?

She was enrolled in a day school forty minutes from home, which operated six days a week and she was able to board for the odd night. When she went to take the entrance exam, she came out with a smile on her face. 'That was a doddle,' she said. 'He left the answers on the side!'

At thirteen, she was ready to join No. 2 and off she went to York. She was always the one that did 'just enough' to get on the next rung of the ladder, and did ok in her GCSE's but decided to come home to the local sixth form college for A levels. She got a place at Sheffield University and has surprised us all. She has actually turned into a bit of a boffin. The company she joined straight from university have allowed her to add to her qualifications and she has worked very hard.

Life has had its ups and downs, and she has kissed a lot of frogs in her time. Eventually one turned into a prince (dare I say he was a long time coming) who knows exactly what makes her tick, and can make her laugh when she has a bee in her bonnet!

She is probably the only one of the four who gave her granny as good as she got, and she always stands up for the underdog. If you have a problem, there is no one better to fight your corner. I know she is a good wife, a good mother, a good sister and a good friend.

She has overcome some serious and ongoing health issues

and is pretty amazing, and I love her!

Phew, I bet you're glad that you've come to the end of that. Sometimes you have to think outside the box, and a bit of reminiscing, can be quite cathartic. I hope I haven't bored you to tears. Onwards and upwards, it will be over and done with one day. Call your friends, renew those old acquaintances, heal those family rifts. For once in our lives, most of us have the time to make some things better x.

The Diary of an Incarcerated Granny. Day 18

My friend in Norfolk is experiencing a lovely sunny day with a slight breeze! I am experiencing quite a grey day with no breeze. She sent me a photo of her smalls blowing in the breeze. She seemed to think there was a hint of sarcasm in my reply!

Consequently, my plans for stripping the bed, pegging out and remaking when dry, have been put on hold! Please note, no mention of any ironing there.

Now on day eighteen, I'm wondering if there is ever going to be a light at the end of this bloody tunnel? There now seems to be a bit of a conflict over whether or not we are tackling this in the right way. 'Herd immunity' seems to be mentioned more and more, and frankly, the chances of that are unachievable if you are locked away on your own.

Being stuck at home in your self-isolating bubble is becoming so far removed from the real world, the horrors that are happening out there seem totally surreal.

I'm a glass half full person, I try and play the joker, I enjoy cheering people up and I am 100% grateful for the life I lead.

However, as with all things, doubt eventually starts to creep in. You suddenly start to realise just how much we all took for granted. Just pottering round, living your everyday life was just the norm. None of us gave it another thought; that was just what we did!

I imagine that there are very few people that don't know someone who has contracted this dreadful disease. Friends who haven't slept for days, worrying about family who are ill, and who are so far away they can do nothing to help them.

I spoke to my four-year-old granddaughter on FaceTime this morning. I could have cried. She was eating Coco Pops playing with Barbie and Ken and telling me that she couldn't see any of her friends and she wasn't allowed to go to nursery. She knows that something isn't quite right out there!

The baby of the group is just over two, she hasn't got a clue, thank goodness, she has got a new slide 'with a very big ladder, Granny' and life is pretty damn good!

The older ones, that are at secondary school and university, must all be starting to get a bit scared. I'm sure being wired into your iPad is suddenly starting to lose its appeal, and all the work that school are sending you must be a bit of a trial. Keep going you lot, love you lots x.

I'm having a big birthday in October. I know a fab family 'away' weekend has been arranged, and I hope to goodness things might be better by then. But none of us know that, do we?

There are a million things I could be doing, but I'm not.

My summer house was badly flooded at the end of last year.

Over eight weeks of constant dehumidifiers and oil-filled radiators resulted in an electricity bill of nearly £500. Some good furniture being stored down there was ruined and it was a bloody mess! Luckily, it has now dried out, but the thought of going down there and giving it a good fettle is beyond me. The updating of the address book, has ground to a halt. The sealing of two quarry tiles every day has never got off the drawing board. As we speak, it's lunchtime. I'm still in my marshmallow dressing gown, I've just eaten my afternoon tea (early) and I'm busy fishing scone crumbs out of my cleavage!

That's enough doom and despair for one day!

I am now showered dressed, and ready to face the rest of the day. 'Hurrah', they all cried, 'we thought she was starting to lose the plot.'

Today's random musing is about cars!

I know sod all about cars, quite a few quite exciting ones have dipped in and out of my life. My father drove a succession of Armstrong Siddeleys which were his pride and joy. He refused to pick me up from Pony Club camp in case the rough tracks in Clumber Park damaged his undercarriage! I had to cadge a lift home in the lorry with the tents.

How mean was that?

My mother also drove (in a fashion!) When I was about eight my father bought her first car. It was an MG two-seater soft top, checked radiator jobby and had to be revved up with a starting handle! I don't think that she ever quite worked out that cars didn't run on fresh air and cigarette smoke. She was always running out of petrol. When I came out of school at the end of the day, I would groan with embarrassment if she was parked outside. There was either no petrol, the battery had gone flat, or she had a flat tyre. She once went to visit some friends and hadn't realised that my pet rabbit had jumped in the back of her car. When it hopped into their kitchen, she remarked how similar it was to the one we had at home!

My mother-in-law was a demon behind the wheel. The only time she ever took her specs off was when she got into her car to drive. She had only two speeds. Stop and full. Red lights never applied to her, she used to leave the top car park at Brentwood and by the time she had careered straight onto Moorgate, she must have been doing at least fifty mph. She wrote off at least two cars with that trick. She nearly met her match in an accident in Australia. Her friend who was driving was killed outright, and she suffered dreadful injuries and it was almost three months until she was deemed fit enough to travel home.

We thought she might have calmed down a bit... but no way. She bought herself an Audi Quattro that went like s...t off a stick, and carried on as normal.

My first car was an MGB, bought from a friend and quite unsuitable for a toddler, a baby in a carrycot and a pair of Gordon Setters! It was nice while it lasted.

Our family cars were rather varied. We went through the list of big 4WD Toyota Landcruisers, quite a few Shoguns and then the ill-fated Range Rover. I was driving back from a weekend in the Cotswolds with some friends and tried to overtake a lorry on the Fosse Way and totally lost the steering. That resulted in one of the worst days of my life. Five of us were pulled out in one piece and one of us was so seriously injured we didn't know if he would make it - he did. The vehicle was a wreck, we were told if we had been in anything else we wouldn't have lived to tell the tale. Enough of that!

We went through a list of Alfa Romeo's, E-Type jags. Land Rover Defenders, BMWs, Mercedes. At one stage, James decided to build himself an AC Cobra. After two years of extremely hard work it was roadworthy. He made a fabulous job of it. British racing green, cream Connolly hide upholstery, with dark green piping. It was magnificent. He was a big guy and the Cobra internally was rather small. We shoehorned him into it and he set off on a test drive. An hour later, after a blast down the motorway, two circuits of Wickersley roundabout, he roared up the drive. We managed to haul him out, he admitted he had frightened himself to death and put it on the market the following week!

Your car, according to a friend of mine, should always make you smile. After buying a house it's probably the most expensive purchase you will ever make.

I had a new car in December. I quite like it but it doesn't make me smile... A soft top Fiat 500c probably would have! Next time maybe?

Have you nodded off? I wouldn't be surprised.

I think today's offering has been a bit miserable to be honest. We all have 'one of those days', maybe this one has been mine?

I'm hoping for sunshine tomorrow, that always lifts the spirits a bit.

Please stay at home and follow the rules, and keep those hard surfaces up to scratch x.

The Diary of an Incarcerated Granny. Day 19

This morning is Sunday... I know that, because *The Archers* omnibus was on the radio. I still wonder if they will include Covid-19 in the storyline? We'll have to wait and see on that one.

The sun is shining today, the bedding is whizzing round in the washer and some of my tulips have just come into flower. What's not to like?

I am on a chat group with some friends, and they were all posting all the amazing things they were having for supper last night. My contribution was a bit lacklustre to be honest. A scampi sandwich and a banana! I guess us singletons don't make as much of an effort?

My friend in Norfolk had her washing out at a very early hour, probably before I had extracted myself from my comfy super king. Of course, she sent me a photo, probably to make me feel guilty.

It didn't.... Just one thing sprang to mind. Vests! Do men still wear vests? These were very white, and there were loads of them. I did ask if her other half teamed them with matching Y-fronts! I haven't had a reply as yet.

My other half didn't do vests, pyjamas, slippers or dressing gowns. Not helpful if you get whisked into hospital at short notice.

However, he did have quite a fetching fleece full bodysuit, complete with a velcro bum flap, that he wore when he was shooting, up in Scotland. A garment that made us all fall about laughing when he modelled it for us. The intricate workings of the bum flap was not for the faint-hearted.

I've had a bit of a disappointment today, and I'm feeling as though I have been exploited. Remember my hard skin foot fettler that came in the post the other day? Today was the day for its first outing. My goodness, what a piece of kit that is. My trotters are as smooth as silk, no complaints there then.

This is the upsetting bit, I started to empty the dishwasher and was putting some things in one of the kitchen drawers. Horror of horrors... nestling in the drawer was my Parmesan grater with the blue handle. It was looking a bit familiar. It's the same as the foot fettler, just a different coloured handle and made by the same bloody company! How very dare they? That's £8.99 down the pan.

Tonight we are having a family quiz. Some app called Zoom will link us all together and we can ask one another questions! I am considering getting dressed for the occasion, firing up the hot brush and maybe even applying a slick of lip-gloss.

I haven't looked forward to anything as much since 2004 when we flew first-class to Barbados for three weeks! All I can say is this had better be good. It will be good to see them all, lots of family banter, which I really miss. My best times ever are when we are all together. I love it!

A lot of people seem to be baking a lot. No. 3 is obviously the proud owner of a flour mountain, she keeps sending me pics of her focaccia, Portuguese rolls and today's offering are finger rolls. How impressive is that? All I'll say is, don't hold your breath waiting for a photo of my scones, because there won't be one.

It's interesting how people are filling their hours. No. 2 and No. 2 Jnr are doing yoga, Pilates, assault courses in the garden, and spending a lot of time on the trampoline. This is to try and exhaust No. 2 Jnr, so that she will at least consider going to bed before 10pm.

No. 1 had a session with the power washer and the patio yesterday, and went a bit overboard, got quite sunburnt and had to rest on the outdoor furniture nursing a Campari. Is Campari the new gin?

Nothing as yet from the 'tall man'. I expect his extra-curricular exploits will be revealed later... or maybe not?

I didn't think Boris looked at all well the other day, hope he recovers soon!

Stay home, unless it's absolutely necessary to go out and keep safe x

The Diary of an Incarcerated Granny. Day 20

Day 20! Yet another day in Paradise. It had rained in the night, quite a lot, judging by the puddle on the lid of my blue bin. How keenly one's powers of observation increase when there is nothing to do. I stood out in the garden this morning and counted the ducks flying over. The same formation as in Hilda Ogden's front room, before she got her Muriel.

Them there ducks are still up to their raucous antics on the river bank. Living here, I've found you have to be politically correct at all times. What actually flows at the bottom of my garden is a dyke. Paper Mill Dyke to be precise. It's not a river, not a stream, not a brook but a dyke! It winds its merry way into Tickhill Mill Dam where all the ducks and stuff congregate. It is not a bloody duck pond! Do you understand?, it's not a duck pond. I have lived here for almost a year and discovered probably the worst mistake you could ever make in Tickhill is to mention the word 'pond' preceded by the word 'duck'. Instant raising of eyebrows, loud tutting, and threats of excommunication abound. Be warned!

I knew Boris wasn't looking good the other day! My suspicions were confirmed when he was hospitalised last night. I doubt we will get the full story as to how ill he really is. I watched TV early this morning and actually felt quite sorry for Nicola Sturgeon. When one of the main members of your team who is wholly responsible for laying down the laws re isolation, blatantly ignores the rules... it's a bit embarrassing, isn't it?

In September, when life was as normal as it ever could be... I went to Scotland for four days. The reason for this visit was a reunion with my friends from college. Four of us turned up, and bearing in mind there were only ten of us on the course. A 40% turnout after nearly fifty years was pretty impressive.

The four of us consisted of two widows, a divorcee and one that is still married to a tax inspector. Apparently he's ok!

We all met at Agricultural College in Berkshire, in the very early seventies. Ten of us, working towards our Veterinary Nursing finals, plus three other girls doing farming related stuff. Thirteen girls in a residential college full of blokes. Not quite as exciting as you would think. We tended to stick together for safety! When we walked into the dining room, all the chaps would stand up and go 'Baaa'! I think we embraced the herd mentality from day one. We had an amazing time, some hilarious incidents and friendships were forged that are still going strong.

Back to the reunion. Scotland was the place of choice. Our hostess still farms high up in the glen above Largs. She is now on her own, so travelling wasn't a possibility for her. The other three were far more flexible. I went up by train from Doncaster via Edinburgh to Glasgow, then caught another train to Largs.

One flew (over the cuckoo's nest!) up from Bristol and one from Gatwick. Our meet up at Glasgow airport was a joy to behold! It was just as though we had seen one another yesterday. The years peeled away and all the memories came flooding back.

We had an absolute blast... the weather was pretty good. We checked out the local ice cream parlour and stuffed our faces with the biggest concoctions you have ever seen. We laughed till we cried. We visited lots of places, ate in, ate out, we even went to see Barbara Dickson in concert. We went for dinner before the concert, and guess who was on the next table... Barbara... I am a huge fan!

One of my most abiding memories of college is of the night we finished our final exams. We walked across the fields (all ten of us) to The Dewdrop, the nearest pub, and we all bought a round. How we ever found our way back is anyone's guess! Some of us at the reunion were able to recall this event, some were not!

If we ever get let out, we will be arranging another meet up ASAP. In fact, it was so good it was on a par with Pony Club camp. There is no higher accolade!

The Family Quiz last night... what can I say about that... it was a bit strange. Five different households trying to log on to an app and waiting to be invited to join the meeting was difficult. By the time we were all up and running, we had used up half of the forty-minute slot we were allowed. A few of us couldn't hear properly, there was a lot of 'typical, how on earth are we supposed to know that?' There was a bit on Disney films and No. 2 Jnr could not resist shouting out the answers. My questions were on the royal family. I had a feeling that some of the assembled crowd had never realised that we had one! One of the questions was, 'how many children did Queen Victoria have?' Shock horror when the answers were read out, how could she possibly have had nine children... you could see them looking around their small broods and breathing a very audible sigh of relief.

My son-in-law is doing a shop today. One of the highlights of the week, bettered only by bin day, which is tomorrow. My fab neighbours do my bins, and I have no complaints at all. How am I supposed to remember which bin's turn it is to go out?

I am debating whether or not to roast a chicken, or make myself a spaghetti carbonara. Decisions all the way, and can I really be bothered to do either? It's getting easier, as the days march on, to procrastinate more and more. The joys of the granny nap are tempting, as it passes an hour.

Even writing this diary seems to be taking longer and longer every day. Sometimes the words seem to flow and you can wax lyrical about a tea bag. Other times (like today) it's a struggle to think of anything at all.

I was cheered to hear that Vera Lynn has re-released 'We'll Meet Again' and it has gone up to number thirty-seven in the charts. It always makes me want to shed a tear... as did the queen in her broadcast last night. Bless her, she's seen it all, hasn't she?

So we must all go forth, and not necessarily multiply, unless by accident. Stay safe x

The Diary of an Incarcerated Granny. Day 21

Gorgeous morning, that's a huge plus in my book! The sun certainly makes a difference. I am currently sitting outside, having a cheeky menthol and swigging from a well-sanitised can of Coke Zero. I wonder if my gin buddies have started already? You know who you are!

Watched a bit of TV, very saddened by the news of Boris. Whatever your political leanings, he is obviously very ill, and the pressure he has been under over the last few months can't have helped. He must be mentally and physically exhausted.

This morning's happenings, loads of phone chats, messages and FaceTimeing. There are not enough hours in the day at the moment.

Annoying things. The kitchen tap has dropped off again! Where is 'Barry the plumber' when you need him? Chatting with a friend this morning, she did remind me that when this happened last time, I was able to prop it up most successfully with a squeezy bottle of Heinz Tomato Ketchup. When I need to use the ketchup, I am experimenting with a Tena Lady to see if it will hold the tap on a temporary basis... just while I assemble my bacon sandwich! They say that necessity is the mother of invention, don't they?

Yesterday, something beastly happened in my little bubble world.

No. 3's husband, my lovely son-in-law, came and delivered my weekly shopping. All rules observed to the letter. Off he tootled home, totally looking forward to his hot Domestos bath and the thought of No. 3 ripping off his kit and boiling it up in a saucepan full of Dettol.

This was not to be... he was pulled over by the police and interrogated. Where was he going, where had he been? He had to sit in their car while they checked out all his car details. They then wanted to know my address. How many sons-in-law know their mother-in-law's address? Why would they? They don't write to you, they pop round occasionally to put up a light fitting and have a spot of lunch, and they know exactly where you live... because they just do! Bless his heart, he finally satisfied their demands by finding my house on Google Earth!

He was released without charge. Apparently they were very nice, and maybe it's a good thing that the boys in blue are keeping tabs on us all.

I felt the need to share this with the rest of the family on our group chat. The response to this bulletin differed considerably.

No. 1 was rather scathing. She said it would have been far more understandable if it were the fashion police that had hauled him in! The fact that he was wearing his 80s shell suit when apprehended was neither here nor there in my opinion.

This is the guy who won the British Formula Renault Championship in 1996, and skied for the GB Team. We know his dress sense is a little bit retro, but we must remember how we all admired him when we were on our family holiday in France. Who else would have wandered nonchalantly down the steps in front of the chateau wearing a lime-green mankini? Answer me that, this guy deserves respect!

The 'tall man' remarked that if they had strip-searched him they might have found a Tena in his pocket! I applauded that.

No. 2 is a sweetheart, she rarely says anything unkind about anybody. When put to the test and asked was there anyone that she wasn't particularly keen on... she did admit that she wasn't a huge fan of Kerry Katona!

On receiving this news, No. 2 was understandably concerned. She is extremely fond of the spouse of No. 3. After a couple of holidays in the South of France she was heard to say, 'if I had to go on holiday every year with the same people... I would always want to go with Mr No. 3. How nice is that, and how lucky are we?

I don't think I have ever had so much grub in my cupboards. I had my sights set on a chicken Caesar salad for this evening's culinary delight. I have a chicken, I have a jar of Cardini's Caesar salad dressing (there is no better, trust me on this one!) I have Parmesan (yes I'm keeping things separate) I have bacon. (No anchovies... evil little sods) and FFS, just discovered no bloody lettuce!

I shall ask Google whether or not I can substitute rhubarb leaves for lettuce. I think I already know the answer to that one. I shall make it anyway and incorporate a 'virtual' lettuce.

I'm now going to watch *Four in a Bed*, just to observe the quality of the poached eggs and later I shall have my supper in the garden.

A very good friend of mine always tells a joke that involves the period after the war. Somebody was asked who her father was, she scratched her head and looked thoughtful, and then replied 'some soldiers'!

Stay safe and spare a thought for Boris.

The Diary of an Incarcerated Granny. Day 22

Overnight observations.

There still seems to be a lot of traffic about. There must be a bump in the road because the house shakes if a lorry goes past.

Poppy insisted on sleeping between my feet, which was not ideal. There is tons of room to spread out in the comfy superking, she was being rude and selfish! I seem to be dreaming a lot more than usual. I woke up at one stage in the middle of a real argument with No. 3! I looked at the clock, (yes, I do have one that works) and it was four-thirty am. I swore and chuntered a bit and then went back to sleep until almost nine am! What a disgrace.

My staircase in the Hobbit House should have come with a government health warning. When I first moved in it had no handrail, that was one of the first jobs on the list. You really have to concentrate hard when climbing both up and down. It has a little twist at the bottom that is just waiting to catch you out and break your neck.

I decided early on that if I needed the loo urgently (when I was much older of course) then it was not ideal. I have a couple of quite attractive outhouses just outside the kitchen. After careful thought, I now have a laundry room, and a downstairs shower room, and I love them.

Upstairs there is a wet room, which has a wall-hanging loo, a washbasin the size of a cereal bowl, and a shower contraption, which involves swinging glass panels. It's all very trendy, it was very expensive (I've seen the bills) and I dislike it intensely.

The downstairs one is a different matter altogether (designed by *moi*). There is a big shower that you can wave your arms around in with a tiled inset shelf to put all your stuff on. Suggested by Fordelicious. A pedestal washbasin that doesn't splash water everywhere, with enough room to wash your smalls if the occasion demanded it. The loo is a proper loo, bolted to the floor, so it doesn't shudder when you sit on it. It has a soft-closing lid and is magnificent. The building is now insulated, replastered, has down lighters, metro tiles, proper flooring and a radiator. My cup runneth over!

My plan was to build a sun room type thing from the kitchen to include the laundry and shower room. A quick word with Rob the builder and we reckoned about £10-12,000.

How naive was I. The first port of call was building regs. A very chirpy little man showed up and declared that if we wanted to put a polystyrene roof on we could start tomorrow!

I don't like polystyrene roofy-things. In that case the next step was to bring someone in from planning to have a look. We made an appointment.

She was four and half hours late, Rob who came over to discuss tactics had to leave eventually. I was not impressed! One thing that all Listers learn very early on in life is the art of punctuality. We don't do late!

She was vaguely apologetic, but pointed out that if she had taken time to phone me, then she would have been even later. I'm still trying to work that one out.

She poked round a bit, took a few photos and then proceeded to tell me her life story. She was here for nearly two hours. No stone was left unturned, there was nothing about her (and all her relatives) that I wasn't party to. I could have gone on

Mastermind, with her as my chosen subject, and wiped the floor with the lot of them.

She floated off into the sunset, convinced I'm sure, that she had made a friend for life.

All went quiet for a few weeks, then a letter arrived stating that the Hobbit House was slap bang in the middle of the conservation area.

This changed the dynamics considerably.

The plans Rob had submitted were not detailed enough. There was a party wall that was an issue and I was told that a qualified architect needed to be brought on board. As luck would have it, we found an architect that we had used before and actually lived nearby.

The conservation issue became a headache, the party wall attachment became a no-no! The planning and architects fees were nudging a thousand pounds. It was then suggested that a party wall surveyor should be appointed! Only another £600 to add to the mix. Suddenly, the little 'project' was galloping towards the ridiculous sum of £30,000 as everything has to match in with existing buildings, which I do understand. Bearing in mind this 'sun room' is not overlooked by anyone, one wonders if I had just gone ahead, if anyone would have been any the wiser? I think not.

At the moment I'm still thinking about it. I managed perfectly well over the winter months, taking two steps from the kitchen to the shower room without getting frostbite. I am not a precious snowflake, I am a granny with attitude and a collection of umbrellas to be used in inclement weather. I'll let you know what I decide.

It's quite warm out. Just had a FaceTime with the West

Sussex branch. Much wearing of skimpy clothing in the garden. No. 2 and No. 2 Jnr were having a picnic in a wigwam with Barbie and Ken. Barbie looked ready for a night at the Oscars, and Ken was wearing a denim jacket and no pants! No. 2 Jnr was tucking into salami, cucumber, carrot sticks and olives and Mummy was bemoaning the fact that they were right out of sesame oil and soy sauce! Life's a bitch.

I have just got my hose-pipe out, one's tubs appear to be drying out pretty fast. The French lavender is putting on a very attractive show, and there is another tulip wafting around.

Today's offering is a little strange, but at least you all have a mental picture of the areas in which to ablute in the Hobbit House.

I am heartened by the fact that Boris seems to be improving slightly. We really do need him back at the helm. I hope you have all had a good day, doing whatever people do, when there is nothing to do. Keep safe and stay at home …

The Diary of an Incarcerated Granny. Day 23

Arghhhhhh! I have had to have a very stern word with myself this morning! Procrastination is my middle name at the moment and this is not boding well. The fact that nobody has crossed the threshold for twenty-four days is beginning to hit home.

Talking of middle names, my middle name is Marguerite. I have connections with the Queen Mother, whose maiden name was Elizabeth Angela Marguerite Bowes-Lyon. Cool or what?

Anyway, after a bit of an unsettled night I vacated my pit at about 8.30, and gingerly negotiated the staircase of doom. Violet-Elizabeth was fast asleep in her basket... but no loud snoring detected! For about a minute I thought she was dead. I couldn't see her breathing and one little eye was a bit open. Scary stuff. I poked her with my foot, she gave an almighty snore, sat up and then pottered off outside for a wee. Panic over, thank goodness. Do you think she might have sleep apnoea? I could have done without that first thing this morning.

When I was last down staying with the West Sussex branch, No. 2 Jnr was being a bit whingy. Granny doesn't do whingy, so whenever she started moaning, I said that this behaviour was becoming unacceptable and I was going to have a word with the queen! Remember folks, always go straight the top! After a totally one-sided telephone conversation with HM we reached a conclusion. No. 2 Jnr was listening with bated breath. 'What did she say, Granny? I said, 'Not much... she said, tell her to get over it!' That worked amazingly well, when she started kicking off, I would raise my eyebrows, give her a Granny stare and she would shrug her shoulders and say, 'I know, get over it!' Try it, I found it rather useful.

I had a FaceTime with No. 3 Jnr this morning. I think her hair is going through what could be described as a difficult stage. (She's nearly two-and-a-half). 'Has anybody brushed your hair this morning,' asked Granny? 'Yes,' she said. Followed by, 'and do you know, Granny, that my hair is strawberry blonde?'

'How lovely, and what colour hair does your daddy have?' I said. 'My daddy's hair is Moroccan sunset with just a little bit of ginger,' she said. How cute is that?

Sorry, I'm waffling a bit. Going back to this morning, I made myself a list of things to do before I had my second cup of coffee. Shower, hair wash, washing put on, dishwasher emptied, clean stuff taken upstairs (un-ironed!) and put away. Lawn poo picked up. Pot plants watered and house insurance sorted online. I always perform better if there is a deadline to work towards. I was ready for that second cup and I actually felt I deserved it! I have decided to reduce my food intake to two meals a day, if this continues on the day of release they will be hauling me out by crane… Brunch and supper from now onwards. It's very easy to comfort eat due to boredom and I think I've been 'troughing'(as we say in Yorkshire!) a little too much over the last couple of weeks. So steps have been taken to slow down.

When I was a child, you had three meals a day (if you were lucky), there was no eating between meals unless it was an apple and absolutely no 'snacking'. The snack culture is paramount… probably one of the first words this latest generation utter is 'snack'.

When I was at school, we had a proper lunch, cooked on the premises and there was no choice. Some days it was ok, other days it was revolting, but you were expected to eat it anyway. I remember being told off soundly for not eating all of my Manchester tart. The skin on the custard was at least a cm thick and sixty years down the line I could still heave when I think about it.

Oh boy, haven't things changed! A lot of households seem to run some sort of restaurant facility. Everybody gets asked what they would like and the à la carte version seems to be cooked accordingly.

Packed lunches seem to be an exercise in keeping up with the Joneses. Gone are the days of the cheese sandwich, bag of crisps and an apple. We are now having to compete with a portion of 'Mummy's world famous quinoa salad' jostling for space with some organically-reared chicken strips. All accompanied by some home-made hummus with crudités and a smattering of cherry tomatoes and olives. A flapjack lovingly created with the finest ingredients known to man, and possibly a slice of watermelon, or a couple of mango slices will complete this delectable feast. All food groups will be represented and the 'lunch box police' will be scoring you marks out of ten. The mummy who slips in a Cadbury's chocolate finger, or, God forbid, a fun-sized Mars bar will be forever ostracised at the school gate, and life will never be the same again! Think about it.

Another thing that seems to have come to the fore is 'keeping hydrated'. In my day I walked to and from school (about a mile and a half) every day. Never at any time, did it ever cross my mind to take a bottle of water in my satchel. Why would I do that? They had taps at school!

Nowadays, they can't get to the bottom of their own drive before pausing for a sip of mineral water. This is just in case dehydration catches them by surprise before they get as far as the traffic lights, where they usually pause again for another refreshing gulp! By the time they get as far as school they have consumed the equivalent of a couple of pints and are feeling a little below par. They then feel the need to get their hands on that flapjack, just on the off chance their sugar levels have dipped.

If you look in the footwell of most cars they are littered with empty water bottles. This is because the amount of water required to drive there and back to the supermarket is colossal.

Yes I do think we need to drink plenty of the clear stuff, but seriously, get a life!

Another weird and not very wonderful ramble. It's not quite as easy as you think.

Hoping for better statistics in the news, sadly I don't think we are quite there yet. I think we all knew that we were due another few weeks of lockdown. If it has the desired affect then so be it!

Stay at home over Easter, because that's what we need to do. Take care and get well soon, Boris. x

The Diary of an Incarcerated Granny. Day 24

Happy Easter everyone. I am now officially on holiday until Tuesday. No mundane household tasks will be on my radar.

However. I will still be writing my diary, if I can think of anything to write.

It's Easter apparently, I should have been in Morecambe for a couple of days visiting a friend... and I'm not! This is the friend who I usually have a little adventure with every year. A couple of years ago we went to Whitby, rented an Airbnb and had a very action-packed couple of days. We both travelled independently by train to York, then travelled together by train as far as Scarborough and then caught the bus to Whitby. I have seriously not been on a bus for maybe thirty years! What a joy, the journey along the coast was amazing, the scenery was breathtaking and the fact that I didn't have to drive was wonderful. (a lot of adjectives creeping in there)!

We had such a laugh, the apartment was perfect and we just ambled about enjoying the weather. Fish and chips on the first night, a couple of nice restaurants followed. We did the touristy bit, Captain Cook's Museum a visit to the jet exhibition. Lots of coffees and drinks and ice creams in the sunshine.

The last evening we even got tickets to go and see the local rep at the Pavilion theatre. All good. We departed on the last morning, still friends, she by train this time, and me on the lovely bus.

The bus to Scarborough was really packed Everybody seemed to be heading home from holiday, so there were suitcases piled up everywhere. A couple got on, slung their case on the top of the pile and went off upstairs.

From that moment on, things began to go downhill, literally! The coast road is a bit bendy, and there were cases falling off the pile and juddering up and down the aisle with gay abandon. Some bloke at the back started issuing 'stacking instructions' in a very loud voice, and a woman near the front, whose shins were now black and blue, was unamused and told him to **** off! I love a good altercation, especially if I am just observing, and have no personal involvement!

This was becoming a bit heated, and even the driver was chipping in with his ten-penneth, he was telling folk to remain in their seats and calm down. 'Mighty mouth' at the back, was well used to ignoring instructions and hauled himself up and began to reorganise the cases. He obviously thought he had done a grand job as he smirked and nodded to everyone on the way back to his seat. I think I may even have heard a faint smattering of applause! The woman in the aisle seat opposite (she of the battered shins) was heard to mutter 'smug bas***d' under her breath!

The best bit was when we were heading downhill towards Robin Hood's Bay. Quite a steep hill. An elderly lady was viewed in the distance, waving her arms about, indicating that she wanted the bus to stop. The driver slammed on his brakes, and the top case on the pile made a break for it. Just as the doors were opening, it shot down to the front, made a neat turn, bounced down the steps, hit the pavement and took off down the road.

The woman waiting to get on glanced round and said, 'Is there anybody with that bugger or not?' The driver retrieved it, and we all sniggered a bit. When we arrived in Scarborough, the couple whose case it was came down the stairs, grabbed their case and headed off home. They had no idea!

I swear that is a true story!

I had a surprise earlier this morning. A ring on the bell and some old friends out walking their dog, left me some lovely fresh eggs on the doorstep. So appreciated, thank you.

I honestly don't know where the time goes.

I try and sit down and get this diary thing over and done with. This is me, on my iPhone typing with one finger and just writing whatever comes into my head. All off the cuff, but sent with love!

I'm now going to have some poached eggs on toast and a cup of tea, decadent or what..

Stay at home guys and keep safe...

The Diary of an Incarcerated Granny. Day 25

It doesn't feel very Eastery does it? Normally we'd be preparing for 'the lunch' tomorrow with family and friends. I suppose if you are in a household of more than one, you can still make a bit of an effort. If you are on your own, I suggest you have a very long lie-in, convince yourself it's Thursday and push the boat out…, add some grated cheese to your beans on toast and garnish with a spoonful of Branston pickle. What's not to like?

I wonder if that would be considered a 'northern' dish?

As families mingle together through marriage, I think the north/south divide is still alive and well, and has its head office in Watford.

I have no problem with the south, I went to college there, No. 1 and No. 2, live there and in my opinion it's fairly ok.

However, some of those hatched in the south seem to have a very dim view of us 'oop north'.

Many years ago, quite a lot of us went to a Round Table weekend in Ruislip. We stayed for the weekend with families, and met up during the day and in the evening for various social do's. I really think that they thought we would be wearing flat caps, eating tripe and onions and be the proud owners of at least one whippet and a loft full of racing pigeons? How did we ever manage to create that impression…? I loathe tripe, not a huge fan of whippets and wouldn't thank you for a flock of pigeons. Total mistaken identity!

On the subject of pigeons, I shall now tell you the favourite joke of my dear departed husband. A brilliant raconteur and a minefield of excellent jokes. I will issue an apology before I start, I hope this won't offend anyone... but it still makes me howl! Ready?

Two punks in Trafalgar Square, Mohican haircuts, rings through everything you can think off and both with a bit of a snuffle. Proper Essex boys.

Lots of people milling around, and loads of pigeons flying around everywhere.

One of the lads looked up at Nelson's column and said to the other, 'Oy John, what, what, what would you do if a bird s**t on your head?' The other guy thought about it for quite a while, then shook his head. 'Well,' he said. 'I don't fink I'd take her out again'!

Thanks sweetheart, still one of the best; I so wish you were here to tell it! X.

Seeing as it's a 'holiday weekend', I made a bit of an effort at 'brunch time'. If you are on your own you can have your meals in any order you like... nobody cares.

Mindful of not wasting anything, I did a bit of crust-munching and jar-scraping.

Two toasted crusts, each one cut into four. A sweet plate and a savoury plate. Jam, lemon curd, honey and marmalade on one. On the other, Marmite, peanut butter, Philadelphia with Branston pickle and four bits of cooked penne with a drizzle of basil oil and a smattering of green pesto! T'was lovely. Necessity is the mother of invention, or so I seem to keep saying!

Some of you will be heaving at this juncture, and some of you may be raiding your cupboard to see if you can recreate this feast.

Bit of a disturbed night last night. I knew I shouldn't have given Poppy some chicken pickings with her dinner! I just knew it. Violet-Elizabeth, on the other hand, has the constitution of the Berlin Wall. (when it was still up, obviously). You could overdose her with a vindaloo curry and a Sainsbury's strawberry trifle, and her internal plumbing would still continue on an even keel.

Poppy woke me up at three-thirty am, and again at just after six am, she desperately needed to go out. That involved several extra encounters with the staircase of doom! Luckily for her she seems to have the ability to go straight back to sleep between bouts. Sadly I don't!

When the dame on *Desert Island Discs* gives me the call, I know which book I'm going to take. *The Wind in the Willows*... Last night, between Poppy's bouts of anxiety, I came across a copy that I was reading to No. 2 Jnr and I began to reread for the umpteenth time. In my humble opinion, it takes a bit of beating. It is closely followed by '*The Boy, The Mole, The Fox and The Horse*', by Charlie Mackesy. If you haven't seen it, get yourself one. Pen and ink illustrations and very little dialogue. I have started buying a copy for all the new little people that are coming into the world in lieu of a babygro. A marvellous first book for their library, and for grown-ups too, and so full of the right sort of things you want to emphasise! It brings a tear to your eye (well mine anyway, but I'm a soft touch!). Trust me on this one!

Enough now, my finger is aching and I have the disappointment of no Easter eggs to face tomorrow.

The Diary of an Incarcerated Granny. Day 26

Happy Easter Sunday everyone. Happy Anniversary to me... one year today, since I moved my decluttered self into The Hobbit House. A move I have never regretted for a moment.

Somehow or other, I found myself watching a black and white Vera Lynn film yesterday afternoon. Everyone was very charming and polite and spoke perfect BBC English. At the end she sang 'We'll Meet Again'... and I cried! Somehow, it brought it all home that we don't know when we will see anyone again. That's scary, and the news is horrific, and none of us can predict the outcome. All I know is, that when we do finally emerge, the world will be a very different place, and priorities will have changed considerably.

I'm not a very religious person, I often wish I was. I do so admire the people who have a strong faith and are able to rely heavily on that to see them through. I try my best to be kind to people, and treat them as I would like to be treated. I will be the first to admit that I have on some occasions, got down on my knees, and begged for something, somewhere to make things better. Who knows? I wish I did!

On a lighter note, I have been racking my brains to come up with some more material. Someone suggested a resumé of group family holidays from a very long time ago. Here we go.

There is safety in numbers!

A very long time ago, the great and the good decided that we would try and have one week a year where we holidayed en masse.

We would pour over the *English Country Cottages* brochure just after Christmas and try and find somewhere that ticked most of our boxes.

The first one was in Devon, a thatched creation within ten yards of the pub. We decided we would take a rosy-cheeked daughter of a farming friend with us to act as a nanny in the evenings. Big mistake, she had never been away from home before, she hated the kids, they were not overly invested in her and it was a recipe for disaster. She spent the majority of the week slumped on the sofa, sucking her thumb and crying because she was homesick! She was sixteen or seventeen, so there was really no excuse! Needless to say, the ladies never made the pub at all, and the chaps managed it every night.

We learned from that one, and decided we needed at least three families to lighten the load! The next venture was a manor house in West Pentire in Cornwall. Much more like it, access to beaches and rock pools. Pub yet again on the doorstep. Village shop on the doorstep that sold everything, we had a magical week. One of the kids bonded with the old lady that ran the little shop and popped in for a chat at least twice a day. When he was taken to say goodbye, we discovered he had been going in every day, not just for a natter but he was actually laying away goods for Christmas! As a parting gesture, he bought two Lyons Individual Fruit Pies as a gift for his grandparents.

We loved it there and returned the following year. One day we headed for St Ives, the chaps and the boy children went mackerel fishing... and the mummies and the little girly people went nearby to look at a stallion that a friend was considering using. On the way to the stud farm we heard a distress rocket go off. The stallion turned out be a magnificent specimen. His owner, less so! The poor woman had the worst case of BO that any of us had ever encountered, we were gasping for air! No. 2, who was probably about five kept asking what the horrid smell was. We left as soon as it was polite to do so.

On our return, it became clear that the mackerel fishers had been called back into the harbour, a squall had got up and it was considered dangerous for them to stay out there. Several people had been seasick, two of our lot had caught one another with their hooks underneath the boat, and nobody had managed to catch anything.

The following year, we rented a big house at Kingsbridge in Devon. It came with a boat and its own jetty. The plan was, to keep sailing over to Salcombe when the tide was right and pick up whatever we needed. What is it they say, 'time and tide wait for no man'. Too bloody right. As we limped into the harbour on our maiden voyage, the 'tall boy' was heard to say, 'Dad, why are we sailing through mud, the water has disappeared?' That was boating out of the equation. One of our party had done his own packing... when his wife opened the case, all it contained was a single flip-flop and a pair of torn swimming trunks! He had to be dispatched to buy a whole new wardrobe!

We then moved on to Somerset. A fabulous house in the village of Coxley, formerly the second home of John le Carré. Still family owned, but now by his ex-wife and her husband who was a diplomat. They lived abroad and let the house out for extra income. The weird thing was, that it was just as though they had all popped out round to the corner shop. All their stuff was everywhere! Clothes in the drawers cupboards and wardrobes, all personal papers still on the desk in the office. Nowhere was locked. It was big and rambling, had a swimming pool and a huge garden, and a magnificent view of Glastonbury Tor from the loo window upstairs. The kids loved it, in the conservatory there were the most amazing 'dressing up' boxes. Proper costumes and props and everything you could think of. I think we had a 'show' most nights. The order of the day was to stick around, do your own thing if you wanted, but always be back around four-ish to start to prepare the evening meal. We had a version of Sunday lunch every night, and then the men sodded off to the pub (bear in mind, this was before the age of the nappy-changing, bottle-feeding, new man!) One recent bride, who was angling for the step-mother of the year award, decided to go with the men to the pub. As she left she issued instructions. Would we make sure that the children showered when they came in after swimming? Would we ensure they were given a warm, milky drink? We laughed... very loudly! I think as responsible citizens we may have done a head count around ten. Thirty just to check they were all alive. Super-step, came back at midnight, pissed as a fart, having drunk the equal of her own weight in good old Somerset Cider! What sort of example did that set? She was very wise to leave the child care to the experts!

We once did a girly week and rented a cottage in Robin Hood's Bay. Not quite as upmarket as those from *English Country Cottages*. The first thing not in its favour was it had a detached kitchen... this was in an outhouse in a yard at the back. Parking was non-existent, so we had to lug every about a mile and a half. It too had not one, but two staircases of doom. The fixtures and fittings were not quite up to standard, and it was home to the biggest spider you have ever seen in your life. One day we went to Scarborough for afternoon tea, that was when No. 3 was manhandled from the dining room at The Royal for continually shouting 'bollocks'. To be fair the tea was nothing special. We booked tickets to see *Snow White and the Seven Dwarves* and it was a jolly good show. Pizza Hut afterwards and then realisation set in. It was nine fifty-five and the car park closed at ten pm. You have never seen anybody move so quickly. We just made it, and sang our way back over the moors in the fog. He of the Individual Fruit pies was heard to remark, 'That was the best thing I have ever seen in my life, I never realised that there were real dwarves!'

The week continued, the kids were increasingly foul, the grown-ups were to be found sitting eating the secret stash of Mars bars in the detached kitchen, sitting on the floor, backs against the door and refusing entry to anyone under thirty! On the last afternoon the spider made its appearance again. I kid you not, it was the size of a bloody donkey. Sitting there in the middle of the armchair rubbing its legs together! We picked up the chair and threw it outside... and we never ever went there again! I could go on, I have only touched the tip of the iceberg but you are most probably yawning, and my index finger has had enough for one day.

I am having crispy duck and pancakes for my supper. I had my Smarties Easter egg for breakfast and all is ok on the Tickhill front.

Stay home! It's the least we can do. Take care and keep safe. X

The Diary of an Incarcerated Granny. Day 27

B it chilly in Paradise this morning! Had the usual phone calls, FaceTime, messenger stuff. Kitchen floor 'dust busted', hard surfaces disinfected, house-owner showered and dressed. Baskervilles checked for 'bum crumbs' (all spick and span) so everything in the Hobbit House is sorted.

Just occurred to me that if you had two of something, like puppies or kittens, you could call them 'Spick' and 'Span'? How cool would that be? If you were the proud parents of twins…, probably not such a good idea!

Observations this morning… there are only two bananas left! The dining room table is cluttered up with everything imaginable. Just read online that Covid-19 can be transmitted by farting! If there ever was a case to ditch those thongs and invest in some big pants this is it!

Right, have discussed today's topics with No. 2 and No. 3 and have their blessing to include a few of their somewhat traumatic moments. Over the years there have been incidents that were dreadful at the time, but thankfully came good in the end. Some that were amusing, but shouldn't have been. We've all had them, and here are a few of mine.

No. 2 was born in a Sheffield Hospital. She was eventually induced as she was quite happy staying put. Several hours later, she arrived. Much jubilation all round. Daddy shot off to inform grannies and family. Mummy was hiked up in the stirrups being sewn back together and then the shit hit the fan!

Buzzers were going off, No. 2 was removed at speed and total chaos ensued.

As she was being delivered (I can actually remember every word of this conversation) the midwife said to her assistant, 'When you see the baby's anterior shoulder, give this injection'.

The injection was a muscle contractor to speed up the appearance of the afterbirth, and sadly the instructions became lost in translation. She gave the injection to the baby instead of me! No. 2 went into spasm and everything stopped. Fortunately they did realise what had happened and No. 2 was rushed to intensive care and put on a ventilator. Daddy arrived back from his 'good news' telephone conversations to complete panic. It was so horrendous. The prognosis was poor, and an hour later we were taken to ICU, along with the hospital chaplain to have her baptised. The plan was to keep her sedated and ventilated until the drug came out of her system. If she survived, then nobody knew what long-term damage there would be. I had every 'big cheese' in the hospital standing round the end of my bed all quaking in their boots, and begging us to keep this quiet! This was nearly forty-two years ago, just imagine in today's culture, we would have sued the pants off them.

All we wanted was a healthy baby, no amount of money would have made the slightest bit of difference.

Eight long days later, we were allowed to go home! There appeared to be no apparent ill effects and she was carefully monitored monthly until she was twelve-months-old. She passed every milestone with flying colours and was considered fit for purpose and discharged. She even got a write up in *The Lancet*! Today, she is a perfect specimen, beautiful, clever, kind, and everything that you would wish for. I suppose you would call that a nightmare with a happy ending?

The other good thing to come out of that experience, is that

I met another mum in there, we clicked, and are still clicking on a very regular basis, nearly forty-two years on. You know who you are!

Another interesting event, we can now look back on with a hint of amusement. Seriously not funny at the time!

My lovely (sadly not with us anymore) other half was an insulin-dependent diabetic. He paid little heed to this condition and never really let it stop him doing anything! Occasionally he got it spectacularly wrong. I woke up in the middle of the night, not sure why, and he was unconscious, freezing cold and wringing wet and out for the count. I tried to hold him up and give him some glucose gel, but he was too far gone. I dialled 999 and sent for an ambulance. I woke up No. 3 and requested her help to try and support him. You couldn't have written the next bit! Suddenly No. 3 flipped back and had an epileptic seizure. She was out for the count as well. So that's two of them unconscious on the bed. In the midst of this mayhem, there was a clatter downstairs, and into the bedroom shot one of the cats with a live rabbit in its mouth. Ring on the doorbell and the ambulance arrived. The outcome of this jolly jape was that they managed to bring James round. They took No. 3 into hospital overnight, and I eventually collared the rabbit (which was hiding under the bed) and let it go outside. The cat was unimpressed.

This story was always a crowd pleaser!

Just one more.

We were camping in the South of France in Argeles. No. 1 was dispatched to the car with some pate that we had bought. We were all in the sea, No. 3 sporting a contraption called a 'David Wilkie Hump'. This was a bit like an inflatable rugby ball on a strap that kept you afloat. We were all sploshing around when somebody noticed that the David Wilkie was floating unaided on the surface. No sign of No. 3... we managed to grab her as she came up for the third time! Not good! David Wilkie was deposited in a nearby dustbin and his name never mentioned again in polite society!

We returned to the car, not only had No. 1 forgotten to lock it, but she had left the pate at the side of the gear stick in the full sun! What a bloody mess. To add insult to injury, we then discovered that someone had been in the car and stolen the travel wallet, all the passports, money and credit cards! This was our last day, we were heading north and luckily had an hotel already booked and paid for. This is where the 'tall boy' came into his own. We had been away for three weeks, he was still in full possession of every halfpenny he had taken as pocket money! What a star, we were able to dine out that evening on the very substantial contents of his wallet. We never called him a tight arse for ages after that!

No. 3 has always had entrepreneurial tendencies! She has had to be forcibly removed from several of her money-making schemes. She was discovered singing on the doorstep outside a restaurant in Sarlat, holding a saucer, and the general public were dropping coins in as they passed by. Granny Lister was with us at the time and was appalled that her granddaughter was begging on the streets. She then moved on to selling Sunday lunch menus for ten pence to diners leaving the hotel. That was stopped in its tracks! The big money-maker was an album she bought for twenty pence at a Ladies Circle Jumble Sale. This contained a very nice collection of leather bookmarks. They were removed with care and gleefully sold on for fifty pence each. She really cleaned up on that one!

Sadly, a fool and his money are soon parted. No. 3 had usually spent all her holiday money at the service station before we had even got on the motorway! The absolute opposite of her big bro!

Done enough now, today's offering was a bit grim in parts. It's good to share all the ups and down though. We all have dodgy times, and we generally manage to reschedule our lives and carry on. I hope this will be the case with the scenario we are facing at the moment. Chin up all of you, stay in, keep safe, and be grateful for everything you've got. X

The Diary of an Incarcerated Granny. Day 28

Day 28! That's a month isn't it? I can't believe it's been so long. The days all seem to have rolled into one. I have to check what day it is, and I am in contact with so many people that I can't remember who I told what!

It's been 'bin day' today. One of the few highlights of the week.

I have had quite a productive morning. I managed to pay my council tax online by bank transfer, so that's sorted for twelve months. I left a voicemail at the GP surgery to reorder my prescription. I keep trying to sort out a Moonpig card for my grandson's birthday, I'm not having much success there.

I thought the response to yesterday's effort was quite enlightening! Most people have periods in their lives which are fairly awful, maybe it makes you realise that you aren't on your own?.

The hospital saga was such a very long time ago, so unless you were around at the time, you probably were unaware that it ever happened.

I'll try and dig deep, and see if I can conjure up any more 'unfortunate incidents that we could have done without'!

Here goes. Many years ago we always used to go down to London just before Christmas, do some shopping, see a show and have a girls weekend.

I remember it well, 17th December 1983 to be precise. Me, my best chum (still is surprisingly!) her daughter, No. 2 (who was five) and the daughter of another friend who was about fifteen. We went down by train and had arranged to stay with a friend of mine from college, who lived in Ealing. We had booked tickets to see *Daisy Pulls It Off* at the theatre on Saturday evening, and the following night we were going to Olympia for the last night of the Christmas horse show. All good so far!

Saturday was good, we did some shopping, I think we went to the Natural History Museum, usual stuff. We then decided to head to Knightsbridge and go to Harrods. The fifteen-year-old wanted to look in Miss Selfridge so she tottered off there, and we arranged to meet her an hour later. We went inside, got on the escalator heading up to the men's department, when a bomb went off! It was terrifying, people were screaming, chunks of plaster were flying around, there was dust and smoke everywhere and panic set in. We were still together (minus one) and we ran back down the escalator, through the food hall and out into Beauchamp Place. There was thick smoke everywhere, and we followed a taxi driver who was climbing into his cab, and we climbed in after him and he drove us away from the mayhem. Police cars, sirens, fire engines were everywhere. The bomb had been placed in a car on the corner of Hans Crescent, which was on the doorstep of Miss Selfridge! One side of the building including the men's department (where I was heading) had been blown out. The police were clearing the area, and there were hundreds of people running around like headless chickens. Remember this was a Saturday just before Christmas and incredibly busy. We were very shaken, covered in dust, but ok. The problem was, that one of our group was missing! We had heard several people had been killed and countless numbers badly injured.

This was in the day before mobile phones, so no way of making any contact. We made it back to Ealing in a state of shock.

Can you imagine ringing your friends and telling them their daughter is missing? All we could do was hope if she was ok that she would ring her parents.

We had arrived the evening before in the dark, I don't think she had a clue where we were staying, so it was all pretty disastrous. That was one of the longest days of my life (and there have been a few!) About four hours later we got a call from her parents. She was ok, very frightened, the public had been pushed further and further away from the scene. Queues were forming at telephone boxes and were constantly being moved on by the police so the chances of phoning home were slim. She was convinced we had all been killed and we were thinking the same about her. She had walked past the car containing the bomb one-and-a-half minutes before it exploded. I can't bear to think about it even now! Eventually we managed to give her mum the address of where we were staying and we arranged to meet her at Ealing Broadway station. All was well. All the theatres were closed, so we never made it to *Daisy Pulls It Off*, but the following evening we did manage to get to Olympia for the Christmas show.

Six people, three police officers and three civilians were killed that day and ninety people were injured. A dreadful day courtesy of the IRA.

My husband was a bit accident-prone! One night in December he had been to a dinner, black tie affair and came rolling home rather the worse for wear - again! He decided to stand on the terrace, smoke a cigarette, let the dog out for a wee and gaze at the stars. All good so far, what he hadn't noticed was that someone had delivered the Christmas tree, encased in a net, and left it outside. Basically, he turned round, fell over it, managed to collide with the wall of the house and hit his head on an iron bolt that was sticking out of the stone work. I was woken by someone standing by the bed, holding a tea towel to his head and blood spurting out everywhere. On further inspection it appeared that most of his forehead was hanging off and it had missed his eye by a mm.

I rang my neighbour who came round and we managed to get him into the car and down to A&E. The wound was so serious that they had to send for a maxillofacial surgeon from Barnsley Hospital to come and sew him back together. They kept him in overnight and he had fifty-six stitches in his face. I went home and surveyed the damage, a trail of blood right through the house, bloody handprints on the walls and up the staircase, very *Hammer House of Horror*!

Two days later it was the end of term carol concert, No. 2 and No. 3 were coming home for the Christmas holidays. I went with a friend to pick them up, my husband was a sight to behold, and not a good one! On 29th December we flew to Fuerteventura with a load of friends for New Year. On the second day he was carrying a mattress, fell down a flight of stone steps and broke two ribs!

He had the most amazing scar on his head, if anyone ever asked how he got it, he always said he'd had a frontal lobotomy. That usually shut them up! We always try and find a positive in a bad situation, the positive in this one was that he never had another headache for the rest of his life!

Enough doom and gloom.

Lovely day here, I'm going to drink my coffee in the sunshine in the garden now.

Stay safe everyone, x.

The Diary of an Incarcerated Granny. Day 29

A lovely day, it just makes you feel that little bit better doesn't it? Me, showered, hair washed, bedding washed, dining room table tidied up, garden poo picked, half-an-hour spent searching for the lead belonging to the nnormous George Foreman grill, I think I found it? Knackered now, coffee in the sunshine. The news from 'out there' is very depressing yet again. I do think all the doubters, trying to lay the blame on the government and anyone else they can target need to do one! This situation is dire, nobody can accurately predict the way forward... and everyone is out there doing their best. So, unless you think you know the answer, then button it!

I've thought long and hard about today's offering. The last couple of days have touched on a few scary moments, but very much part of my life.

Today, I'm going to tell you all about my best friend! When she reads this later, which I know she will, she will be groaning, quaking in her boots and secretly quite chuffed.

We met about forty-six years ago. We were invited for Sunday lunch, and I was a bit apprehensive. Some people have an aura of capability, and I was pretty sure she was one of them. What is it they say, appearances can be deceptive? Bless her, we sat down to lunch, stuffing, apple sauce on the table, out came the joint... and it turned out to be lamb! Whoops, an easy mistake, especially when your other half is a butcher! We never looked back, she ticked all my boxes.

Remembering all the things we have shared over the years is tremendous. We can be around one another, and never feel the need to utter a single word. I'm sure we have never had a cross word... although, we were once on a ferry going to Bruges when I asked what language they spoke in Belgium. She had obviously answered and I wasn't paying attention, so I asked again. She looked at me and bellowed 'Walloon' in a very angry voice! That's the only time she got cross, ever! We have spent dozens of holidays together, both with family and just us and the kids. At once stage we were approached to write a book entitled '472 meals with mince'!

We were once in France and trudging round the palace of Versailles on a very hot day. Me, eight months pregnant. Frankly we'd had enough, we escaped and slipped out and found a cafe and bought ourselves a hot chocolate. That was all we could afford between us! We were in quite a lot of trouble over that one, search parties were out in force, just in case my waters had broken and I had been rushed to hospital.

We once borrowed Auntie Edith's caravan and took the kids camping in North Yorkshire. I think it had been manufactured between the wars, and looked very much like a small Hovis loaf. You opened the door and it was a wall to wall bed. I think we all just slept in a heap and decided it wasn't one of our better ideas.

We spent weekends in Stow on the Wold for the horse fair, happy days at Chatsworth for the horse trials and The Game Fair.

We once removed ourselves from a trip to Ascot for Ladies Day. The excuse was, I had piles! Which I did, but only small ones. Really, we couldn't be faffed to get tarted up so we went to a farm auction instead and I bought a horse!

She once dragged me out to The Pony Cub AGM, it was a filthy winter's night and freezing cold and took an hour to get there. We soon discovered that we were a month too late. She owed me for that one, for ages!

She was there when my arches fell in Florence, she was with me when I bought the stupid boat, and the pony trailer that looked as though Heath Robinson had assembled it in his lunch hour.

We were in Brighton when I had my first Big Mac, in Harrods when the bomb went off. At her daughter's wedding, when I accidentally overdosed on champagne! An incident I have never been allowed to forget.

We were on holiday in Devon, minding our own business, when a concerned passer-by asked if we had realised that the two youngest were playing in a sewage outlet! Who knew?

She was the first person to visit me when No. 3 was born. She wandered into the hospital, (a private birth experience, after all the hassle with No. 2) gave the sprog in the box a quick glance, gave me a copy of *Homes and Gardens* and proceeded to tell me that it had all worked out pretty well. Twenty-four hours earlier and she would have been born in a caravan in Appletreewick!

We were at the top of the big wheel at the fair when her car keys fell out of her pocket, we never found them!

She was at my wedding (still have the Le Creuset dish) She was there when my mother-in-law passed away on the terrace. I was there when her dog was run over by a Ferrari. Together we have survived births, deaths, marriages, divorces, some hilarious times and some pretty desperate ones.

One of her party tricks is falling down stairs, and she has made quite a career out of it. The last one resulted in a broken shoulder and a double fracture of her wrist! Attention seeking, I call it!

I don't think either of us would have ever been nominated for the 'mother of the year' awards... but we always did our best.

I am a sensitive soul, she hides it well! One of the few times I have seen her cry was at the film *The Way We Were*! I was astonished, I thought it was pretty cheesy to be honest. It has been my good fortune to have someone around that has always had my back. For all the snippets you have read today, there are a million more.

We are going through some scary times at the moment and it's a time to reflect on the good things in our lives.

British stiff upper lip, often makes us uncomfortable to say what we really feel. Well, I think some things need saying.

Thanks for always being there for me, you have dragged me through some horrible times and I love you! Not in a pervy way obvs.

I assume she'll realise who I'm talking about?

Helen Keller said, 'I would rather walk with a friend in the dark, than alone in the light' and I agree with her.

We are having a family competition. There is a group called 'Recreate art works, with things you find at home'. This is my son-in-law having a stab at being Henry VIII. The naan bread on his head is a particularly clever idea.

Take care everyone. X

Best Friends. Joan and Me

King Henry VIII of England and David Cook

The Diary of an Incarcerated Granny. Day 30

Lovely day in Tickhill-land. Ducks and ducklings every-where. Some nowhere near the Mill Dam! This is all so far removed from what is happening out in the big wide world. Very hard to comprehend.

Did a bit of gardening, watered some pots and removed a couple of dandelions. My BF always says, that a weed is just a flower growing in the wrong place. I am very much inclined to agree. Titchmarsh and Sons swept by yesterday. They came in through the side gate, the cheque was left in an envelope sellotaped to the dustbin, so no social distancing rules were broken and the lawn was mowed. Granted some of the stripes were a bit wiggly, but who's complaining?

The Baskervilles are enjoying sunbathing today.

Roald Dahl wrote a lot of books for both adults and children (big favourites of No. 2 Jnr).

I was just wondering what to do about my lunch, when I thought I might write an update on *James and the Giant Peach*. Here goes.

'Granny and the Giant Quiche'.

My lovely son-in-law, you know the one? He who is a dead ringer for Henry Vlll, has his own Wikipedia page, and has been known to wear a lime green tankini on the odd occasion... that one!

For his sins, he is the only one of the four who live anywhere near me. So his fate was settled before the ink had even dried on his marriage certificate! Because of the present situation, he is designated (or coerced by No. 3?) to take care of the shopping needs of the incarcerated granny. I message them a list, he heads for the shops and delivers later in the day, bags left on the steps inside the front gate, all rules adhered to. Last week, I had a hankering (nice word, don't often get those) for a cheese and onion quiche. Never a Quiche Lorraine, as I'm always a bit doubtful about the provenance of the bacon bits! Anyway, the shopping arrived, and in one of the bags was a very large cardboard box. Inside the box was a cheese and onion quiche the size of a dustbin lid! Seriously, this was of catering-sized proportions. If it had been served at 'The Last Supper' with a side salad and a jacket potato, it would have done them all proud, and with enough left over for a picnic lunch the following day, wherever they were heading! This was a quiche that almost filled one of the drawers in my freezer.

This was no ordinary quiche, this had been baked by an artisan. The parsley on the top had been sprinkled with love, the pastry was crisp and delicious and you couldn't fault it, a joy to behold in quiche circles. The sensible person would have cut it into portions and frozen them. Why did I never think of that? The first night I heated it up in the oven and had it with new potatoes and salad. Very nice it was too. Day two, I warmed it up in the microwave and ate it with some beans. Day three, I had it for lunch cold with some potato salad and beetroot. Day four, (I'm struggling to look upon it with any affection by this time) I cut the crust off and ate a middle bit. Day five (today) I binned the lot! There was still enough left for The Famous Five to have had it for lunch, along with a hard-boiled egg and lashings of ginger beer!

The moral of this story is, always divide food into portions and freeze the spare ones for another time. Try and convey to your son-in-law that this is lockdown, you are not having a Tupperware party for twelve and providing them with supper! You are at home... alone. Apart from yet another missing Greek yoghurt (he found it in the boot of the car when he got home.) He has been fantastic, and I couldn't have done without him. He was hand-picked for his even temperament, sunny nature, fabulous sense of humour and his ability to live in total harmony with No. 3, who can be very bossy! We also love the colour of his hair, which has been described as 'Moroccan sunset'. Total winner!

What a list of credentials eh!

I am anxious to see the rest of the 'Recreate art works' attempts. I think I know even now who will have a go and who won't. On New Year's Eve, my portrayal of 'Grotbags' achieved international acclaim, so they have a very hard act to follow. I suppose if push came to shove I could have a go at *Whistler's Mother*? She doesn't look much fun though!

This has been one of my 'thinking days', very useful for giving yourself an excuse for just doing the basics. I think I know full well that another three weeks is on the cards so there isn't much rush, is there?

Stay in, Be safe x

The Diary of an Incarcerated Granny. Day 31

It's 3pm and I've only just put finger to iPhone! Not very sure where this morning has gone, I certainly haven't done anything of any consequence.

I woke up quite early, and came down the stairs of doom just before seven. Coffee made, dogs out, TV on. I then woke up on the sofa at 10.15! What's all that about? There is always someone out there that makes you feel better by saying, 'you must have needed it'!

Life has taken on an air of jubilance since the Hobbit House became a quiche-free zone. I am no longer hesitating when I open the fridge, although I do seem to have accumulated a bit of a bacon mountain.

No. 3 is rather a good cook, as are they all to be fair. A Lister child will never be late and will never starve! Last night involved No. 3 sending a lot of photos on messenger, highlighting the manufacture of the individual beef Wellingtons, fresh asparagus and Hasselback potatoes, with a red wine and blackberry jus, closely followed by a raspberry and strawberry pavlova! That was cruel and uncalled for and looked bloody delicious. I soldiered forth with my mound of bacon sandwiches and delicious banana, and sent her a message telling her to 'Sod Off'!

No. 2 is heavily involved in a cabinet reshuffle.

No. 2 Jnr has been promoted to one of the big bedrooms. This is centred around a king-size French bed with Bergère panels (bought from a family member when they emptied their French villa in order to sell it last year) and brought back to the UK along with some other very pretty French furniture. No. 2 is a bit of a bargain hunter and wouldn't thank you for a Billy bookcase from Ikea. How much involvement No. 2 Jnr will have in the finished result is anyone's guess, but I can guarantee it will be pretty special. Dressing tables, mirrors, chests of drawers are all being relocated and rearranged. Annie Sloane chalk paint is at the ready to tone in with the Farrow and Ball walls. This is all going to happen over the next few days apparently! From the photos that were sent this morning the place looks as though it has been burgled and ransacked.

Piles of stuff for the attic, for the charity shop and the bin are piled up everywhere. The dishwasher is on the blink again, so the kitchen has looked better. No. 1 would not be happy!

My only comment was, 'while he's at it could you put a mirror in the downstairs loo, and a bolt on the big bathroom door?' I somehow don't think that went down that well! My theory is, if you have decided to get your toolbox out, you should attend to as many things as you possibly can, before the novelty wears off!

That's enough of domestic bliss!

When the 'tall man' and the Lister sisters 1, 2 and 3 had all left university and gone out to conquer the world, we decided it was our turn. Having spent huge amounts of time in France over the years, we thought it was time we branched out.

We booked our first holiday with a travel company called Page and Moy entitled 'Cape Cod and the White Mountains'. What a joy it was. New England in the fall, and all that jazz! We started off in Provincetown and went whale watching. Fabulous, apart from the fact that on that particular day the whales had obviously been double booked and were on another gig further up the coast. Easily done!

Undaunted, we set off the following day on a journey along the Kancamagus Highway, this runs from Lincoln to Conway and passes through the White Mountain forest. Beautiful scenery and absolute 'Moose Country'. Every 100 yards or so was a sign with a picture of a moose on it. Our tour guide was 100% sure that a moose would appear around every corner and was getting quite excited. We, who had suffered the day of the absent whales were less convinced, and how right we were! Not a sign, not even a pile of moose poo on the road to indicate one had passed that way in the last six months The tour guide whipped out a hat with moose antlers on, stuck it on her head and turned to face the open road. We felt that this had happened on many other occasions.

We chummed up with a lady travelling on her own called Mavis. If you have ever watched *Shirley Valentine* it was a bit like that in reverse. Shall we say to be totally accurate, that Mavis chummed up with us! Mavis loved us, no beating about the bush, had a *ménage à trois* been on the cards, one felt she would happily have made up the numbers! Don't get me wrong, she was lovely, but we didn't feel the need to occupy her every waking hour. We moved between a succession of very good hotels. Some days you could decide in the morning which trip you wanted to take. Seeing as Mavis leapt out from behind the potted plants most mornings, therefore joining us for breakfast, we wised up to this! First question of the day was 'and where are you going today, Mavis?'

Wherever she had decided, we chose the opposite! Hence our visit to Ben and Jerry's ice cream factory. The home of the original Cherry Garcia. It was fab, we thoroughly enjoyed and really it was all down to Mavis!

We went to Newport, Rhode Island, stuffed ourselves with lobster and champagne, visited the Church of St Mary's where JFK and Jackie were married, spent the afternoon in Martha's Vineyard.

We saw the 'covered bridges' (not of Madison County but similar) in Vermont, and even went to Morse Farm in Montpelier to see how they harvested maple syrup. We went up the mountain in a ski lift, to see where the world downhill ski championships had been held.

New England was a delight, villages of clapperboard houses and wooden churches with pointy spires, white picket fences, straight out of *Ann of Green Gables*. So far removed from the hustle and bustle of New York. (that's another story.) The final days were spent in Boston. We have friends who live in Concord and Pam is a district attorney in Boston. They had visited us in England about three months before and we must have mentioned we were planning this trip later in the year. We pulled into the carpark outside Quincy Market in the centre of Boston, and there they were! They had taken a day from work to meet us and show us the sights. What a day that was, marvellous lunch, off the tourist trail in a very swish restaurant. A ride on the famous swan boats in the park, a walk up Beacon Hill, the statue of Paul Revere and a lovely wander round the famous Quincy Market. The following day we flew home from Boston, we had such a good time, and that became the first of many trips all over the world.

Mavis was obviously sad to lose us, but on our occasional forays without her, she had met up with a very nice couple from Wigan. They ticked all her boxes and vice versa. A good time was had by all.

Phew, that was an epic instalment. The dogs are wanting their dinner and I am swamped with memories.

Keep on doing whatever it is you do in these strange times. X

The Diary of an Incarcerated Granny. Day 32

Raining! My funky 'Prue Leith' red specs fell off my head into the dogs water bowl... twice! I have found that since being incarcerated I do swear much more... Do you? Two crumpets for brunch and the obligatory banana. My mother always said you could go to war on a banana! At this moment in time, I'd be happy to go anywhere.

Bit of excitement in West Sussex, the new (old) dressing table, mirror and stool had just been delivered. The spouse of No. 2 was conscientiously washing it down, with a bucket full of hot soapy.

No. 2 Jnr. When asked if she thought the new bedroom was looking good, was heard to remark that it could do with a bit more pink! She's four, so I suppose she has a point!

Just had a long conversation with No. 1, she is struggling to come up with anything for the 'Recreate art works' competition tomorrow. To be honest, No. 3's vision of Henry VIII will take some beating, and apparently there is more to come!

I think I have brain numbness today! My creative juices are not flowing in the slightest... help!

I have just signed a petition to award Captain Tom with a knighthood. I do feel that he is somewhat more deserving than all those Z-list celebrities that keep popping up in the New Year Honours list. After seeing him interviewed the other morning I tried to get onto the JustGiving site to make a donation. I eventually managed it two days later, think the site kept crashing due to unprecedented demand.

I normally wear a watch, but for some reason at eight pm last Thursday I wasn't! So I missed the clapping bit. I wonder how long that will continue, or if it will start to fizzle out, as most things do eventually?

I am generally quite hot in bed! Temperature-wise of course, (the alternative is a very distant memory!) and I remembered that last summer I had bought a one tog duvet and never got round to using it. What a revelation, I hunted it out and had one of the best night's sleep I've had in ages! Poppy has no complaints either.

I have a bit of a 'thing' about bedding, and I do tend to buy quite a lot. Since No. 2 married Mr No. 2 there has been an enormous upsurge in the purchase of Egyptian cotton!

It appears that Mr No. 2 cannot slumber with any success if there is a hint of polyester incorporated in the weave of his bedding! Who knew? I had always trotted off to M&S and

Dunelm and bought whatever I liked the look of. When Laura Ashley jumped on the bandwagon, there was no stopping her. I never read the small print on the packaging and I certainly never discussed the breathability of different thread counts with my peers. How wrong I was! When you look back at the seriously awful bedding you liked back in the day, it makes you cringe - well it does me, anyway!

No. 2 is the world's leading authority on Egyptian cotton bedding. We can while away many a happy hour, waiting with bated breath for The White Company sale to be announced, or some tasty bargains to be had on the Brand Alley site. The pros and cons of 'Housewife' and 'Oxford' pillowcases are a subject in themselves and a mattress protector that isn't 100% cotton would not pass muster. Nowadays, 'white' seems to tick all the boxes as far as No. 2 is concerned. A hint of the palest pink on the border of the Oxford pillowcase might just make the grade, but it has to be pale, and this only makes an appearance in the bed chamber of No. 2 Jnr. Nowhere else!

How different thing we're back in the day.

I recall with great fondness the flannelette candy-striped sheets in winter, the top sheet, the layers of wool blankets, the bedspread and then the eiderdown. It took a while for anyone to realise that if the eiderdown had been a bit bigger, we could dispense with everything else.

My first experience of a 'continental quilt' was in Italy, on a school trip in 1964. What an eye opener, they were hung out of the windows to air during the day and that was it. A bottom sheet, a bolster and the job was a good'un!

It took a lot of years before they were renamed 'duvets' and eventually became acceptable to the masses.

Let's talk towels! The bigger, the thicker the better. I still have some that the girls had at school, complete with name tapes (one at each end and a hanging loop in the centre of the long side), No. 3 left school in 1996, and they are still going strong. I am a bit of a fan of Hamman towels, perfect for holidays, the beach and little trips into the unknown. Very absorbent and they dry really quickly. I have lots.

I don't think I have ever written such a load of drivel. I know its crap... just couldn't get my act together today.

I'm having meatballs for supper. So I'm going on a secret date with Lloyd Grossman to learn how to make the sauce!

Stay home, check your linen cupboard and clap on Thursday. I'm off to meet Lloyd. X

The Diary of an Incarcerated Granny. Day 33

Sunny day in Paradise, with just a hint of a breeze. Reminds me of Mrs Cropley in *The Vicar of Dibley*... when she produced a cake at one of the meetings, they asked her what sort it was. 'Chocolate with a hint of liver' was the reply!

I discovered yesterday evening that I don't know how to spell flannelette!

The shame!

People out there are working hard to reduce the carbon footprint, I am working equally as hard trying to reduce the bacon mountain! In fact I am starting to get 'giant quiche' flashbacks whenever I open the fridge. Shopping list day tomorrow... there are two items that definitely won't be going on the list.

I was/am and will continue to be an 'only one'! I have no complaints whatsoever. What you don't have, you don't miss, and I think that is absolutely true. My late husband was an only child as well... how we ended up with such a brood still baffles me! A family weekend can easily rustle up eighteen of us... and is the best time ever. Crumbsnatchers ranging from two to twenty-two are all thrown into the mix and everybody does their bit.

I am hoping and praying that we will be let out before October. I am having a significant birthday and many secret phone calls are in the pipeline, (all orchestrated by No. 1), for three nights in a country house, indoor pool, games room etc all are required to attend... and I apparently don't have to do anything, apart from show up. Sounds like a plan! We will have had three significant family birthdays this year. My daughter-in-law reached the big fifty in March. No. 3 will be paying homage to the big forty in September, and yours truly, hitting the ground running towards the big seventy in October. I was saying this morning to Number 2, that we may just manage it... who knows. All their holiday plans have been put on hold, and my trip to Chester Zoo may never happen!

I have a 'bad back', what a dreadful phrase! I won't go into the whys and wherefores, but a lot of walking is out of the question. A trip to Chester last year with a friend, resulted in me hiring a mobility scooter for the day. Said friend has been blackmailing me for a year and threatening to make the photos public!

I've said it now, I've told the world... I am probably feeling the huge surge of relief that Phillip Schofield felt when he came out on *This Morning*.

Accompanying friend was wired up to one of those things that tells you how many steps you have walked. We calculated about six miles all together. My back would have seized up after a mile, so I did exactly the right thing. The scooter was amazing... you could make it go quite fast on a clear stretch of path. I almost squashed a small child, but I do feel if we are apportioning blame it was probably fifty/fifty. His mother seemed to think it was all his fault and gave him a clout for not looking where he was going! There was also the very forgiving couple that I kneecapped outside the chimpanzee enclosure. It was an easy mistake and I think they would only have suffered superficial bruising. They took it on the chin, or if we are being very specific, on the shin, they were almost apologetic! Honestly, if you ever get a chance, hire one. Don't feel shame or embarrassment, it's just like driving a bumper car, but on the open road! I think I know how Toad felt in *The Wind in the Willows* when he fell in love with a motor car.

Talking of cars, mine is sitting outside, costing me an arm and a leg every month, and it is not even making me smile! Am I supposed to go out and start it up, or take it for a little road trip... or just leave it and hope the battery doesn't go flat? Not sure about that. I am doing random subjects today because it's Sunday. *The Archers* was reduced by fifteen minutes, the ketchup is still holding the tap up, and I could kill for a Coke Zero.

I am outside now soaking up the rays, just had a pic from No. 2 resplendent in a bikini. I haven't gone that far and I doubt that I ever will again! The big knicker is alive and well and living in Granny-land!

I feel that this is now the time to introduce you all, to the interesting life you may have in store if you ever have a stairlift installed.

A couple of years after we came back from France, things were starting to go downhill pretty quickly. We decided that it was high time to install a stairlift, or make some serious changes downstairs.

James was rushed into hospital on the Wednesday night. The following morning they came and fitted the stairlift. A week later still in hospital and things were desperate

He was extremely ill, had a gangrenous foot, sepsis, and pneumonia. We had the 'family round the bedside' meeting, and it seemed there were no options available. He needed his leg amputating, but his heart condition was so severe he would be unable to cope with the anaesthetic.

He was eventually sent to a local nursing home on an end of life plan!

They were marvellous, the treatment was incredible and can you believe it, eighteen months later he came back home to live. He was not the easiest of inmates and they had their work cut out believe me! (Thanks Mo and Co, you were the best!)

I think he was the only person ever to leave the place in a vertical position!

For the six months before he came back full-time, I collected him every day after lunch, brought him home, cooked his supper and then took him back every evening for nine o'clock. Everybody said I couldn't manage full-time, but I was determined to at least give it a try. The week before he came back home to live, I took the girls to Venice and we had a fabulous few days. I think they call it the lull before the storm! Luckily we had the stairlift in place (gathering dust for eighteen months) we had bath lifts, Zimmer frames, wheelchairs and every contraption known to man. Someone came to dress his foot twice a week, and beyond that I did it myself. Hence the bad back!

He had an all-singing all-dancing chair that fully reclined and also brought him up to a standing position. One night he was going up on the stairlift when the seat snapped off, face planting him full stretch on the second flight of stairs. He couldn't move, and I couldn't move him. Dialled 999... the paramedics arrived and eventually managed to manhandle him back downstairs and into his chair.

He had to sleep in the chair for four nights until a new seat was fitted. What a bloody performance. In his favour, he never ever complained, and somewhere in there, even with vascular dementia, he could still raise a smile. What a guy!

I told you today was random! Keep safe, bin day on Tuesday. Hurrah!

James Lister delivering a speech at one of his daughter's weddings. Looks like the punchline of one of his infamous jokes. Probably.

Shopping delivery today, and bin collection tomorrow. My cup runneth over!

I have spent virtually all morning ringing people. After the sixth call you realise that you are saying exactly the same thing to everyone! Poppy has had a Houdini moment. She had managed to get through the gate at the bottom of the garden, to the riverbank, where the ducks are. She then pushed her way through a hedge and ended up in next doors garden! Very naughty. I've had to do a bit of barricading with upturned water butts and the odd log. Starting to look a bit like Steptoe's yard down there.

I have come to the conclusion that I am coping slightly better than some! Familywise there are a few that are tearing their hair out. Teenage meltdowns, four-year-old mega tantrums, and terrible twos, starting to strop over nothing! We've all been there, so get a grip, and pick your battles!

Looking back I can't ever remember having a row with my parents. It wasn't in the manifesto. My mother would have knocked me into the middle of next week if I had ever answered her back... so I never even dipped my toe in the water! Nowadays the little blighters have a direct connection to Childline if you so much as give them a sideways glance. How the world has changed. My prep school, had the cane. I doubt it was ever used, but it was a wonderful deterrent. If anyone was caught telling lies, they were marched to the cloakroom to wash out their mouths with liquid soap. It sounds quite barbaric in this day and age... but life is a pathway of choices, and there are always consequences if you go down the wrong path.

I went to an all-girls Grammar School, and I really liked it. It was pretty strict, but you knew exactly where you were. If you were seen in town not wearing your hat you were reported, and you got a detention. Your choice! I think things were far more black and white then, too many grey areas nowadays. They say that eventually everything goes full circle, so bring it on!

I wonder when all this comes to a close, if we will start to adopt a more frugal lifestyle? I think we may realise that we really don't need tons of stuff. The decluttering lockdown will have changed the way of thinking for a lot of people. So many people structured their lives based on the acquisition of 'things'! The mantra was, 'Happiness is just another purchase away!' If this last five weeks has taught us anything at all, it's that is a load of cobblers!

We want to see our friends and our families and spend time with them. If we live in a mansion or a hovel, those feelings still ring true. The human race was not designed for solitary confinement, so the sooner we get back to normal the better.

My shopping has just been delivered, I'm going to indulge myself with the biggest bowlful of Greek yoghurt, granola, blueberries and strawberries you have ever seen! Probably followed by a Diet Coke and a granny nap. Sorry today's is a bit short, I've actually been a little bit busy!

Keep safe x

Day thirty-five! How can this possibly be? Nice day again, I have just dropped a full bag of granola all over the kitchen floor. I am assuming birds like granola?

Usual FaceTimeing and the odd phone call and emptying of dishwasher. Having dealt with the giant quiche and making satisfactory progress with the bacon mountain... I now seem to be the proud owner of a banana plantation! Eleven at the last count!

The most marvellous news filtered through the Tickhill website yesterday. The highly acclaimed Tickhill Chippy reopened last night. I think it's telephone ordering only and social distancing when collecting, but hey, that's a step in the right direction. I haven't had a chip for five weeks!

Had a little chat with No. 2 Jnr earlier. She was balanced rather precariously on a stool at the kitchen island, dressed as Rapunzel and eating Rice Krispies whilst wearing a very fetching straw hat. She did tell me that she had decided to wear her vest, as her Rapunzel dress was a bit scratchy! It made sense to me. I have the same problem with most of my dressing up clothes, especially my Elsa from Frozen outfit!

Every conversation with my friends seems to include a discussion about the hairdresser. It will be so interesting to see what people's natural hair colour really is! I am very lucky, my hair has made its own arrangements and produced (all by itself) a most acceptable shade of platinum blonde. So other than the occasional chop, it's very easy to live with.

I have a very good friend who went to the hairdresser always twice, sometimes three times a week! Until this latest debacle, I don't think she had washed her own hair for at least fifty years. You can imagine the turmoil she is experiencing. Apparently in Australia, the hairdressing industry is still up and running. I would have thought washing and cutting hair, whilst social distancing must be awkward to say the least... unless you have exceedingly long arms?

Going back to my fiftieth birthday; (nearly twenty years ago, when fish and chips were still wrapped in newspaper, and Heinz Tomato Ketchup came in glass bottles.) I had a party at our cottage in France, lots of people flew out and we managed to find beds for everyone and we had a hilarious time. The evening of my birthday we booked a table at an hotel in Montignac. We used this place quite a lot, and the food was good. Madame was a sweetheart, always flustered, a fan of a very eclectic mix of garments. Velvet plus fours, the odd length of curtaining draped artfully over her shoulder, or tied in a rakish fashion around her waist. Velvet slippers with curved pointy toes, dozens of brooches and bracelets, she was a star. Somehow or other she always managed to pull the look together. She was so 'French chic' it oozed from every pore. Basically, she would have looked good in a bin liner. The hotel was shabby chic, huge emphasis on the shabby, but again it worked beautifully. Nothing matched, there were bare wires hanging from the ceilings, the odd table leg propped up with a glass paperweight. If you can imagine eating dinner in a warehouse for architectural antiques you would be very close. The food was fabulous and she had even made me a birthday gateau as a surprise. A charming person! We always described her as an out-of-work principal boy!

About eight weeks later, James and I decided to have a few days in Toronto. Ten days before Christmas, -8 degrees, and dare I say it, 'absolutely fabulous'. All the Christmas lights were white, skating rinks in the squares, it was beautiful. Yong street, the longest street in the world, the biggest book shop on the planet, wonderful restaurants, and an expedition right to the top of the CN Tower with the world famous glass floor! 553 metres of scariness, followed by lunch in the revolving restaurant.

That was an interesting one, James didn't do heights and once had a very dodgy half an hour trying to navigate Filey Brigg! He coped pretty well, but the glass floor was a step too far!

We had a day and a night at Niagara Falls. The falls were of course spectacular, the town was a dump! Just as one would imagine a very run-down English seaside town

A big disappointment, we went to the Hershey shop and bought a load of chocolate to bring home. Never eaten such disgusting stuff in my life. We went to a burger restaurant called Wendy's. That was naff as well! A Wimpy bar under a different name, that particular smell of grease is still with me! I once lived in a shared flat, where all the crockery and cutlery had been nicked from Wimpy bars! Not by me, I hasten to add, when I grew up I became a magistrate!

We were delighted to get back to Toronto for the final day and do some Christmas shopping and have a farewell dinner. He who didn't like heights bought me a new watch as a belated fiftieth present, it's still going strong, unlike him sadly!

Would I go to Toronto again? In a flash, we loved it. Niagara Falls? No rush there!

Keep going folks, be like Captain Tom!

The Diary of an Incarcerated Granny. Day 36

'The sun is out, the sky is blue, there's nothing there to spoil the view... but it's raining, raining in my heart!' Who the hell wrote that? Miserable sods!

I now have a glut of Greek yoghurt, in view of the fact I dropped all the granola all over the kitchen floor. I know in the scheme of things it's a 'First World problem', but it rankles nevertheless! When discussing with a friend last night my surfeit of bananas, she commented, 'you could always make a banana loaf'. My reply was 'I could, and I could also run naked through Clumber Park by moonlight!'

'I have pigeons nesting in my conifer!' A dinner party conversation starter for ten, if ever there was one? On the subject of pigeons, have you ever seen a baby one? I haven't! I think they must hatch and dispatch in the space of a couple of days!

The French aristocracy loved a good pigeon pie. There are very few chateaux or manoirs that don't have a pigeonnier in the grounds. Always a guaranteed source of meat through the winter, or when you were under siege.

During the Spring of 1987 we decided to buy a little bolt hole in the Dordogne. We saw an advert in *The Lady* magazine and contacted the vendors. They lived in East Sussex and were selling a cottage and a barn. They suggested we went over to take a look, as there was a lot of interest! (as if!)

I was in the middle of my magistrates training, so I couldn't go. James went, picked up his cousin David in Gerrard's Cross, and armed with a video camera they set off to view! It took them thirteen hours to get there, as directions were sketchy to say the least. Arriving in the dark, they weren't exactly enamoured by what was on offer! The next morning the sun was shining and big plus was that the properties were in a tiny hamlet with its own little chateau, lovely golden stone (very Cotswold-esque) buildings, and a total step back in time. The guy who was selling was an architect and had done the biggest bodge job you have ever seen. He was no more an architect, than I am Audrey Hepburn's financial advisor, I'm sure you get the drift!

Anyway, the barn was soon dismissed as a money pit, but the cottage, although in a bit of a state, had distinct possibilities.

Much negotiating over the phone and a price was agreed.

Fast-forward to half term week in October, of we went *en famille* to do the deed! This was the week after the dreadful storms when Michael Fish got it wrong. We drove through a path of destruction in Brighton and on to Newhaven to get the ferry. Landed in Dieppe and headed down towards the promised land. We were in a seven-seater Shogun with a seriously overloaded trailer hitched on the back. We also had an empty Thornton's Continental box containing £10,000 in cash! Those were the days! We made it down in eleven hours without a wrong turn. We dumped the stuff and went out in search of a restaurant. We found a restaurant, had a very welcome meal, and then got spectacularly lost on the way back! Think rural France, pitch black, it took us two hours to find our way back to the cottage.

James kept saying, 'if you're not sure, we'll pack up and go.'

We didn't! The following day 'architect of the year' and his other half turned up. They had been hiding in the barn, and swapping all the half decent bits round, so we got all the rubbish.

In France the *notaire* does all the legal stuff, acting for both parties. In those days, half way through the transaction the *notaire* would leave the office for five minutes. That was when you handed over the 'under the table' cash! And only declared the other amount for tax purposes! All legal and above board, except that it wasn't!

It was ours, and there was no going back and it turned out to be one of the best things we ever did. There was a patio where we could eat out, a pergola with a grapevine, a big garden with walnut and fig trees. We turned an attached pig-sty into a bedroom, we put in a great big wood-burning stove in the massive inglenook fireplace We hung a rope from the beam over the staircase, to hang on to so we didn't break our necks! We bought a sofa bed so that we could sleep eight if push came to shove We really made it a home from home, in a rather rustic way.

We went over for two weeks every Easter, a month every summer and every October half term. We let it when we weren't there, so it covered its costs. Everybody and their grandmothers came to stay, either with us or with their friends and families. Some of our friends liked it so much, they bought their own properties nearby, which made it even more fun if we were all there at the same time.

When we sold the business and retired, we decided to move to France full-time. We found the dream 'big house' and decided to sell the cottage. Big mistake! After four years, health issues were causing great concern and we sold up and came back to live in the UK.

How I wish I still had The Little Cottage, a huge part of our lives for so many years, and the provider of so many happy memories. It makes me sad to think we let it go.

I have just searched high and low for some photos of the cottage, found a couple, so here it is!

Keep safe! X.

The Little Cottage, Marsingeas.

The Diary of an Incarcerated Granny. Day 37

I've decided to restructure my day, by getting the diary done as early as possible. Thus giving me the rest of the day to do 'not a lot'!

You will be delighted to know that I am motoring down the bananas in a very structured manner. Fried bananas with bacon… who would have thought of that combination, unless you were desperate?

Try it, you may well be surprised!

Had a bit of an issue with the dust buster last night. I have apparently been busting a lot of dust in the last week or so and I could see that the collection chamber was almost full. Could I work out how to empty the damn thing, could I thump! Why is it that I am so rubbish at certain things these days? Years ago, when we had a couple of student houses in Sheffield, I could assemble an Ikea Billy bookcase in about thirty seconds from scratch! Have I lost my spatial awareness, I wonder? I am still hunting for the dust buster instructions. I sincerely hope they didn't go the same way as the attachments or I am lost!

I have a few favourite places on the planet, the main one is of course the Hobbit House, perfect for me in so many ways. Home is where the heart is, it's a testimony to the life you have lived, it contains all the items that make your memory bank work overtime, and most of all, it houses your knicker drawer!

Someone once asked me if I had to do the same thing every day for the rest of my life… what would it be?

I doubt I would ever get bored doing this, I am a people-watcher, and no two days would ever be the same!

The number 1 waterbus in Venice and the journey up and down the Grand Canal. I have been captivated by Venice from my first visit when I was fourteen. I have probably been close to a dozen times over the years. It is the most beautiful city in the world, and it holds my heart! I have been with James (just us two), with family, with friends and it never fails to delight.

The joy of getting up really early and wandering into St Mark's Square, when the sun is just coming up, when the Venetians are preparing for the day ahead, and before the hordes of tourists arrive... is priceless.

A late night trip down the Grand Canal in the dark, when you can see through the windows, the chandeliers glowing and a sense that you have stepped back in time.

I have found the perfect hotel, four doors down from the Danielli (and a quarter of the price!) three minutes' walk from St Mark's and the Doge's Palace and in the same run of buildings as Vivaldi's Church, where he was choir master!

You would struggle to ever get lost in Venice, all signs lead to San Marco or Rialto and it is a place to amble freely. Our little hotel has a tiny roof terrace looking out over the lagoon, and is the most perfect place to watch the world go by. I wonder if Venice, which relies so heavily on tourism, will survive and manage to reinvent itself when this world gets back to normal?

My late mother-in-law was an intrepid traveller. You could almost say that if she hadn't been, it wasn't worth a visit!

She once said that when the doors open on the plane, you stand at the top of the steps, and 'you can smell Africa'. I know what she meant!

We were lucky enough to travel to Kenya in 2004. We flew to Mombasa. I remember the pilot coming on the loud speaker, and saying 'ladies and gentlemen, if you look out to the left, we are just about to fly over Mount Kilimanjaro.' For some reason I thought that was marvellous. We stayed at an Hotel called Hemingway's in Watamu which was amazing. We also went on a four-day safari and did the 'Out of Africa' bit staying in game lodges in the Tsavo national parks. We went with a couple of friends, had our own personal jeep and driver and saw everything there was to see! That was a holiday of a lifetime and one I will never forget... and she was right, you can smell Africa!

Barbados, St James's beach, West Coast.

Pina colada... what's not to like? 'Beam me up Scotty!'

That was a good trip down memory lane, close your eyes and you can take yourself anywhere. So when you are finding all this hard, do just that!

Another little trick of mine in the middle of a sleepless night, is to recast *The Archers*, using people I know! Guaranteed hours of fun!

Still trying to avoid the news as much as possible... I do not wish to be depressed. I'm doing as I'm told so I can't alter what is going out there!

Having a FaceTime with No. 2 this morning and a chat with No. 2 Jnr, who has just discovered jokes! 'Granny, why did the chicken cross the road?'

I came up with a few guesses, all wrong of course! The answer, with much rolling around and guffawing was, 'because it had a caterpillar in its armpit!'

Out of the mouths...

I am now going to contemplate lunch, no bananas will be involved thank goodness. or bacon for that matter.

I hope you are all staying positive, if this carries on much longer we will all be domestically institutionalised, so we won't want to go out anyway. Perish the thought!

Keep safe.

The Diary of an Incarcerated Granny. Day 38

Rumour has it that it's Friday... again! The weeks seem to be whizzing by at an alarming rate.

It's eleven am now, I got up just before eight, made coffee, sat on the sofa and fell asleep again? My body clock has freaked out. I rarely go to bed before one am... I then read for at least an hour. Usually I wake up at about four am, still propped up on three pillows, with my specs welded into my face. I then adjust my collection of pillows, (I have five, all with very differing attributes!) and eventually I turn the light off.

Sometimes I go back to sleep, and sometimes I don't. Life it seems is a lottery, even if you don't buy a ticket!

It's a lovely sunny day, for which I am grateful, I always open the French doors in the kitchen as soon as I come down in the morning. This allows The Baskervilles to structure their day as they think fit. Violet-Elizabeth sunbathes mostly. Poppy requires me to throw the ball down the garden, rather a lot. She retrieves rather nicely for a Shih-Tzu. Violet doesn't do balls!

When I was in my early twenties, I had a wish list. It consisted of two things... a cottage with beams and a Gordon Setter!

How lucky was, the acquisition of a husband and four children seemed to have evolved later... they were never on the original list! In the last forty-four years I have moved eight times. Some amazing houses, and quite a lot with beams! Where else are you supposed to display your Christmas cards?

Gordon Setters, we had four over the years, and what a joy they were. Still my absolute favourite breed.

How we ever ended up with two Shih-Tzu I still find a bit

confusing. They are stubborn, quite difficult to house train (in Poppy's case!) they get on your chair the second you get off it. Basically if they had two fingers, they would stick them up at you! However, they are loving and affectionate, prone to 'bum crumbs', slightly fussy eaters, have a tendency to yap (mine don't!) and I wouldn't be without them.

Reminds me of a joke!

If you shut your wife and your dog in the boot of your car for the afternoon, when you let them out, your dog would be overjoyed to see you!

Question, what are you supposed to do about your car whilst all this hoo-ha is going on? I had a new car in December, it has done approx. 600 miles (one careful lady owner!) and it hasn't been anywhere for nearly six weeks! Am I supposed to go out and start it up? Should I take it for a drive? Will the battery go flat if it just sits there? it's costing me £300 a month for the pleasure! Millions of other folk in the same boat I know, and a first world problem. Shut up, Granny!

Just had a cheese (mature cheddar) and tomato sandwich and guess what? ...an apple! Gotcha!

Not a huge fan of tomatoes... they add a pop of colour to the proceedings, but generally they are a bit uninspiring. However, I have encountered three tomato experiences that were worthy of mention.

1) a friend who had a villa in Fuerteventura grew the most delicious tomatoes.

2) Afternoon tea at Hemingway's in Kenya, their tiny tomato sandwiches were to die for. Just tomato, nothing else!

3) Lunchtime buffet on the Sonesta St George 1 on the Nile. I think I ate my body weight in tomatoes every day!

The River Nile and all who sail on her!

The year after we moved back to England we decided a little trip would be good.

James was wheelchair-bound, but most of his other issues were more or less under control. I had never had any inclination to go on a cruise. Far too many people, a plethora of organised fun, and all in the confines of an enormous tin can, on the ocean waves! Not for me (no offence to you professional cruisers out there) just not my bag!

Anyway, after much consultation with travel agents (still had them in those days!) we decided to embark on a Nile Cruise.

We settled on a boat called The Sonesta St George 1, less than fifty cabins and a few suites for the rich and famous (never spotted any of those!) and away we went. We flew to Luxor and were picked up at the airport and swiftly taken to the boat. 'By heck', as they say in Yorkshire, it was magnificent. The cabin, wasn't really a cabin, it was a big bedroom with a huge en-suite. The service was out of this world, the staff were delightful and insisted on pushing James everywhere in his wheelchair. We were on a table of six in the dining room. Always a bit of trepidation sharing with people you don't know! No worries on that score! There were two very rich widows from Birmingham. One who was embarking on marriage number five the week after we got back. The other had amassed a serious fortune and felt no need to wander down the aisle ever again! They were hilarious. The other two were a charming couple from Wiltshire, celebrating their silver wedding anniversary and in possession of a brilliant sense of humour! The food on board was first-rate. You could send your knickers to the laundry after lunch, and they would be back, ironed and wrapped in tissue paper in time for tea! No subject was taboo, and we romped our way through the most bizarre selection of topics.

We did a lot of sight-seeing, although it wasn't ideal for James. Being pushed for a couple of hours on very uneven ground in a wheelchair was uncomfortable for all concerned. (I once took him to Hodsock Priory to see the snowdrops and almost tipped him into a stream! It was eventually decided that he would be far happier left on the top deck, next to the bar with someone to wait on him hand and foot!

The Nile was just as I imagined, slow and peaceful, and almost biblical. The temples were awe-inspiring, how on earth they built them with only manpower is unimaginable. Like most places, us tourists generally only see the ancient wonders. We don't see the poverty and depravity. Off the boat was a very different ball game. You were followed everywhere, pushed and hassled to buy things and almost dragged into market stalls and shops. That was the other side of the coin, one which you know exists and the difference in the two extremes is vast.

Saying that, we had a very interesting experience, met some lovely people, and arrived home in one piece. Who could ask for more?

Just watching a bit of news! I see Donald has put his foot in it yet again! There are bound to be some idiots out there that will see fit to inject themselves with Jeyes Fluid! Nice one Donald!

I think that's it for now, I feel a Coke Zero coming on, and Poppy needs me to go and play ball. Bit mixed again today, but I don't have to write it, and you don't have to read it!

Stay safe, I really do wish I was on the Number 1 waterbus… but not today x

Violet

Poppy

The Diary of an Incarcerated Granny. Day 39

Feeling a bit lacklustre today! I'm really starting to think that I have had 'Covid toes'!

I have just read up on it, and I seem to have ticked all the boxes. Luckily, it seems to have almost disappeared and I still feel ok.

I have just spoken to No. 2 and No. 2 Jnr, they both have dreadful coughs and are barking away like a pair of Jack Russell Terriers.

Something seems to have gone pear-shaped with the TV. I can't get access to Netflix, and I was midway through watching something, so I'm having a 'bit of a strop' as No. 2 Jnr would say. She is well-versed in the art of the strop. They are very unpredictable, and can manifest themselves within seconds! The word 'no' seems to be the main catalyst.

There are considerably more cars on the road today and I think people are starting to escape. I'm not sure how easy it will be to keep tabs on everyone. Maybe the persistent escapees should be sent fruit picking? They appear to have a need to be out and about, so wouldn't it kill two birds with one stone?

It's very lazy to sit here tapping a few words out on the old iPhone. The kitchen is in great need of a good fettle, and it would probably take me fifteen minutes max... but I can't be bothered! I have to keep setting myself little goals or I doubt I would achieve anything at all. The only structured bit of the day is having to write the diary. In fact, I thought this morning that if I had a day off, the world wouldn't come to an end, but I think for my own sanity I need to keeping going!

I was reading an article about the chef James Martin. He was bemoaning the fact that his biggest regret was that he had sacrificed his chance of marriage and children to pursue his career. Rubbish! Jamie and Gordon managed to produce five each whilst the dough was proving! Surely it would have been more honest to say he couldn't be faffed?

I have convinced myself that I need to sort the kitchen. Catch you later!

All done, I feel better for that. Sandwich in the garden, a bit of ball-throwing for Poppy. Hard surfaces dealt with... I have to hold my hand up, and say I only do them once a day.

Nobody has crossed my threshold for forty-two days, so I doubt there is much viral activity going on in the Hobbit House! Unless of course, I'm the 'not so proud' host of Covid toes!

I think I read somewhere that garden centres will be starting to do limited openings. I can't see why not, providing the usual rules are in place. Shocking to think all the thousands of plants were just going to waste. I think I may even invest in a tomato plant or two...!

We were big fans of north Yorkshire. A family member had a cottage in a village called Marton, very near to Helmsley, and we spent a lot of happy weekends there. Incredible lunches at The Star Inn, Harome, well worth a twirl! My mother and stepfather often stayed at the Feversham Arms in Helmsley, slightly more formal, but very good indeed. There was an ice cream shop in Helmsley that sold stem-ginger ice cream, don't knock until you've tried it! The Mallyan Spout in Goathland, always a good lunch on offer.

Fish and chips in Whitby, either at The Magpie or Trenchers.

I think The Magpie is slightly ahead in my book. Fresh crab sandwiches at The Hart in Sandsend... the best!

We spent quite a lot of weekends at 'The White Swan' in Pickering, it was owned by friends of ours and I'm pretty sure it's still in the family. The White Horse and Griffin in Whitby, used to be good for a night away, and their restaurant was superb. Not heard it mentioned over the last year or so, maybe it's gone off the boil? This is a very condensed list of good eateries up in the wild and woolly north... so if we ever get let out and you've never been, head that way!

Another of my favourite haunts is the Cotswolds. It always reminds me of the Dordogne with the honey-coloured stone. I love Stow on the Wold, and I think Burford is probably my favourite. No. 2 and husband, (before the arrival of No. 2 Jnr) once spent a weekend at The Bull in Burford, and reported back that the food was some of the finest they had ever had. Praise indeed! The Lygon Arms in Broadway was another haunt of my parents, they liked formal!

We were once having lunch at The Bay Tree in Burford, when Douglas Hurd came in with his family. At the time he was either home secretary or foreign secretary in Maggie's government and the MP for Witney. The security was very much in evidence and fooled nobody! Interesting to be there though! Last but not least, we spent our honeymoon at The Plough Inn at Clanfield. It was owned at the time by a couple called Jean and Harry Norton who had a regular column in *The Caterer* magazine! Fame!

We are talking well over forty years ago, we had a four poster bed and I dropped a blob of creme fraiche on the lapel of my new, blue, velvet jacket! I remember one of the puddings was called 'Elizabeth Moxon's Lemon Posset'. And there were prunes at breakfast!

We had a lovely time! X

If all else fails, you now have a list of eateries and places to stay!

Keep safe, no escaping because it's a sunny Saturday! X.

The Diary of an Incarcerated Granny. Day 40

Day forty, that seems to put things into a whole new league! I always think of St Swithin's Day. Rain for forty days and forty nights, now that would be bad news!

It's eight am, my goal is to get this done, before *The Archers* at ten am!

Bit grey this morning, and a 'top coat' chillier! I might do something with mince today, or I might not! The choice is mine. I had a Donald Russell delivery just before lockdown, and I need to chomp my way through some of it. I occasionally buy from them if they have an offer on, and have been known to send them to the 'tall man' and his sisters when I have been feeling particularly generous!

When No. 3 and her other half produced No. 3 Jnr I wanted to buy them something as a welcome home present. Nothing baby related, just something for them. In the end I settled on a Chateaubriand from my local butcher. It cost an arm and a leg, and couldn't have been more appreciated!

Might have a foodie chat today!

I don't think I ever said, but we had a hotel and restaurant.

In the family for three generations… hence the food obsession and the need to check out other establishments.

The best cauliflower cheese I have ever had in my life, was in a restaurant called Masseys Chop House, on Beauchamp Place in Knightsbridge. We were down in London for the Horse of the Year show (still at Wembley in those days) I can't remember the chop, which presumably came with it, but I was seriously enamoured by the cauliflower cheese. I also, remember the restaurant next door was called Borscht and Tears.

When we were living in France we tootled off to the Ile d'Oleran for a couple of days. We stayed in a little hotel overlooking the harbour. Lobster is a bit of a favourite of mine, so I was pleased to see it was on the menu. Lobster Thermidor was duly served and was quite good. It wasn't until we checked out the next morning that we discovered they had charged the equivalent of £65 for the bloody lobster. I think the next day we went to McDonald's by way of protest!

I am still of the opinion that sometimes 'only a Big Mac' will do!

The best creme brûlée was in a restaurant in Roque St Christophe in the Dordogne. Someone who I hope will be reading this will remember it well (JB?)

We were on holiday in Kingsbridge in Devon and bought a leg of English lamb that was the best I have ever tasted - with onion sauce of course!

In New York, James was keen to try a real American hotdog. What a let-down that was, very disappointing!

We once rented a villa in Carveiro in Portugal for three weeks. I think No. 3 was about eight months old. We did eat out most of the time. The 'tall boy' was sharing a room with

No. 1. He acquired food poisoning and managed to projectile vomit from one side of the room to the other luckily avoiding his sister who was fast asleep in a bed between him and the unfortunate wall!

We had friends staying with us in France and they took us out for dinner as a thank you for having them stay. An amazing menu, when we got to the main course there was a 'floppy' bit of something doing the rounds on my plate! I couldn't quite bring myself to give it a try. When they cleared the plates I asked the waiter what it was. A cock's comb! So glad I didn't go there.

In Menorca many moons ago we found a little beach bar that produced the most delicious barbecued tiny shoulders of lamb. When we came home we tried so hard to recreate the flavours but we never ever managed it!

One of the worst things I have ever seen being eaten is Surstromming.

We were staying in Sweden and it was Midsummer's Day, there was a bit of a party going on, and the national delicacy was suggested. This consisted of a large tin (blown and ready to explode) of fermented herring. We all stood round in the garden as the tin was punctured. The stench was indescribable. Sea gulls were circling overhead and it was all very surreal. Those brave enough, tried it on a crispbread with a slices of new potato. It was disgusting! The Swedes pretend they like it, but I think they are telling pork pies!

We took the kids to London to see *Me and My Girl.* Stayed at The Waldorf, which was very nice - I think we got a good deal! We had lunch sitting on a balcony overlooking the ballroom where there was a tea dance taking place. I can't remember what we ordered, other than the 'chips' were the size of fish fingers, perfectly golden brown and stacked in a sort of tower. We still talk about them now!

We were in Perigueux and called at the ice cream parlour. A vast selection of flavours - although I don't think there was any liquorice! We managed a couple of *boules* each, apart from the 'tall man' who managed four! He is still referred to by family and friends as 'Monsieur Quatre Boule'!

One of my favourite meals in France is without a doubt a perfectly executed *confit de canard*. The lovely Maria in Thenon made the best potatoes to accompany the confit. Thinly sliced, fried in duck fat, with garlic and parsley, delicious! The kids used to love Maria's 'stale bread soup' as they called it, they could get through gallons of it.

Where else could you get four courses including wine for five francs a head - a very long time ago! Happy days! I'm sure there are many more memorable eating experiences I could dredge up, and probably will.

The Archers is nearly finished, I was listening with one ear! That took longer than I thought. The news is still depressing, I personally don't think we are ready to ease up on the lockdown... but what do I know? Better be safe than sorry in my book, however annoying and boring it may be!

Have an interesting Sunday, have a dip into the memory bank and focus on those special meals, good or bad... and share them with the rest of us. Carry on regardless! X

The Diary of an Incarcerated Granny Day 41

Not feeling the love this morning! Someone posted a YouTube video, Vera Lynn and the all the casts of the West End Shows, singing 'We'll Meet Again'. Ashamed to report I was reduced to a blubbering wreck!

I think as I've said before, I'm fine 99% of the time, but once in a while it hits me like a ton of bricks! This morning has been the 'once in a while'.

The news is depressing, people are starting to do their own thing, and it's all going to backfire if we aren't careful. Stay at home you morons!

Rant over! My nose is running, is it because I've been crying or have I got a cold starting?

I still have plenty of foodie tales up my sleeve!

One of the best dining experiences I have ever had (and it was free!)

When we had the hotel, we dealt with the Champagne House, Pommery. Champagne is big business and the different companies try very hard to keep you on board.

We were invited by Pommery to a luncheon at the Devonshire Arms, Bolton Abbey. (Coincidentally the wedding venue of No. 1, a few years later!)

I think there were only about forty guests, and oh boy did they push the boat out! I am not a big drinker, but I can always manage a few glasses of the bubbly stuff!

I remember it being a glorious summer's day, and the Devonshire Arms was the perfect backdrop and I seem to recall we ate outside. A helicopter landed in the grounds, and we were told that the foie gras had just been flown in from France. Nice touch methinks?

The waiters were hovering round with canapés, the obligatory smoked salmon, and the quite exceptional beluga caviar with sour cream and blinis. I can't actually remember what we had for the main course or pudding, but whatever it was it was superb. I recall floating off (by taxi) in a champagne haze to stay overnight with some friends who lived nearby. The rest is a bit of a blur!

Now for the other side of the coin.

When we had the cottage we spent most of the summer holidays in France. A very rural area, dotted with tiny hamlets, and very much a farming community.

We heard via the grapevine, that the wife of a local farmer had started cooking dinner in the evenings.

Pre-booking only, one menu, as much wine as you could drink, and seven euros a head. It would have been rude not to give it a go!

You have to imagine the scene, a very dilapidated farmhouse. A farmyard full of rusty ploughs, hens, ducks, geese and mud, in equal quantities. A flight of stone steps leading up to the door, with a red geranium on every step. I think there were about ten of us... so full up!

We filed into the house, just the one big room. There was a huge table with a plastic cloth, an assortment of odd chairs and stools and an enormous fire in a big inglenook fireplace. A selection of mustard jar glasses on the table with a heap of mismatched cutlery, and the warmest welcome you could ever have wished for!

Madame didn't have a single word of English, her husband

Bernard possessed two! 'Very' and 'Gooood'! Between us all we had a fair bit of French, and managed to keep the conversation flowing.

Gesiere salad for starters. yum, I love a good gizzard salad! (May I point out that this was all home-produced, including the lettuce under which I managed to hide my gizzards!)

Soup next, which I think was ok, some of the bowls were a bit cracked, but what the hell! The bread was lovely!

Bernard was multi-tasking, he seemed to be busy doing something outdoors involving cows and possibly tractors? There was a lot of mooing going on and his hands were covered in oil and cow muck. In between that he was serving drinks! His own wine, purple (with a hint of vinegar) was flowing freely. He served it with aplomb, his black, filthy thumbnail wedged into the spout of the jug to prevent it pouring too quickly. Whilst performing this task, he was grinning from ear to ear and bellowing, 'very goooood' in an extremely loud voice.

In the fireplace quite a lot of action was taking place. Ten of the biggest duck breasts you have ever seen were being burnt to a crisp on what appeared to be a metal foot-scraper. Madame was flapping her pinny about, trying to get rid of some of the smoke and their son aged about eighteen was sitting in the only armchair in the corner, smoking a Gauloise and trying to watch TV. French domestic bliss at its finest.

'Bernard the thumb' popped back in from the cow shed and managed to quell the flames and rescue the duck, and harmony was restored.

The main course turned out far better than we could have hoped for. Served with khaki-coloured peas and fried potatoes.

The French are brilliant at potatoes, all duck fat and garlicky and delicious.

Not 100% sure what the pudding was? A sort of omelette/ yorkshire pudding/*clafoutis* concoction it came with alcohol infused Mirabel plums and tots of Bernard's home-made *Eau de vie*. The whole evening was a triumph, we laughed from start to finish. This was rural France and this was as good as it got. Environmental health would have imprisoned Bernard on the spot. Health and safety would have had a field day and the whole caboosh would have been closed down immediately... but do you know what?

That was one of the most fun evenings we ever had, nobody got food poisoning. In fact, if I'm not mistaken we might even have gone back for a second dose!

We lived just a few minutes from the hamlet and the farm. We often drove up the lane and encountered Bernard bringing in his cows. We would always stop and say hello. He would give us a thumbs up (filthy nail still in situ) a big smile and a loud 'very gooood'!

My lovely pal has just left me a cottage pie on the wall... how very kind.

You will be pleased to know that I am feeling much more cheered now. T'was nowt but a blip!

Stay safe everyone x

The Diary of an Incarcerated Granny. Day 42

I slept very well, Poppy expressed no desire to go for a wee in the middle of the night, Violet-Elizabeth was snoring away downstairs… so ten/ten on the slumber scale.

I'm feeling much more chipper today, I've had several long telephone conversations and a FaceTime with No. 2 and No. 2 Jnr.

Yesterday was big shop delivery day… the excitement was up there with going to a Beatles concert at Sheffield City Hall, when I was twelve!

Let's talk music today. In my middle-to-late teens I was very into the folk scene. I spent a lot of time with my head down, my eyes closed and one hand over my ear! Try it… it's very easy to slip back into the groove.

I went to lots of folk concerts and was a big fan of Tom Paxton, Fairport Convention, Leonard Cohen to name but a few!

I was, and still am a loyal fan of Barbara Dickson, in fact I saw her in Scotland last September, if you get the chance, do it… you won't be disappointed.

I think I have an eclectic taste… I don't care who sings it as long as it floats my boat. I love choir and organ music, I love hymns and I love a bit of Pavarotti and Queen.

When I ordered my new car, I specifically requested a CD player as I have so many things I love to listen to.

I like my music full blast, and when in the car, if I have to stop at traffic lights, I always wind down the windows. It's good to share, and it makes people jump!

I did play piano as a small person, then swapped it for a pony! No. 2 was pretty good on the flute, and can play quite well by ear. I'm hoping No. 2 Jnr will have a musical bent. Her daddy is musical, head chorister at St George's Chapel, Windsor, and still plays the piano rather well. No. 3 had a bash at every instrument going, and was notoriously bad at them all! I think if push came to shove she could manage a rendition of 'Little Donkey' on the recorder! No. 3 Jnr is, I fear cast from the same mould... therefore all hopes are firmly at the feet of No. 2 Jnr!

Yonks ago when picnics in the park were all the rage, I was in my Pavarotti phase. When I'm in a phase, I'm pretty hard to live with. I become slightly obsessed and probably very annoying. Having shuffled off to a myriad of Michael Ball outdoor concerts and similar at Castle Howard and Harewood House, I decided to give it a go at home!

You've all been there, whoever is starring is a mere speck on a stage a mile away, and you can always hear the music because they put speakers everywhere. Basically, you speak very loudly to whoever you have gone with as you can't really hear them because the music is so loud!

I was into Pavarotti, it was summer, the weather forecast was good so we had a bit of a ring round. We wired up a few speakers, stuck some lights round the garden, lit a big BBQ and provided a couple of dustbins. Job done! We ended up with nearly fifty people who brought all their own stuff! Out came the tables and chairs, cool boxes full of the bubbly stuff. granny's candelabras, picnic hampers bursting with the finer things in life. We fired up a big BBQ for those who couldn't survive a Saturday night without a fillet steak or a couple of sausages.

It turned into a brilliant evening, Pavarotti was belting out 'Nessun Dorma', everybody was singing along and getting more and more inebriated! I think we kept going until about one am. So the moral of this story is, if you provide the venue and some music, then all your pals will bring all their own booze and food, and spend the next six months telling you how marvellous it all was!

Try it once they let us out!

Have you ever done your list for *Desert Island Discs*? Just in case you get the call? Here are mine in no particular order:

1) Queen – 'Love of my life'
2) Bruno Mars. – 'When I was your man'
3) Barbara Dickson - 'Caravans'
4) Hubert Parry – 'I was glad'
5) 'Duet' from the Pearl Fishers
6) Simon and Garfunkel – 'Homeward Bound'
7) Peter Skellern – 'Still Magic'
8) Mozart. – 'Ave Verum Corpus'

Have a listen on YouTube if you so desire.

Stay safe x

The Diary of an Incarcerated Granny. Day 43

Ooh, much cooler this morning and a bit wet as well. I think it's Wednesday? I always have lunch with the aunties on Wednesdays, well I did before all this hoo-hah! Oh how we took it all for granted.

It has become apparent that I shall have to do some dog grooming ASAP. Violet-Elizabeth looks like a mop, I'm struggling to tell which end is which! She also needs her nails cutting, which she dislikes intensely.

Normally they both go to the beauty parlour every six weeks, bath, haircut, nails clipped, anointed with aromatic oils etc.

I'm debating whether or not to buy some electric clippers, I don't have a bath in the Hobbit House and I don't think my back would withstand trying to wash them in the shower. A slight dilemma is presenting itself!

Where shall we go today?

Determined to broaden our horizons, we decided to take a trip with some friends to Sri Lanka in 2002.

It's a very long way, I am tallish, and economy seats don't do it for me on long-haul journeys!

I can't remember where we flew from, but I can remember where we landed. I had a bit of an issue during lunch on the plane, I munched my way through a whole and very hot chilli, cunningly disguising itself as a green bean!

We landed in Colombo, we were herded onto an apology for a bus, and set off on a seventy km drive to Ahungalla on the West Coast. It was probably one of the worst journeys of my life. Driving through Colombo was a nightmare. The traffic and noise were dreadful, there were a few emergency stops, screeching of brakes and everyone seemed to drive with their hands permanently on their horns. We eventually left the city and headed south. I don't think I have ever seen such poverty and filth as we saw driving through some of the little towns and villages. It was heart-breaking and disgusting in equal measures. There were open sewers running down the side of the roads. Cattle meandering everywhere, stalls selling fish and meat covered in flies and all in an unbearable heat. We didn't like it one bit.

I think it probably took about two hours to get to the hotel, progress was slow, the condition of the roads was abysmal and there was no aircon on the bus.

We stayed at the hotel Triton, which was destroyed by the Boxing Day Tsunami in 2004 and finally rebuilt in 2008. It was a beautiful hotel, as with all these places, a different world to what was happening on the other side of the well-guarded gates! You couldn't really fault the hotel, the staff were lovely, the food and accommodation were first-class, but I don't think we ever felt really safe. I think the highlight of the holiday for me was the Madu Ganga River Safari. It was a different world, water monitors criss-crossing in front of the boat, cormorant fishermen, beautiful birds, monkeys screeching in the trees. We travelled through the mangrove swamps and the little guy on the boat was constantly spotting things and pointing to what he had seen. I can see and hear him now clutching at James's sleeve and saying, 'Look sir, look sir, kingfisher sir, kingfisher sir!' Hmmm that brought a tear to the eye. That was a memorable day.

We were sitting having a drink after dinner one evening, when one of the waiters beckoned us. There was a huge turtle laying her eggs in the sand only a few feet from where we were sitting. We watched her for a very long time. Suddenly she stopped, clumsily covered her eggs with sand and then slipped soundlessly back into the ocean. Magical.

This then led to a visit to the turtle sanctuary a couple of days later. Sea turtles are part of a huge conservation project in Sri Lanka. The sanctuary was fascinating and we were able to see the tiny turtles as they were just hatching until they were deemed old enough to be released back into the ocean. That was something not to be missed.

As I'm trying to write this, I'm getting a photograph every two minutes from No. 2, who is having a wardrobe audit, she seems to need my input on which items I think she should hang on to. She's the classy one, works up in London (or did) a couple of days a week and likes her clothes! I'm fairly sure she will take no notice of me any way. No. 2 Jnr is proving to be quite fashion conscious as well, obviously takes after her mummy and not her granny!

Back to Sri Lanka!

We took a taxi to the fort at Galle, which was well worth a visit, the taxi driver insisted on taking us to his 'uncle's' jewellery shop. We were hassled and jostled until it all became a bit too much! I lost my cool, doesn't happen often but when it does it's epic! I do not like to be coerced into anything. Those times away from the hotel, just wandering around were ones I wouldn't want to repeat. The beach at the hotel was a public beach, patrolled by hotel guards. The locals were constantly trying to attract attention by waving white shawls and scarves. We called them 'the white water wafters'!

So, in a nutshell, that was our visit to Sri Lanka. We were all of the opinion that we had no desire ever to return. The hotel was lovely, and we were all so upset at the devastation and huge loss of life caused by the tsunami. It could just as easily have been us.

Having just given the thumbs up to a lovely dress and matching jacket from Zara, I fear I've done enough for one day. Stay safe, oh and congratulations to Boris!

Somewhere in the dim and very distant past, I thought that if I stayed at home for fourteen days, showed no symptoms, I would be out and about as per normal! I got that wrong, didn't I?

It's a bit dull this morning, I've just 'poo picked' the lawn, just on the off chance Titchmarsh and Sons make a surprise appearance. That will be the highlight of the day if that happens, an extra burst of excitement after bin day' on Tuesdays!

First of May tomorrow, the second of May would have been my forty-third wedding anniversary. What a long time ago that seems, and indeed is!

Speaking to the 'tall man' the other day, I was saying what a struggle it was to keep thinking of something to write every day. He suggested I write about 'our' family... so here we go!

We got married when I was twenty-six. I was an only one, never been within fifty yards of a child, and suddenly became a stepmother to a two-year-old and a four-year-old (cunningly disguised as the 'tall man' and 'No. 1'). Scary times indeed! They had moved away with their mum and stayed with us every other weekend. Looking back you wonder how you coped, but you did. It was in the days of the 'not very hands-on' Dad period. No criticism there, that's just the way it was in those days. They were brilliant, I never tried to be 'Mum', why would I? They had a perfectly good one already. I was never anything to do with the marriage break-up, and I think that does make a difference. There was very little animosity and a great deal of flexibility. I'm sure there were times when we bit our tongues and kept quiet, but doesn't that happen in any relationships?

Their mum remarried to a great guy, who has been a marvellous stepfather, and still is!

We made a point of never criticising the other side, and that too makes a hell of a difference. Here were two little people, whose wellbeing and happiness were paramount in a not quite ideal scenario.

Fairly soon, No. 2 came along and was welcomed into the fold with open arms. Over the Pennines a new baby brother arrived, followed six months later by No. 3 on our side of the border! Suddenly there were quite a few people in the mix. We all met regularly, we actually got on extremely well. When we bought our French cottage they all came to stay and liked it so much they bought one a couple of miles away. That heralded several years of family holidays in France.

I think if you asked the eldest two, they can't remember anything other than how it is now.

We shuffled around very happily, their friends came to stay with us, new girlfriends were brought over for inspection. We shared school fees, they bought the cars, we paid the car insurance, we made it work!

When James was very, very ill, a close friend said that she wondered if when he died, if I would still see the eldest two! That nearly broke my heart. We were at home waiting for more bad news and I mentioned this conversation to the 'tall man'. I think he was just as upset as I was! As far as he was concerned he was a damn sight luckier than most. Two sets of parents that loved him, supported him and wanted nothing but the best for him... and two lots of birthday and Christmas presents. What's not to like?

When No. 1 got married, both dads walked her down the aisle, while both mums sniffled in the front row, and shared a tissue! We were all there at the graduations, an occasional Christmas, the twenty-first parties and the weddings and sadly the funeral. Big bro gave No. 2 away when she got married, her daddy was there, but in a wheelchair. When No. 3 got married her daddy was no longer with us, but big bro did the honours yet again.

James was so proud of them all, they all went to university, they have all worked hard, done well, and most of all they have all married lovely people that do the family thing!

We are now into the second generation of fabulous grandchildren. The 'tall man' has two, a boy and a girl. No. I has two lovely girls. No. 2 has one little girl, but inherited a wonderful brother for No. 2 Jnr, who is loved by us all, and adores his little sister. He's twenty-two! He also has an amazing girlfriend who we all love to bits, and she's part of our family too.

No. 3 has a little girl, and also inherited a big girl who is nearly fourteen and was overjoyed to have a baby sister. That's not a bad tally from two only ones is it?

There is just the one boy who will carry on the Lister name, what a responsibility, Max! He will inherit the family number plate, LI5TAR, it was the nearest we could manage!

I was chatting to 'the other mother' on the phone the other day, and I said I was thinking about writing about us all, and what did she think? She said, 'you go for it, we did a bloody good job!' Too right we did, and that's something that makes us all very proud!

So there you have an insight into my family, none of us are perfect, but we will always love and take care of one another.

You can see now why we need to hire a chateau for a family holiday!

Life is far too short to harbour grudges, especially where children are involved. There is so much game playing out there, and so much anger could be resolved by putting the past in the past, and concentrating on the ones that really matter!

That's it then, that's my family, and I love them all, and I know how lucky I am!

I have a feeling that Boris is going to tell us all to stay put... so I will, and I hope you will as well. One day this will all be filed in the memory bank, so hang on in there. x

The Diary of an Incarcerated Granny. Day 45

Covid 19 Much sunnier this morning, I took a stroll down the garden, and found five boy ducks (aka drakes) asleep on the roof of the summer house. I think maybe they were hiding from their wives and kids?

I was watching *The Real Marigold Hotel* last night on BBC 1. Probably because I had read that Barbara Dickson was in it. I quite enjoyed it, an interesting mix of celebrity pensioners. They were all being quite charming to one another in episode 1, I wonder if three weeks down the line they will be feeling quite so chummy when they have all been living cheek by jowl. We'll have to wait and see on that one.

Years of group holidays have made me quite aware that you choose your companions very carefully.

I had a lovely message from 'the other mum' this morning, after yesterday's diary. She said it made her cry reading it, and it made me cry writing it. What a daft pair, eh?

I found yesterday's news quite unsettling. I knew that lockdown would be extended, but I just had the feeling that if they are waiting for a vaccine to be developed it could be months and months before we see daylight!

I had a little parcel in the post this morning… I love getting parcels! It was a little wooden sign which said 'Welcome to The Hobbit House'. How lovely is that? I think I have an idea who sent it… I may find out at 10pm this evening?

I'm trying to think where else I've been that I haven't bored you with already!

Lake Garda.

We went to Lake Garda with Page and Moy to celebrate our Silver Wedding Anniversary.

We stayed in a small but very nice hotel in the pretty little town of Limone. Famous for its lemon groves, olive oil and very long-living inhabitants! Lake Garda is beautiful, we loved it. We had opted to eat out in the evenings and really just use the hotel as a base to sleep and have breakfast. You could catch a boat that visited the other towns on the lake. We spent a day in Malcesine which was fascinating, I remember buying James a tiny original oil painting as an anniversary present. Lord knows what happened to that, I can't remember having seen it for years.

We visited Riva, right at the northern end of the lake and had a lovely day, just wandering, the weather was perfect and we ambled!

I couldn't miss a trip to Venice, even if it was just for the day. I'm sure you all know by now it's my best place on the planet. There is a certain satisfaction to be gained by going to somewhere that you know quite well. The ability to find 'that' restaurant, or that special church or the alley that cuts right through somewhere and saves you a ten-minute walk. All very handy if you are only there for the day. I always feel very sad when I leave Venice, as you travel away across the water, the last thing you can make out is the pointed top of the Campanile in St Mark's Square. It brings a lump to my throat every time!

So, a magical day in Venice, the next little adventure was a journey to the Dolomites. Gorgeous weather in Limone, we climbed higher and higher up the mountains in a coach that only just managed to negotiate the hairpin bends. It was getting quite foggy and much colder. I can't say the views were spectacular because it was far too misty to see anything. The further we climbed, the snow became more evident. A bizarre feeling after the scene we had left behind in Limone.

We had lunch in a hotel restaurant where Sylvester Stallone had stayed when he was filming *Cliffhanger*, that was the about the most exciting bit of the day, and that only ranked a three/ten! Ruined by the weather! We could have spent the day in Verona in the sunshine, hoping to bump into the two gentlemen! Can I recommend Lake Garda? A definite yes. Lots of pretty towns and interesting buildings and history plenty to see and do. A very popular destination for tourists providing a touch of refinement. No 'kiss me quick' hats or rock! Would I go back? Maybe not!

One other place I would go back to tomorrow is Barbados.

We took No. 2 and No. 3 just before No. 3 went away to school. I think they had spent so much time in France over the last seven or eight years that they were desperate to go somewhere else... just for once!

We had a friend who was in the travel business, and he recommended a recently opened hotel in Holetown. All-inclusive, but with a dine around facility to some very good restaurants. It was an incredible hotel and had been open only a few months. We met two couples whose offspring were virtually the same age and we all had a ball. I think we hired a car for a couple of days and did some sightseeing. We were on the West Coast, St James' which is the Caribbean side. The East coast is the Atlantic and very different. We hardly saw the children, they made friends and did everything together. Still in touch on Facebook! Us oldies took a cab to Sandy Lane one evening, just to have a drink and a nosey. It was very nice, but I'm not really sure what all the fuss was about. We thought that Mango Bay was just as good! I have never had a finer Pina Colada anywhere else in the world! That was the first time I ever had any Hershey's chocolate, disgusting stuff. There was a department store called Cave Shepherd in Holetown that sold some very nice things. Bridgetown was interesting, the old plantation houses well worth a visit. The thing that struck us the most was that you felt safe. I knew people that had been to Jamaica and never ventured beyond the hotel complex. The only downside of the whole holiday was that No. 2 got a sandworm in her foot. It started itching as we boarded the plane, by the time we reached Manchester her foot had swollen to twice the size. It was a mess! Our doctor even called the Institute of Tropical medicine in London. There was a drug that would kill it, but the side effects were dreadful. She was given antibiotics to guard against infection, but the general opinion was to leave it and it would die eventually as she wasn't the natural host! Horror of horrors. It was still going strong when they went back to school wearing a giant flip flop. She had to go to the san twice a day to have it looked at! As with all things, it pegged out eventually, but it wasn't a good experience.

Many years later, when they were all paddling their own canoes, James and I got a mega deal. Three weeks in Barbados, West Coast, suites in two great hotels, and upper class flights with Virgin! Now that was one for the grown-ups! We really loved that!

Both No. 2 and No. 3 have returned since the initial family holiday. In fact No. 3 spent her honeymoon there.

Would I go again? Not half! Loved every second - apart from the worm!

I'm running out of exciting trips! I did once sleep overnight in a car park in Filey... but I doubt you would find that very interesting!

Keep safe and things. X

The Diary of an Incarcerated Granny. Day 46

Same old this morning, is it ever any different? Wondering what to spread on your toast is about as good as it gets! Lemon curd this morning. I forgot about lemon curd for about twenty years, then suddenly remembered it a week into lockdown. It now rates quite highly on my list of 'things to spread when you've only got bread'. Yes, I have poetic tendencies as well!

A family crisis hit yesterday! No. 2 is furloughed, No. 2 Jnr's nursery is closed. Daddy is working from home and very busy. The girls decided to walk down to the beach, ten minutes max if you dawdle.

No. 2 Jnr insisted on taking her scooter, her helmet, a drink, a snack and her cardigan!

It was all going well to begin with, I don't think 2 Jnr will ever scoot for the nation, but she was managing to keep on the pavement which was a vast improvement on earlier expeditions.

She suddenly got 'a bit hot'. This required the journey to be put on hold for a minute or two. The helmet was removed, the cardigan was removed, a refreshing drink was then required to stave off dehydration. All good so far. 2 Jnr clambered back onto her scooter. Mummy reinstated the helmet, and then 2 Jnr started to scream and scream and scream! She was jumping around like a demented trout, when No. 2 suddenly realised that not only had she fastened the helmet, she had trapped a chunk of Jnr's skin in the plastic clip. Concerned passers-by were asking from a distance what was wrong. Jnr was still wailing and shouting, 'I want to go home' and No. 2 was convinced they thought she had been kidnapped! They went home, Jnr had calmed down a bit, but No. 2 was so horrified that she had hurt her, that she began to cry as well! By the time they reached home No. 2 was sobbing, Jnr was wailing again because Mummy was crying. Daddy was on a conference call in the dining room and rushed out, wondering if the world had come to an end and nobody had let him know. What a performance!

Eventually they all calmed down and equilibrium was restored. Later in the day 2 Jnr announced that she might go into the garden and ride her bicycle, and would Daddy please come and help her with her helmet as Mummy was not allowed to touch it ever again! We had a FaceTime this morning, 2. Jnr was much recovered, and sporting an Elastoplast the size of half a postage stamp under her chin. No. 2 was still looking upset, but had slept well under the circumstances! What are they like?

Quite a few folk have suggested that I tell a few stories of things that happened when we owned the hotel.

Quick overview, it was bought just after the war by James's grandparents. Basically a big Victorian mansion previously owned by an industrialist. I think it was run as an upmarket boarding house to begin with, and as time evolved it grew bigger and better and passed through three generations. When we sold at the end of the nineties it had forty-six bedrooms, a fine restaurant and an excellent reputation.

It was an amazing place, it provided us with an enviable lifestyle, it educated our children and it took care of us all!

I prefer not to go back to visit, I think it has changed hands several times, and now is part of a chain providing food from freezer, to microwave, to plate! I accept that times have changed and that we were lucky enough to have been part of an era where old-fashioned values still counted. Before I begin with the anecdotes, I need to introduce my mother-in-law, she was, in my eyes, what it was all about!

My mother-in-law, once retired, still had lunch at the hotel every day. She took no prisoners, was always immaculate and a great judge of character. If you had ever rattled her cage, you would be acknowledged, as that was the polite thing to do, but she never forgot and she never forgave!

She was generous to a fault, it was dangerous to ever mention something that you had seen that you liked or admired. You could guarantee that it would arrive within the week! She was a devoted granny, but was always quite critical and very honest with her likes and dislikes. I remember us all turning up for a family lunch one Sunday and No. 1 was sporting a new pair of Doc Martin boots. The look said it all, followed by the comment, 'what on earth are they? I never realised you had two club feet!'

Christmas and birthdays for the kids were always a bit of a gamble. They were never sure when the envelope was handed over, whether it would contain a £5 note or a cheque for £500! She liked to keep people on their toes. We had a lot of staff at the hotel, where she was always referred to as Mrs Lister, and there were very few other people that were brave enough to call her by her Christian name. She had been widowed before she was fifty and had run her own ship for a long time… consequently she was always right!

She travelled extensively and always occupied the same cabin on the Canberra. She drove a fast car, and when she went to London, she always stayed at her club! Christmas day was always frantically busy, fully booked from one year to the next. James would leave home at 7 to pick up staff, there would be two sittings for lunch. I would spend the morning at home with the girls and then drive down to the hotel later for lunch.. There would probably be around ten or twelve of us in one of the front little dining rooms. Every Christmas day, she made No. 3 cry… it became almost a tradition. She wasn't sitting up straight, she wasn't holding her fork correctly, she had her elbows on the table, why wasn't she using her napkin? All quite heavy stuff really. As the years rolled by they reached a sort of truce. I think in the history of the family, No. 3 was the only one that was brave enough to voice her opinions and I think she was secretly admired for that.

In 1984, Mrs L was seriously injured in a car accident in Perth, Australia. Her friend who was driving was killed outright and Mil suffered terrible injuries. I remember getting the phone call, James was at the hotel at a Round Table Meeting. He flew out two days later and was gone for a month. She was in intensive care for three weeks and it was very much touch and go. The day she had the accident was the day No. 2 swam a mile, she was six! Sorry just thought of that!

James came back and flew out two months later to bring her home. Things were never really the same after that. She could no longer play golf which she enjoyed very much. She had lived in a lovely apartment in the Mews at the back of the hotel. We bought a bungalow nearby and she moved there, as she could no longer manage the stairs easily. She still continued to travel but not as far and certainly not for so long. She loved the bungalow, she had a beautiful garden and still had her lunch at the hotel every day. Time marched on and she did amazingly well for a very long time.

She had a stroke and recovered reasonably well. She then had another stroke the day No. 2 was taking her History of Art A level. We limped on for a few more months. She was coming to stay with us for a while and waited until No. 3 had gone back to school. The day she arrived, James was at the hotel in the evening. I cooked dinner and my BF came over for a couple of hours. We were chatting, and she said she felt sick and needed some fresh air. She sat on a chair on the terrace and she died! It was almost as if she had waited for Rachel to be out of the way before it happened. It was a big shock for us all, the end of an era, and the passing of a very complex character, who underneath the crusty exterior had a heart of gold!

There are many stories to follow that will amuse you, I'm sure, just had to get this one off my chest!

Onwards and upwards!

This was taken at the end of November. The first time No. 2 (on the left) has been back since we sold. There is now a 'Lister' banqueting room and there are still a couple our old staff still working there! They were good days! X

The Brentwood Hotel Rotherham

The Diary of an Incarcerated Granny. Day 47

Sunday, so rumour has it? I know it is because of *The Archers*. That was the last omnibus for a month. What is the world coming to?

Yesterday I found a canister of Mr Sheen under the sink. Later on, I might shine umpteen things clean! Or I might not, it's Sunday after all.

Other than a couple of FaceTime's yesterday, I didn't telephone anyone! There's nothing to say really is there, all you seem to do is reiterate something that you heard on the news or saw in the newspaper! I don't have a newspaper, I sometimes read 'The Daily Fail' online, and then discount most of it.

I used to love Sundays, always a proper lunch with friends and family, *The Sunday Times*, which would last you most of the week, and usually something reasonable on the TV.

When you find yourself on your own, the weekends are always the worst time of the week. I can happily fill most days during the week, seeing friends, meeting for lunches and generally bobbing around.

Out of our tribe, 'the tall man' lives up in Clitheroe, No. 1 lives in Reigate in Surrey, and No. 2 lives in Worthing, West Sussex. That leaves poor old No. 3, who is unfortunate enough to live the nearest to the Granny. Twenty minutes away if you put your foot down!

No. 3 and Mr 3 have demanding jobs, both often work late, and in No. 3's case she is sometimes away from home overnight. They have a toddler, who has an older sister who stays with them most weekends, so they are busy bees. They invite me a lot, and I decline a lot! They have very little time together in the week, so their weekends are precious. I have a friend who is on her own, and often stays with me for the weekend. We are Yorkshire's leading authority on the best places to dine out for Sunday lunch, and now we are all locked up for lord knows how long! Arghhhhhhhh! Rant over.

As for the tales of my mother-in-law. Here's another!

One weekend, Mrs I was standing in reception at the hotel talking to the receptionist. A rather scruffy-looking guy walked in with an equally scruffy-looking young lady. He asked if he could book a room for one night and wanted to pay in cash there and then. They had no luggage and they didn't want a reservation in the restaurant for dinner. They were shown up to their room and Mrs L's antennae started to twitch, and she was not a happy bunny. An hour later, the car park was full of police cars, there were armed officers in the bushes surrounding the hotel and everyone was asked to leave the building. The police stormed upstairs and kicked in the door of the room where the chap and his lady were staying! Mrs L's take on this was a) he had a Northern Irish accent. b) this was in the middle of all the problems with the IRA. c) he was going to plant a bomb and blow up her hotel. She had phoned the police and told them there was a terrorist in the building!

The true story was... he was a bloke from Northern Ireland who had been working on the motorways round here, laying tarmac. He had just been paid a big wad of cash, so he had found himself a prostitute and booked a room overnight, nothing more than that! He was caught in a compromising position by the police when they kicked the door in, and his lady friend did not appreciate having a gun pointed at her.

They got dressed, and a bit like Elvis, they left the building! Peace was restored, Mrs I was congratulated for her vigilance (always better to be safe than sorry) and we got a hefty bill for a new bedroom door!

Her one and only comment was, 'I will not have my premises being used as a brothel.'

She was unrepentant!

She didn't really have many close friends when I think about it. She was popular, and had a lot of acquaintances, and was invited everywhere because of who she was. I could never see her baring her soul, and discussing personal things with anyone, that just wouldn't have happened!

I got on very well with her, far better than James did. They were maybe far too alike in some ways?

I think I'm going to wind it up for today, I have dusting to do! I may reward myself with an Indian takeaway later. Shopping list day tomorrow, hurrah. Bins on Tuesday, what's not to like? I hope you are all keeping to the straight and narrow, and still rinsing your tins for the recycling bin?

We must all do our bit! Keep safe x.

The Diary of an Incarcerated Granny. Day 48

Today I thought I would tell you about my old cleaner. I originally wrote this on Facebook for my friends just after she left and they enjoyed hearing about her so much I thought I would share the post. I would like to be know that this is all true!

Today after four-and-a-half years my cleaner didn't come, she has buggered off back to Wales and left me for the land of the leeks. Officially she was the worst cleaner on the planet, but she was also reliable, very kind, and totally trustworthy.

She was recruited via a postcard in the local newsagent's window. I would like to say that I was inundated with people wishing to clean and polish the Lister residence, but sadly she was the only person who applied for the position. The interview went something like this... she screeched into the courtyard in a clapped out Ford Fiesta, parked diagonally in front of the garage and clambered out through the passenger door. Apparently her son had bolted the driver's door shut as the handles on the inside had all snapped off. She was wearing a woolly hat, a fleece covered in straw, and an extremely large pair of shit-covered hiking boots. She was, I thought, about ten years older than me, but turned out to be five years younger. At the time she was living in a caravan on a farm near Doncaster where she kept her Shetland pony, three dogs, five cats, a guinea pig and various rescued wild animals. I had put in the advert that I wanted someone that was used to animals... so she fitted the bill in that respect. Violet and Poppy adored her from the word go and Foo and the now sadly departed Jeffery suffered her hugs and kissed with alacrity. All good so far... she assured me that her dedication to the duster and the hoover was paramount and we agreed terms, every Thursday nine am until one pm. We arranged for her to start the following Thursday.

In the early days, punctuality was never a problem, at least for the arrival time! The first hurdle to overcome was the shit-encrusted hiking boots. A polite suggestion that they weren't entirely suitable for marching throughout the house on cream carpets was met with a vigorous nod of agreement. The following week a pair of lime green velour mules with a bell on each toe joined the household and took pride of place on the utility room shelf. We rubbed along for the first few weeks and it became obvious that Hilary's preferred 'weapon of choice' on the cleansing front was without doubt the feather duster. She got through them at an alarming rate, little shocking pink and cat sick-yellow feathery wisps were to be found clinging on for dear life in the strangest of places! She would don the velour mules and leap out of the utility room with all the poise and agility of Margot Fonteyn landing centre stage in *Swan Lake*. This was a woman on a mission... slipper bells jingling... she wafted and flapped, twisted and twirled, leapt into corners, and according to her, had 'given them shutters a right seeing to today'. It was apparent that the 'bog standard' Tesco feather dusters were not up to such strenuous and enthusiastic application. Soon afterwards I was in the DIY shop in Bawtry and came across the Rolls Royce of feather dusters... ostrich feathers with a stout hardwood handle and the gob-smacking price tag of £11.50! I wrapped it up and left it on the kitchen table. When she arrived I handed it over and said 'there's a present there for you'. She unwrapped it and her eyes filled with tears. 'Oh thanks Ang, that's bloody lovely that is'... and to her it was!

Now, some people can think on their feet, others have never had an original thought in their lives. Hilary, bless her, fell into the second category. New cleaning products made her nervous, things with lots of wires made her jittery, and the mechanics of the vacuum cleaner brought her out in a cold sweat. Life became dotted with suggestions. What if... instead of cleaning the bathrooms with neat Stardrops we dilute it into a bucket full of hot water?! What if... we move the mats in the kitchen and then we can sweep and mop underneath them.? What if... we don't empty the crap from the hoover into the kitchen bin and all over the floor when we have just mopped it?! What if we empty the bathroom bins and put a bin liner in? What if... we replace the loo rolls in the bathrooms when they are running out? How about we don't clean all the windows in the house with Beeswax furniture polish, even though, as you point out 'it smells bloody lovely'?! Do you not think that maybe cleaning the mark on the bedroom carpet with neat bleach was a bit of a rash move?!

Could the reason my shoes are sticking to the kitchen floor be anything to do with the fact you have squirted it all over with Cif and forgotten to wash it off? How about we remove the bottom sheet on the spare bed when we change it, rather than putting a clean one over the top? Is there any particular reason you have filled up the dog's bowls with cat biscuits? No need for you to bother watering my houseplants, the roots appear to have started to rot.

Tactical avoidance... This took quite some time to perfect, in fact four years on I still hadn't quite cracked it. She had the same enthusiasm for idle chit chat as she had for her feather duster... she loved it.! Clutching a mug of tea, she would wedge herself companionably in the kitchen doorway and launch into the ups and downs of her weekly traumas. The forthcoming court appearances of close members of her family was a favourite topic of discussion. She was fiercely loyal and firmly believed that most of the offences that resulted in their arrests were simply due to mistaken identity. Bail, conditional and unconditional was a minefield that she couldn't get to grips with no matter how much I tried to explain things. In a former life she knew I had been a magistrate, and was convinced that I would be able to accurately predict the likely sentencing outcomes for her nearest and dearest's court appearances. The way round that was to say that the powers of the magistrates' court were limited, as her brood were obviously professional criminals and at the top of their game, the Crown Court was the only place fitting for them to receive their just desserts. This appeared to cheer her up no end. The old adage 'It doesn't matter what you are good at, as long as you are good at something' seemed to foster a glimmer of maternal pride!

The stair lift to Heaven... The day they came to fit the stair lift was a Thursday. The day before James was rushed into hospital and none of us ever imagined that it would be eighteen months before he would come home. Bad timing all round! Hilary arrived that morning and viewed the installation of the stair lift with huge excitement. She positioned the ironing board at an angle in the kitchen doorway so that she could keep tabs on what was happening in the hall. She chatted non-stop to the engineer about how it would turn the corners and how fast it was likely to go. Periodically, she abandoned the iron and popped into the hall, hands on hips, cheeks puffed out and head bowed in awe as she charted the progress of the rails up the stairs. This to her was a really big deal, the erection of a scaled-down version of the Eiffel Tower on the top landing wouldn't have come close! In her eyes, this contraption was the domestic equivalent of the Nemesis rollercoaster at Alton Towers! She was enthralled! When the installation was completed, she was invited to take the driver's seat, press the magic button and set off on the maiden voyage of exploration. Up the first set of stairs, along the half landing and then the final speed gathering rush up to the first floor. She negotiated the return journey with aplomb, face flushed pink and the bells on her slippers jingling with the exertion of it all. She alighted gracefully and stood transfixed with a huge smile on her face... 'Bugger me Ang,' she said eventually...'That was effing marvellous'!

Transport through the ages... For the first few months the old Fiesta rattled and spluttered its way into the courtyard every Thursday morning. Various parts had in effect left the building and made alternative arrangements. Plenty of duct tape was in evidence, especially on the windscreen wipers. She was still getting in and out through the passenger door and the writing was on the wall. One night in November the engine gave a final shudder and the poor old thing passed away painlessly up to its axles in mud at the side of the caravan.

The following Thursday she arrived looking a bit hot and bothered. She came into the kitchen wearing her woolly hat, a bright orange cagoule and a pair of grey jogging bottoms covered in oil. She flopped down on one of the kitchen chairs, wriggled her way out of the straps of an enormous rucksack and took of her hiking boots. 'Car's fucked,' she said, and went into the utility room to find her slippers. Over a cup of tea, I asked her if she was going to sell it for scrap. She looked at me as if I had suggested she joined me for a naked picnic at Glyndebourne... 'am I buggery,' she said, 'I'm buying some chickens!' When I looked outside, an ancient racing bike was leaning drunkenly up against the house. A well-worn green and white umbrella was tied firmly to the cross bar with orange baler twine. All future inclement weather conditions were catered for. The bike soldiered on for quite a few weeks until she rolled up late one morning with two black eyes and a huge plaster on her nose. Sorry I'm late she said, 'I had to come on the buzz. I hate bloody buzzes!' I asked what had happened to the bike... She rolled her eyes and sighed... 'Bleeding potholes,' she said. 'Effing wheel buckled and I went arse over tit and landed on me face!' She looked at her mug of tea and shook her head, 'I'll just have to get the sodding buzz from now on'!

Biddling for Beginners. A couple of years down the line we had a very, very harsh winter. Life in a thirty-year-old, four-berth touring caravan was no picnic. The roof had started to leak, everything was damp and it was bloody freezing! She started to look a bit peaky, I don't think she was eating properly and I think she struggled to afford to buy the gas canisters for the caravan heater. She came in one morning muffled up with scarves and gloves and a streaming cold. She warmed her hands on her mug of tea, looked me straight in the eye and said, 'That bastard caravan will be the end of me! I can't do another winter like this one'. She soon warmed up and started to look quite cheerful. 'I'm going to biddle,' she said, and nodded her head thoughtfully. 'Sounds good, where's that then?' I said. 'Are you going on the train?' She gave me an old-fashioned look and rolled her eyes. "It's not a place you daft bugger, it's something you have to do!' 'You better explain,' I said, 'because I don't have a clue what you are on about'. She told me that earlier in the week she had been to the doctors and got chatting to another patient in the waiting room. The conversation soon gathered pace and Hilary told her about the problems with the caravan. Apparently she had been on the council housing list for several years, but had never bothered to contact them. "This woman said that if I want a flat I can ring the council, go down to the office and look at the empty ones, then If I see one I like I can put a biddle in and if no one else wants it, then my biddle might win'! 'Gotcha' I said... 'that sort of biddle...' Over the next few weeks 'whether to biddle or not to biddle' occupied every waking moment. She would arrive with a clutch of A4 printed sheets showing the desirable residences on offer... each one only 'a biddle' away! I helped her draw up a shortlist. As she would be moving with enough livestock to set up a small zoo, then a) it must be on the ground floor, b) it must have a garden or some outside space, and c) it must be close to a 'buzz stop'. Four weeks on she found the ideal place... went to have a look and put in her 'biddle'! She rang from a payphone a few days later. 'Ang, Ang...I've done it Ang... I've effing done it' I've got the flat... my biddles won!'

Hallelujah...

The Diary of an Incarcerated Granny. Day 49

Hotel stories seem quite popular, so I have unearthed a couple.

The hotel had two permanent residents for many years. One was a local solicitor, and the other the Home Office Pathologist for Sheffield. Both bachelors and as different as chalk and cheese. The solicitor was a very reserved gentleman, who kept himself to himself and the situation suited him admirably.

Dr Dick was a different animal, an avid walker and explorer, a keen sailor, (he taught James how to sail) a great raconteur and a very interesting man.

We had a chambermaid called Evelyn, who had worked at the hotel for years. She had a calliper on one of her legs and wore a surgical boot, but that held her back not one jot! Evelyn was to cleaning, like Sir Steve Redgrave was to rowing! Unsurpassed!

On one occasion she was sorting out a newly decorated bedroom, right up on the top floor in the converted apple lofts. She had gone up there mid-morning and was giving the room a 'right good fettle'! Around four in the afternoon a very agitated Mr Evelyn phoned reception. She was usually home around two pm, hadn't turned up and he was very worried about her. Staff that had left around lunchtime were contacted and nobody could remember having seen her after the morning tea break. Someone then remembered that she had gone up to sort that room in the apple loft. A search party was sent out and as they climbed the last flight of stairs a little voice could be heard shouting 'help'!

Evelyn had decided to move a wardrobe, and as she wrestled with it, it had spun round on one of its legs and trapped her in the corner under the eaves! She had been there for hours! Lots of hot sweet tea was provided and a lift home from the boss! After that a sign in, sign out system was put into place. The staircase at the hotel was quite grand, it had a wonderful curved stained-glass window on the half landing, and very high ceilings. Evelyn was walking through the hall one day and looked up to see a pair of legs swinging from the top of the staircase! She started to scream and people came running. All she could say was 'Dr Dick has hung himself.' She was in a dreadful state. Someone shot upstairs, to see a rather bemused looking Dr Dick climbing back over the banisters. He had been hanging by his fingertips and allowing his body weight to stretch his spine! Poor Evelyn, more hot sweet tea, and a big box of chocolates from Dr Dick by way of an apology!

Dougie and George.

George was the 'yard man' all things outside, other than the gardens and greenhouses were George's domain! He swept and disinfected the yards, he took care of all the hotel drains, he was responsible for the cleanliness of the store-rooms, and the removal and stacking of all the rubbish. His particularly favourite job was keeping his swill bins up to scratch. In those days all edible waste was collected in a huge galvanised bin. A local farmer would collect the bin twice weekly and feed the contents to his pigs. The farmer in question was called Philip, and he was affectionately known as 'Phil the Swill'! One day the bin was removed and a spare one left in its place. It hadn't been cleaned properly and George was not a happy man. He marched up to the office, demanded that Phil the Swill be contacted ASAP, the bin replaced with a clean one, or he was resigning forthwith! There were not many Georges out there, or Phil the Swills for that matter. The incident had to be handled with great sensitivity. Apologies were given and accepted and eventually things got back on track. To have lost them both would have been a nightmare!

Dougie was the CEO of the 'pot wash' in the back kitchens. He presided over his stainless-steel empire with pride. There were two enormous sinks, both big enough to bath a donkey. Shelves and plate racks and duck boards on the floor. Nobody could scour a pan the size of a cauldron better than Dougie. He was a perfectionist. He had a bevvy of assistants that came and went, but he was a hard taskmaster. He and George were good buddies. They had the 'eradication of all germs' in common, and Jeyes fluid and bleach were a much discussed topic.

One Wednesday it was, as ever, Rotary Club lunch. George and Dougie always ate their staff lunch in the little out building called the Miller House. It was where the chefs got changed and it had a couple of easy chairs. Dougie was a little perturbed that one of his monster sinks seemed to be draining slowly and George agreed to take a look. They prodded and rodded, and eventually found a container of drain cleaning stuff and about a gallon of bleach, Dougie was hanging over the sink, and George was outside with his head over the drain. What neither of them realised was that the combination of the two substances produced a chemical reaction and gave off a very toxic gas. Both Dougie and George passed out! As luck would have it, there were several doctors at Rotary lunch. An ambulance was called ASAP and they were blue lighted to the local hospital. They were both kept in for observation for a couple of days, happily in adjoining beds. Luckily, they were back in harness after a few days, and very thankfully none the worse for wear. A cautionary tale!

I think that is roughly what you would have got yesterday.

I shall now have a shower, wash my hair and dust!

Going off on a tangent, do Campbell's still make condensed chicken soup? I have a recipe for a tuna fish pie (sounds gross but isn't!) and nowhere seems to have it!

Stay safe x

The Diary of an Incarcerated Granny. Day 50

A very lovely sunny morning, coffee outside, and the dogs are sunbathing!

I read last night that one of the TV doctors had produced a list of things we should be eating to boost our immune systems. Baked beans, Greek yoghurt, bananas, and a vitamin D supplement. I eat all those things and I do take extra vitamin D. I am obviously an example to you all!

Done the usual FaceTime this morning. No. 2 Jnr was sitting at the piano and couldn't get her head round the fact that it didn't just play whatever tune she was thinking about. We tried to explain that you have to learn how to play, it doesn't just happen! She was getting crosser and crosser, so I bid a hasty retreat. I know her argument will be that it plays everything for Daddy!

No. 3 Jnr is hilarious, she's just two-and-a-half, she has picked up a few French phrases, and is learning to sign. She sings a lot, very loudly, always out of tune, and should never be allowed within fifty metres of a recorder! Don't you just love them?

You seemed to enjoy the stories of the hotel staff, so here are a few more.

Grace worked for us for many, many years. In fact she didn't retire until she was eighty!

She was a bit of a busybody, she was a leading authority on everything concerning waitressing and silver service. She thought the sun shone out of my mother-in-law, and considered her a close confidante. Grace worked two or three shifts a week. She always did Wednesdays, which was Rotary lunch. Sunday lunch, and Saturdays if there was a wedding.

Grace knew all the members of Rotary, and considered them to be 'her boys'! They all used to make a fuss of her, and her stock reply to anything she was asked was 'definitely'. As time marched on, Grace's control of the gravy boat lessened. It reached a stage where the cost of the cleaning bills had started to exceed the profit made on Rotary lunch. I'm fairly sure that by the time she retired there wasn't a single Rotarian that hadn't been splattered by Grace's gravy and enthusiasm.

She was the leading authority on weddings, and the guardian of the cake knife! She hid it in a secret place known only to her, and it was considered as precious as the Crown Jewels. One Saturday, Grace rang in sick, and was unable to mastermind the wedding. She requested a personal phone call from my mother-in-law, as she was the only person to whom she would divulge the whereabouts of the cake knife. What a performance! Grace was 'old school', she had been widowed for many years, and her little job at the hotel was the highlight of her life... she was Amazing!

We went through a period of cars being broken into in the car park. Wednesday lunch time was a particular target day.

The assistant chief constable came to give a talk at the Rotary meeting as to how South Yorkshire Police were tackling this problem. It was just a tiny bit amusing that while he was making his speech, five cars were broken into, including his! Whoops!

The hotel was pretty big and it became more cost effective to have a full-time decorator... a bit like the Forth Bridge!

We got Barry, late fifties, Elvis look-alike, winkle picker

shoes, dyed black hair with huge sideburns, and fully confident that he was the babe magnet of the Western world! I think I had him down as a bit of a creep, early doors. To give him his due, he was a reasonable decorator (an incident in the home of my mother-in-law would refute that!) and he pottered along quite happily. The time arose that the kitchens needed repainting, so Barry was asked to do a week of nightshifts. We had a very pretty, newly married receptionist who stayed overnight when on a late shift. The receptionist's bedroom window looked out onto the flat roof of an annexe with fire escape access. (you can see where this is going can't you?) Barry painting away in the kitchen, receptionist went up to bed. After about fifteen minutes she thought she heard something outside the window, this happened on two consecutive nights and she was getting a bit unsettled. She told her husband what had happened. On the third night, business as usual! Apart from the fact that an extremely strong and fit young husband was hiding in the bushes.

Barry crept through the garden, climbed up the fire escape and was enjoying himself looking through the chink in the curtains!

Not for long... shall we just say he was given a 'proper pasting'. James was called in and he was dismissed on the spot. I'm not sure who finished decorating the kitchen!

The next decorator, funnily enough, was also called Barry. He was a sweetheart. Mrs Barry obviously washed his overalls in Persil, attended to the trimming of his nasal hair, and scrubbed him within an inch of his life before he boarded the bus to work every morning. He was immaculate and an absolute perfectionist. His hobby was calligraphy!

I have managed to get a slot... not for the supermarket, but to get the Baskervilles clipped next week! They will be collected and dropped off. Such a relief, I'm not 100% sure which way Violet is facing!

Romped through it today, so I may well read by book outside in the sunshine!

Keep safe everyone x.

The Diary of an Incarcerated Granny. Day 51

I am having a lazy day today! I haven't slept very well for the last couple of nights, not sure why! I go to bed far too late around one am, then I read until I fall asleep. I'm usually up and about around eight am, mainly because Poppy sits on my head, which signifies she needs to go out! I usually read the news online, FaceTime somebody, the usual stuff. I need to be up for a while before I have any breakfast. Can't eat straight away. Then somehow or other it's fast-forwarded itself to eleven o'clock!

I can't say I find the days long, because I really don't. Someone said the other day that she was alone, but not lonely! I think that applies to me as well.

The hotel seems to have been a popular subject to write about, and endless little stories spring to mind!

New Year's Eve... always one of the big nights of the year. Never a favourite of mine, I always find it quite a sad time, wondering what the next year has in store for us all! Crikey, that sounds really miserable doesn't it?

New Year's Eve was a special night, black tie, posh frocks, music, champagne, and the culmination of a very busy few weeks. Staff wise, everyone was on their knees and looking forward to a break.

For some people, New Year's Eve is the time to let your hair down and celebrate with friends. Christmas can be quite fraught, with families dutifully hosting relatives for several days. Tempers are easily frayed, and by the time everybody waves goodbye to their nearest and not necessarily dearest, they are ready to blow a gasket! (Please be aware that this is in some cases, not all!)

NYE in a lot of cases seems to be an excuse to get hammered. All that champagne flowing usually renders one member of a couple getting blotto early doors! This causes a simmering resentment from the other, who is starting to feel embarrassed at being shown up in front of a load of strangers! Before you know it, insults are exchanged, all the tensions of the past couple of weeks come to the surface and they have as they say in Yorkshire 'a right Barney'! Then their friends start to chip in, (this not a wise course of action!) incidents that have rankled over the last twelve months bubble to the surface and before you know it World War III is in its infancy!

I rarely drink, I never reach the happy stage, it just makes me feel ill, and I have to retire to a darkened room with some paracetamol. So over the years I began to observe instead! I think I have witnessed every type of inebriation. There are the ones that smile a lot, kiss everybody and proclaim their love and devotion to the world at large. They eventually slide under the table, and can usually be left there until home time. There are the ones that get a bit too flirty and make a move on someone who clearly isn't interested. They say a refusal often offends, and this tends to make them a bit defensive.

They then start swaggering, and become quite obnoxious. Then we get the ones that fall into the 'loud' category. They become fuelled by the sound of their own voice. The louder they get, the more confident they seem to become and the more ridiculous they look.

We get the ones whose eyes start to cross and refuse to uncross, and this makes them cry. They sob uncontrollably, they have no clue what they are upset about, and this makes them cry even harder. They are best being removed post-haste, as crying appears to be catching, when you get a whole row of them sobbing in a corner, you don't want to be there... trust me!

There is always the 'angry' one! They can barely stand, and boy are they cross! Any attempt to calm them down results in a tirade of abuse. Everything and everybody pisses them off, they threaten to flatten anybody that looks at them and of course they know everything and they are always right. They will argue with themselves if nobody else is available.

The violent ones are the worst, their fists are always clenched, they destroy things, they threaten and they intimidate. They develop a super human strength and can leave a trail of destruction in their wake. They need leaving to the experts!

I have often wondered if you filmed them in action, what their reaction would be if you played it back when they had sobered up?

I think I tottered off on a tangent a bit there!

NYE was usually a very successful night, most people booked from year to year and a lot of the time it went like a dream, and sometimes on the odd occasion... it didn't!

We once had Sir Chris Bonnington staying at the hotel for a few nights. He was on a lecture tour in the area and was a really nice chap.

Mother-in-law was ecstatic, I think he ranked up there with Margaret Thatcher in her list of 'the most admired people on the planet!' She greeted him personally and probably left a chocolate on his pillow! (She didn't.)

When he eventually moved on, he left a pair of trousers in his bedroom. She tried to contact him, but to no avail. So, she kept them! I don't think it was the actual trousers, but the thought of the legs that had been in them, which had reached the summit of Mount Everest four times! Years later I did ask her what ever happened to Chris Bonnington's trousers, and believe it or not she still had them!

Clement Freud stayed with us for a weekend.

As those of you who have ever worked in the hospitality industry will know... playing the 'do you know who I am' card, is a big mistake! He was probably one of the most arrogant people I had ever met. Nothing suited him and he was a pain in the arse. Nobody raises their arm and clicks their fingers at me, I looked straight through him, and ignored him from then on!

My other half was a brilliant 'mine host', he was charming and funny and a very popular guy. I once asked him how he managed to keep his cool in awkward situations.

His theory was, that there was more than one way of killing a cat... and in his view, the preferred method was to choke the bastard with cream! It stood him in good stead, and it works!

I think that's it for today folks, a very mixed bag. I just have to type it as it comes into my head, I don't do notes, so what you see is what crossed my mind at the time.

Almost dog's dinner time, Violet-Elizabeth is squinting at me out of her one good eye! If left to her own devices she will attempt her meerkat impression which involved waving her front paws in the air and trying not to fall over! She's fifteen, so I'm delighted that she still makes the effort.

I hope most of you had a good day, it's not easy is it? I think might stay under wraps even if Boris says we can go out. I feel safe at home!

You all take care! x

The Diary of an Incarcerated Granny. Day 52

I slept ok! That's quite a bonus. Hung out some washing, and then had my Greek yogurt, Granola and blueberries sitting outside. Very civilised!

Apparently it's a Bank Holiday today... I didn't have a clue! VE Day as well, I don't possess any bunting, and neither am I the proud owner of a flag pole. The chances are I will be celebrating very quietly. HM the Queen, Vera Lyn, and a box of tissues!

Trying to remember little bits and bobs from the hotel days. I think these will become even more random as the thoughts pop into my head, or one of the offspring reminds me of something!

This I thought was amusing. The hotel acquired a black and white cat called Tigger, he wandered in one day and decided to move in on a permanent basis. He had worked out that he was only allowed in the hall and the residents lounge. He was fed in the yard outside the kitchens, and the food on offer was extremely tasty. He had landed on his feet, which cats tend to do anyway! The time came for him to visit the vets and have certain parts of his anatomy removed and all was well. The invoice from the vets was kept, and was eventually put through the books as 'a modification to rat trap'! It was never queried either. Creative accountancy at its best!

We decided to sell the hotel at the end of the nineties, when it was still doing very well, but the competition from the 'hotel groups' were starting to change the dynamics.

We sold quickly, and within six months they made it fit their mould! The tennis court and croquet lawns gave way to an enormous 'pirate ship' and children's playground, right outside the big windows of the main dining room. The food was ordered at the bar, fresh from the freezer, to the microwave, to the plate! No longer a head waiter with a flambé lamp cooking at your table, no more fillet steak Diane, tornedos Rossini, scampi Carlos and crepe suzettes. All finished!

When I moved recently, I came across one of the flambé lamps stored away. I think it found its way down to West Sussex to join the champagne buckets in No. 2's dining room.

We kicked our heels for a few months, trying to decide what to do next.

We eventually bought a pub in Derbyshire, just outside the village of Ashover. It belonged to friends of ours, they had retired to Cornwall several years before and put in managers who were doing them no favours! It was a very pretty little place, beams, open fires, and quite a popular restaurant, but with a limited menu.

We booked a table, just the two of us and went incognito to suss it out. The first thing I remember as we walked through the door was the smell of Frytol! Frytol is a long-life cooking oil, produced in Ghana which has an odour all of its own. We looked at one another, wrinkled our noses and said Frytol under our breath!

The place was a typical country pub, but the restaurant side was quite busy. I think this was a Tuesday evening. You never go spying on Fridays and Saturdays... most places can generate a few bookings over the weekend!

We quite liked what we saw, and a very lengthy period of negotiation took place!

We kept on all the staff, sadly, the new brooms start to sweep things very clean! The manager and his wife had been given a free rein for three or four years, and they were clearly feathering their own nest, and providing free meals for three idle daughters and most of their friends. We observed from a distance for a few weeks, and we didn't rock any boats!

It reminded me of the time No. 2 and No. 3's school in York changed headmaster. The previous one was very gregarious, quite the showman and someone who certainly had his favourites in the staff room. The new chap was quiet, unassuming, a bit of a nonentity, or so we thought. For a whole term he sat back and observed! He watched and he listened and he took note of everything that was happening. Right at the end of his first term, he made his move, he cracked his whip, and said 'jump', the ones that didn't ask 'how high' were conspicuous by their absence at the start of the new school year!

This was exactly the way we played it at the pub. During the observation period we had got people lined up to takeover if the present incumbents were not prepared to toe the line! They weren't! We brought in a couple of our good friends to manage the place. They were keen to have a change of scene, the kids had flown the nest, so they rented out their house and moved in. We made a lot of changes in the kitchens, new head chef and a brand new menu. We travelled over at the weekends and a couple of times during the week. Even No. 3 got roped in to do some waitressing if she was home on a Saturday evening!

It did well, in fact I think we almost created a monster! We were spending far more time out there than we envisaged. I was staying over for at least one night a week as it was so busy. One Sunday it was all hands to the pumps, and so many customers. We drove home exhausted, and that night James had his first heart attack! That shone a totally different light on the whole thing. We decided to put it on the market and there were several interested parties. It flew off the shelf very quickly. Our friends decided if we were no longer involved that they would return home, which they did - still best chums by the way!

James went on to have another heart attack followed by a triple heart bypass and we decided that the catering industry was no longer for us. We were in and out of the pub within twelve months... and luckily we didn't lose out!

Watch this space for the next chapter of our lives! Another time though!

It's VE Day, so enjoy yourselves and remember the social distancing!

Keep safe x.

The Diary of an Incarcerated Granny. Day 53

How can it possibly be Day 53? I looked on my calendar in the kitchen, the only entries for May are three birthdays! I enjoyed the VE programme last night, and of course the words of encouragement from HM the Q. Did anyone notice she seemed to have broken a tooth, on the bottom, at the front?

My observational powers are off the scale at the moment!

I have a very good memory for trivia. For example, someone I went to school with when I was five, I can still remember the name of her guinea pig! No. 2 rang a couple of weeks ago and said could I remember the name of her friend's mother? I have met the friend twice, and never set eyes on her mother, but I knew what she was called. We once won a quiz, due to the fact that I knew what a Buff Orpington was! For the uninitiated, it is breed of chicken, much admired by the late Queen Mother! Why would I know that? As Alice said 'curiouser and curiouser'!

Today's dregs from the bottom of the bucket!

Property, I love it, always have and probably always will. My father was a builder and also owned a lot of rental property. Some of my favourite memories as a little girl was to go with him to the auctions to bid for furniture for the properties. His mantra was always 'put your money in bricks and mortar' it always stood him in good stead!

When No. 2 and the now Mr 2 decided to join forces they had two properties to sell. She had a flat in Brighton and he had a house in Worthing. They were both working full-time and had little time to explore the market. I was requested to trawl the sites to find them something to buy together. Such joy, nothing I like better than house hunting! There were a few conditions, period features, detached, off-road parking, and a garden big enough to play badminton in, oh, and a doer-upper! I trawled Rightmove and similar, for weeks, checked in several times a day just to see if anything new had come on. We found a few likely candidates, but nothing that really excited them. No. 2 works in up in London two days a week. I was perusing the internet one morning, and suddenly there it was. I rang No. 2 and sent her a link, she rang Mr No. 2 and he rang the agents straight away. The agent was a bit mystified as it had only been posted in the last ten minutes. This illustrates the power of the Yorkshire Granny! Mr No. 2 viewed that afternoon, rang No. 2 in London and said, 'I think this could be the one'. She was due back from that evening and she viewed the house at nine o clock the following morning. They say you know within fifteen seconds if it's the one for you. Of course they loved it, and funnily enough so did a lot of other people! By the weekend they had shown eighteen prospective purchasers round with more booked in the following week.

It was owned by the Church of England and it had been the local Rectory for many years, when the last Rector retired, the diocese decided to sell. It was also going to sealed bids! That's a very nail-biting scenario. The Brighton flat was sold, and there were good offers on the other house. It became clear that the Rectory was going to go for well over the asking price, and they needed every penny they could find. I had a tearful phone call from No. 2. Mother-in-law had left her a beautiful emerald and diamond ring when she died and she wondered if she should sell it to boost the coffers. I said yes, and I knew Mil would have given her blessing. She took it up to London and sold it to a Bond Street jeweller. We are convinced that was what made the difference!

The day of the sealed bids arrived. They both took the day off and went and sat in the waiting room at the estate agents. No. 2 said she felt sick. The phones were ringing and the bids were coming in. The agent walked through the waiting room and dropped a piece of paper on the table in front of them, then walked straight back into his office. If they wanted it they needed to exceed the sum written down! They did, and it was theirs. A bit naughty, but he knew how badly they wanted it. No. 2 said that she had always felt that it was going to be ok. They had looked round several times, and she had hidden a little wooden boomerang under the carpet upstairs. It was a present from her best friend who now lives in Australia and signified that she would always return! Weird thinking but I got where she was coming from. I was waiting at home when the call came through, I cried, she cried. All over a blooming house!

They moved in eight years ago, and it has been a labour of love, blood, sweat and tears!

The house has beautiful original fireplaces, arches and cornicing stained glass and all the bells and whistles. There were three marble fireplaces upstairs, boarded up and painted. All now stripped back to the original.

They knew exactly what they wanted and they bought all sorts of things at the right price, and stockpiled them until they could afford to use them. Everything they could do themselves they did. Mr No. 2 has created a lovely garden, put in a new driveway, built rows of bookcases, spent days atop a cherry picker, painting and repairing everything. Every bit of decorating they have done themselves. In the midst of all this they found time to get married, and four years ago welcomed the arrival of No. 2 Jnr. Two days before she arrived, the carpets for the stairs and the upstairs were fitted. They had lived with bare floorboards and a few borrowed rugs for four years!

Looking back at the photographs you remember how it was originally, and it makes you shudder to think of the mess they have lived through! You have to be able to recognise potential, and not everyone has the ability to do that; luckily they did.

They are almost there, still a bit to go, but what they have created is a lovely house, always flooded with sunshine and with plenty of room to put the whole family up! It suits us all fine! I'm very proud of them both. X

Well how interesting was that? Probably not very, but I enjoyed it. If you need me to house-hunt on your behalf, just let me know, it will be my pleasure! Another not very interesting snippet.

The road on which the house stands is named after the Bard. In recognition of that fact, they got married on Midsummer's Day, and No.2 Jnr's middle name is Helena, from a character in 'A Midsummer Night's Dream'. Searching back many years in the archives the house was originally called Verona House, obviously a nod to the 'two gentlemen'!

You can wake up now, I've finished!

I'm wondering what delights Boris will have in store for us tomorrow? I'm prepared to stay put if that's what it takes! X

The Diary of an Incarcerated Granny. Day 54

Morning all, it's a bit dull in Paradise this morning! Very little has changed since yesterday, the Heinz Tomato Ketchup bottle is still doing a fine job holding up the kitchen tap! I have zoomed around and cleaned the bathrooms (shower rooms... I have no bath), I've spoken to numerous people on the phone, on FaceTime and via messenger. No Archers Omnibus this morning, apparently they won't be recording again until June.

I am having Sunday lunch delivered from The Ship in Bawtry at one pm. I chose turkey of which I'm rather fond, followed by rhubarb crumble and custard! I am so looking forward to it.

No. 2 was very pleased that yesterday's tale was all about their house. People do relate to a good house story. There are an awful lot of frustrated estate agents and developers out there. Me included!

Moving swiftly on... After the episode with the pub in Derbyshire, and after the triple bypass, we were scratching our heads yet again for something to do.

We decided to go down the student route. All our lot had been in student accommodation, so we knew the pitfalls. In fact when No. 2 was in her second year, just outside London, we bought a flat and her friends moved in with her. It was a good buy, and several years after she left university, we were still renting it out very successfully. It was only when we were think-ing of moving to France full-time, and our tenants after three years were moving on, we decided to sell. Very nice outcome!

Going back to student houses, we worked out that if you

provided somewhere decent, then they were far more likely to take care of it. We bought a pair of brand new (off plan) semi-detached houses. Within fifteen minutes' walk of Sheffield Hallam University. A bit of reconfiguring was required and each house then had four bedrooms, three doubles and a reasonably sized single. A well-equipped kitchen, with extra fridge and a big freezer. A communal sitting/ dining room and a not bad bathroom, with bath and shower. There was a paved area at the front with plenty of parking, and a good-sized lawned area at the back.

It came fully carpeted and curtained, and we headed straight for IKEA. Such fun! eight beds, eight desks, eight chests of drawers, eight wardrobes, and eight of everything else, including eight Billy bookcases! We roped in our friends and had a few flat pack parties and got everything put together and ship-shape. I became an expert in assembling a Billy bookcase in the shortest possible time. We kitted out the kitchens and provided everything they could possibly need, including an iron and ironing board! All they needed to do was bring, themselves, clothes, bedding and food.

We had contacted the university and they gave us a list of dates when they brought round prospective tenants by mini-bus to view the properties. On the first viewing date we were over there in good time. We didn't really know quite what to expect, and frankly we were a bit nervous! It was really quite hilarious, the mini buses arrived, the sliding doors were opened, and about twenty of them all fell out into the middle of the road! They were all over the houses like a rash... They arrived at ten-thirty, and by midday every room was taken, and we were busy sorting out all their contracts and details for the coming year. There were a few that were rather disappointed, and left their names and numbers in case anybody backed out. It was a very successful venture. We didn't rip them off rent-wise, and they had a very decent place to stay. Some stayed for the whole of their degree course, others moved out after a year. One or two actually moved back in for their final year. If there are disadvantages, one is that you do have to be 'on tap' a lot of the time. They are a bit clueless on occasion, DIY is a step too far, and sometimes the changing of a lightbulb becomes far too challenging!

We carried on until we made the decision to move out to France permanently, and then we either had to employ letting agents, or move them on. We sold them almost as 'a going concern' and it was a period of our lives that we really enjoyed.

I think that will do us all for today, it is Sunday after all, and I'm quite full after a very good lunch including rhubarb crumble and custard! Maybe a granny nap will be on the cards? I do hope Boris is wearing his sensible hat this evening!

Tomorrow, I might tell you what we did next!

The Diary of an Incarcerated Granny. Day 55

The window cleaner has just been, and said I owed him for last time as well! I don't remember 'a last time', as I haven't been through the door for eight weeks? I haven't opened my purse for eight weeks either, that was exciting! I rather expected moths to fly out, but they didn't. Anyway, I gave him the benefit of the doubt, he is very respectful, he likes the dogs and he always fastens the gates with the utmost care. That's well worth an extra fiver.

On the subject of money, I really dislike the shiny, plasticky notes. When they first turned up, I thought they were ok. I soon changed my mind. They don't sit still, they refuse to fold nicely and the minute you open your purse they push their way out and throw themselves all over the floor. I once missed one that had escaped onto the floor, I slipped on it, wearing my socks and nearly knocked myself out! I was all for contacting the Bank of England, and insisting that they were withdrawn immediately! I was talked out of that, and reminded that it would be a waste of a first-class stamp... true enough, on reflection they were most unlikely to cease production on account of my grazed chin and bruised ego!

I always have a ten pound note in tucked into the sun visor of my car... for emergencies only.

Emergencies could include running out of petrol, (obviously) the overwhelming desire for fish and chips, which can overpower you at any time, and the wherewithal to buy a bag of pegs if accosted by gipsies. The latter being by far the most important. I have an ingrained fear of being cursed, and therefore I am an incredibly soft touch. I once ended up with a drawer in the hall table, full of pegs, scraps of lace, and enough 'lucky heather' to open a garden centre! I don't do tarot cards, fortune tellers, runes, tea leaves, and certainly not Ouija boards. I am a wimp and that sort of thing freaks me out more than you could imagine. No. 3 would dabble left to her own devices, in fact she did go and see a clairvoyant a few years ago with some of her in-laws. I imagine that a lot of things can easily apply to most people. The only thing that this woman said that did bear fruit, was the suggestion to go and get her vitamin D levels checked out.

She has regular blood tests anyway, so asked for this to be included. We were down in West Sussex for a few days, and she received a call from her GP asking her to go ASAP to the surgery! As I'm sure you know, most of the vitamin D we absorb is due to being exposed to sunlight. Poor old No. 3 was doing no absorbing whatsoever! She was filled to the brim with vit D post-haste, and still is on a fairly hefty dose. So was the clairvoyant seeing something we didn't? Or if we all had our vit D levels checked. (it's not done as standard) would most of us be deficient? I take it anyway, along with Greek yoghurt, beans and bananas to hopefully boost my immunity!

My son-in-law has just delivered my shopping, the bins are being emptied tomorrow, and The Baskervilles are being collected for a shampoo and set at eight-thirty in the morning. Far too much excitement after all this time under lock and key.

No. 3 is working from home most of the time, so Mr No. 3 came in her car to give it a run out. He also took my keys and started mine up which was fine.

What's your take on personalised number plates? I have had the same number plate for nearly thirty years, it's been on a lot of different cars, and it almost spells my surname and I always remember it. Some people regard them as a bit naff, one of my son-in-law's falls into that category, I still like him though!

Wrapping up for today, stay safe x

The Diary of an Incarcerated Granny. Day 56

I have realised this morning how much I talk to my dogs. They were both picked up just after eight am this morning by the groomers, and they won't be dropped off until this afternoon!

It's a very strange feeling, and so quiet. Violet is usually snoring loudly in the background and Poppy spends a lot of time rolling her ball underneath the furniture. I have a walking stick at the side of my chair, which is perfect for hooking the ball out. The trouble is she does it on purpose, I think it's an attention-seeking tactic!

My cleaner is coming on Friday to blitz the summer house, she is coming through the side gate, bringing all her own kit and will have no contact with me. It was flooded badly when we had all the continuous rain, and I had dehumidifiers working round the clock for over two months to try and dry it out. I have a pair of very nice armchairs and a sofa down there, plus a row of bookshelves. All the books on the bottom shelf were floating in a foot of water. So much for living on the river bank! My garden is very long, so the water never got as far as the house, thank goodness. Quite a lot of Tickhill residents had their houses flooded and some have still not been able to move back in. I know the mess it made in the summer house, and the thought of that, actually in your house is a nightmare. So I'm the scheme of things I consider myself lucky.

I've just had a long FaceTime with No. 2. She works up in London for two days a week, and is furloughed at the moment. They had a call yesterday and this will continue until July. Maybe we will be able to see the wood for the trees by then?

Let's hope so.

No. 2 Jnr aged four, is allowed half an hour on her iPad once she is ready for bed. Apparently the volume was a bit high and she was asked by Daddy to please turn it down.

She fixed him with a stare, and then said, 'Oh for goodness sake, I'll just have to go and listen to it in another room' and flounced off into the playroom! She has an answer for everything at the moment, and I fear it will only get worse!

I have just had a text from the dog groomer, The Baskervilles will be home by 3pm. When they go to somewhere new, you never quite know what to expect when they come home. They went to the same lovely lady for eight years and then she retired. Poppy came back from one encounter looking like a gremlin! I have high hopes, seeing as I've just transferred £75 into their bank account! Not bad in the scheme of things especially as they have been taxied both ways. I might even send you a pic if they look halfway decent!

I have just been and read the gas and electricity meters. Martin Lewis keeps saying it's time for a change, so I might have a look. I've been with Bulb for a couple of years and they have been fine. I had a whacker of an electricity bill after the flood, but we seem to be back on track now. Has anyone used the guys that were on *Dragon's Den*? They move you automatically to the best tariffs, and you don't have to get involved! Anyone?

My girls are home, they smell like a tart's hanky, but even that is an improvement!

As I was up and around very early (for me) this morning. I tuned in to *Good Morning Britain*. Piers Morgan is an extremely aggressive interviewer. I'm not really surprised that members of the government aren't queuing up to be annihilated by him.

On this morning's episode they appeared to have tempted Edwina Currie out of retirement, and let's be honest, a lot of people will show up for the opening of an envelope, providing you cross their palms with silver! I doubt the heated exchange will have affected Edwina very much. She was one of Maggie's army, so is impervious to criticism and thrives on a bit of mud-slinging.

Back in the day, my BF's kids were at Denstone College with Edwina's daughters. This was at the time of the 'salmonella in eggs' debacle. There were no eggs for breakfast for a very long time, and those poor girls were given a really hard time!

I'm still not 100% clear on guidelines, they still seem very open for interpretation! Am I a bit dim or what? All I know is, that when we get the go ahead, No. 3 and co, plus the Granny will be heading down West Sussex for a few days with No. 2 and family. I haven't seen them since New Year and that is far too long!

Talking to my friend in Norfolk (which we do every Friday at ten o'clock) we were discussing where we should go for a few days break, if the occasion ever arises again! If us ancient ladies are not allowed to fly, can we go by ferry to the Channel Islands for a few days?

I went to both Guernsey and Jersey as a little girl several times, but I don't really remember much. Or the Scilly Isles maybe?

Bit uninteresting today, so my apologies. I'll see if I can dig up an adventure for tomorrow!

I got up far too early for my own good this morning.

Keep safe x.

The Diary of an Incarcerated Granny. Day 57

Sorry guys there isn't one today. Had a really dizzy 'do' this morning. Balance all over the place. I decided a day away from the small screen was in order. I've slept virtually all day and feel sort of ok now.

Take care, back to normal tomorrow I hope x. Most people think I'm unbalanced anyway!

The Diary of an Incarcerated Granny. Day 58

Hello, sorry about yesterday, I seem to be ok this morning. Trying to negotiate the staircase of doom was a bit scary, not to be encouraged when you've got a 'wobble' on!

Quite a sunny one today, Titchmarsh and Sons came yesterday so it's all looking rather smart out there. My friends left me some tomato plants and a cucumber plant on the wall yesterday. It looks as though market gardening will be my next hobby!

A long discussion with No. 2 this morning, I am under instructions to trawl the internet for a Victorian mahogany dressing table with bevelled mirror, not duchesse style. They are too lumpy apparently. I love looking for things on the internet, especially houses and things to fill them with. When I moved to the Hobbit House, which is tiny, I brought very little furniture with me (other than the comfy super-king bed, with room for a pony!) I spent a lot of time looking for antique pine pieces, that would complement the beams, which are pitch pine. I have a niche in the dining room, which has a stained-glass window, set at an angle to reflect the light from the kitchen. I searched high and low and eventually found a small pine settle that fits exactly, that and a pine pew and two chapel chairs (with bible holders at the back) give me seating for four. I found the little scrubbed table on eBay.

I have rather a lot of hats. I managed to pick up a hanging rail, made from a very old spirit level, which now holds my hats above the angled-window in the dining room.

I love things with a bit of history and a story to tell. In my little sitting room at the side of the fireplace was an arch, which was rather wonky and offended my eye somewhat.

I measured up and found a pair of old pine cupboard doors that fitted in front of the arch perfectly. They don't open, but give the impression that there is a cupboard behind. A pair of antique handles and the jobs a good'un!

I'm not a fan of curtains, so I have wooden plantation shutters at all the windows. A friend came and measured up, ordered, and then fitted them for me when they arrived.

I had them at my last house as well. I love them!

I'm lucky in the fact that No. 2's house is big and she likes old stuff as well. She has absorbed plenty of mine!

Thirty years ago we were in France at an antique market. We came across a walnut bateau lit (boat bed, one side goes against the wall) which we thought would be just the job for No. 3's room. Duly bought and transported back to the cottage, with the long bits poking out of the sun roof on the Shogun.

We brought it back to England and had a mattress made to fit. These beds are four-foot wide and just six-foot long. No. 3

slumbered happily in it for several years. Eight years ago No. 2 moved into what had been the Rectory. One of the guest rooms has a central fireplace with a four-foot space at either side. They came to stay with me at Christmas, and I said I would give them the original bateau lit, if they could find a matching one on eBay. Our luck was in, something very similar with a memory foam mattress was up for auction ending on Boxing Day. Needless to say, we watched it like a hawk and picked it up for the starting price. That was a great result, who goes on eBay on Boxing Day? In another of their bedrooms they have a pair of low armchairs, that James's granny bought from a contents sale at Wentworth Woodhouse, just after the war. I guess she was trying to fill the hotel!

Mr No. 2's brother has an antique shop and restoration workshop at Brockenhurst in the New Forest, so he is always available to restore and repair things. He removed the original front door, and took it away for six weeks and completely rebuilt it. A very handy man to know, and generally if we can't find it, he can!

So, there you have me, lover of all things not new. Anything with a history, furniture made with real wood and proper joints. I can't tell you how much fun I've had, filling the Hobbit House with bits and pieces that are just to my taste. I must now return to the dressing table search.

Bit of a 'nowt nor summat' today, but I've enjoyed!

Take care all of you, if you think you have deciphered Boris's rules and regs, please let me know. In the meantime, I'm staying put!

The Diary of an Incarcerated Granny. Day 59

The sun is shining in the Hobbit House garden this morning. My cleaner has come, via the side gate and is trying to restore order to my summer house. She brings all her own kit and I won't be anywhere near her. Sounds like a plan!

Just discovered a good pal of mine is selling a couple of Lloyd Loom chairs. I snapped them up PDQ, I love them for in the garden in the summer! Feeling pleased about that!

Last night I think I dreamt I had an ear infection, which was the cause of my wobble the other day... I could feel the pain. It must have been on my mind, and as we all know, the mind is a very peculiar thing. Well, mine is anyway!

Friday again, how did that happen? This week has flown by yet again. Day 60 tomorrow of the diary... I really thought two or three weeks would see it done and dusted!

As James would have said, 'it's not often you're right, and you're wrong again.'

I would quite like to write children's books. I'm sure if the duchess of York can keep churning them out, then I can have a bash.

Maybe I could do some Vera books? She has a wild and interesting life, I'll give that one some thought!

What can I tell you today?

We've touched on hotel life, the short encounter with the Derbyshire pub, the student accommodation, I have to think hard about what came next!

Alongside the student houses we had built up a bit of a rental property portfolio. The time came when we had lost the last of our parents, and we were spending more and more time in France. We decided to move over there full-time.

The cottage was fabulous, but we wanted a proper house. We searched the internet, drew up a shortlist, and got my BF, who lived out there, to go and have a look on our behalf. She has known me for a very long time and she knows what I like.

There was a list of must haves.

Plenty of bedrooms and bathrooms. Utility room, study, swimming pool, garages, outbuildings and at least an acre of land.

Not too far from a pretty town with restaurants and good shops, great views and no more than twenty minutes' drive from the cottage and all our friends.

The one we settled on was a gem, well at least we thought so! Not even that old, but the French have a way of making things look right. It was high up in the hills overlooking the little town of Terrasson-Lavilledieu on the river Vezere. We knew the place well, ate there often, visited the market every week and knew our way around.

The house had been built by a local businessman who had really put his heart and soul into it. His relationship had gone wrong and he had to sell, and the sooner the better!

Up we popped. Good timing yet again!

You must remember, that at that time you could buy a manor house in France for the same price as a one-bed flat in Fulham. Thinking about it, you probably still can!

The house sat on a plot of about an acre. Three-quarters in front, and a lovely cherry orchard at the back. A big pool at the side of what the French call a '*cuisine d'été*' (summer kitchen!) This was a separate building with a tiled roof and open at the front. It had a complete kitchen with electric grills, BBQ, oven, fridge freezer, units and work surfaces. (far bigger than my kitchen here!) There was room for a big dining table and a seating area. Underneath was an air conditioned wine cellar. *Très magnifique!*

We spent a lot of our time out there.

The house was large, with a tower and a pointed roof. A marble-floored hall and a sweeping marble staircase. (very different from the staircase of doom!) five sets of French windows leading from sitting rooms and bedrooms onto the terrace.

We actually did the garden ourselves! All lawns and a ride on mower, what's not to like?

Being us we had to fiddle with it a bit, and opened up a huge loft space, and ended up creating a vast master bedroom with en-suite and a walk-in wardrobe and a view to die for.

I think the first year we were there we had forty-six different lots of visitors (some more than once) Good and cheap flights to Limoges, which was an hour's drive away. The kids came and brought their friends, lots of friends who were touring the Dordogne stopped off for a night or two. It was a golden summer. Winter over there can be very different, James used to say, 'they roll up the pavements at tea time'. Very quiet every-where, sometimes freezing cold and an excuse for enormous log fires! We had deer in the garden, red squirrels, pine martens, and incredible bird life. It was amazing!

More tomorrow… x.

The Diary of an Incarcerated Granny. Day 60

Day 60! The gestation period for dogs is approx. sixty-three days. Were I from the canine species, I would be looking forward to the safe arrival of a litter of puppies next Tuesday... just saying!

Quite pleasant this morning in Paradise. The toaster has conked out, well, two of the four slots have.

The summer house was given five hours of attention yesterday. Still not quite finished, but looking great. It's more like a studio really, I think a former owner gave art lessons down there, so it's double-glazed, wood-floored, spotlights, TV aerial and telephone points, and overlooks the babbling brook... quite bucolic! I might go and live down there if I ever have an argument with myself, and if I write a book I might go and do it down there.

I now have to dispose of seven big plastic crates of ruined books. Heart-breaking, thank you, babbling brook!

I have a pair of very nice armchairs down there, originally they were going to go in the cottage, but they were a bit big. Me being me, I bought them on eBay, they had come from a shop on the Kings Road in Chelsea. The lady who was selling had moved to Bexhill on Sea to retire, and they were in the way. Bought them for a song, but then had to get them up here. Shiply are the way forward, you put in your postcodes and people bid to pick up and drop off whatever you want moving. I think I had them delivered for £60. Bexhill isn't a million miles from the abode of No. 2 and family. I did wonder if I could be transported from Tickhill to Worthing, for sixty pounds, half the price of a rail ticket... and I don't mind sitting in a removal van, I am adaptable, if nothing else! The chairs have just about lived to tell the tale. They have tall legs with bun feet, so the upholstery wasn't too badly damaged. There is a big Duresta sofa down there as well. It got well and truly soaked. It has loose covers so I might give them a wash and see if they recover, if not it's skip time! I am a skip expert, I hired so many when I was clearing out the last house, it would have been cheaper to have bought my own!

I might buy a sofa bed for down there and it will be handy for the older grandchildren to have a sleepover.

Just before lockdown I found a set of photographs of the French house, I have searched everywhere and I just can't locate them anywhere. I really don't know how I can lose things in a two up, two down?

I have been lucky to have lived in some lovely houses, and equally as fortunate to travel to some amazing places... but the real thing that keeps us all going is family and friends, without them none of the material things matter. As I think I've said before, home is where you keep your knicker drawer, and at the end of the day you can only be in one room at once!

Back to Maraval Haut, French bathroom fittings are rather an acquired taste. The French aren't big on having a loo in an en-suite bathroom, and to be fair you can sort of see where they are coming from! One of our upstairs bathrooms was enormous, it had a hexagonal bath that you could get six adults in! This was a dry run I hasten to add. It was ludicrous, we eventually had a shower unit rigged up over it and used the bath as a gigantic shower tray.

Things I have found whilst searching for the photographs:

My Radley sunglasses, great find!
4 Egyptian cotton pillowcases 400 tc
2 old Valentine's cards
An unopened bag of gravy bones
A packet of Baylis and Harding foot soak
About 6 TV remotes
3,000 carrier bags
A bag of duck food

I could go on, I have looked everywhere!

Tada, found the blighters in the back of the corner cupboard, underneath some table mats! Sadly no pic of the pond-sized bath! I know I have one somewhere…

I have been rather distracted today, shopping lists to write, distance-waving to No. 3 and No. 3 Jnr. Mr No. 3 has taken a load of bags full of damaged books to dispose of. He will not be dumping them on a country lane, just in case anyone was wondering.

Bit disjointed today, I seem to have been quite busy! Hope you are all ok and limiting the gin!

The Diary of an Incarcerated Granny. Day 61

A little bit dull in Paradise this morning, I had a very peaceful night. Shopping day tomorrow, and I don't seem to be eating my bananas quickly enough. I give my list in for the week, so if I get it wrong I'm stuffed! I have started buying Cravendale milk as it lasts far longer.

Sunday today, the day of rest... so don't expect too much. I love it the way you lot have started chatting amongst yourselves. Let's hope we may all have made a few new friends during lockdown. Once this trial is over, I shall most certainly have a meet up at the Hobbit House for those near enough to pop in. It would be amazing to put faces to names. You would all have to be labelled of course, to avoid confusion. A sticker on your forehead saying, 'Guess who?' will not be deemed acceptable!

I will be a nervous wreck, wondering if everyone shows up, how I will manage to bake 865 scones?

As most of my friends will be most anxious to point out, half-a-dozen scones would be out of my comfort zone. Therefore, it would be better if you bring your own picnic, glasses and fizz!

Will that be ok?

I could entertain you with my playlist, which is already written down, for when I get the call from *Desert Island Discs*! Just playing in the background, obviously, as you will all want to be chatting noisily.

I'm getting quite excited just thinking about it!

Looking at the photographs yesterday, I found a painting of a soldier wearing a red uniform. James's father bought it in an auction years ago. He took pride of place in the main dining room at Brentwood for over thirty years. After the hotel was sold, we had him in our house in Old Ravenfield, we then took him with us to France. He came back with us to Bawtry and now resides in Worthing, in the dining room of No. 2. He was far too big for the Hobbit House! I have a photo (here she goes again!) of grandson Ben, No. 2 Jnr's big brother, illustrating the low doorways, and lack of ceiling height in the Hobbit House!

The painting came with a fair history. The subject is a

Captain R.W. Pearson of Brandsby Hall near York. He was known for writing a book on 'Military Planning' of which a copy came with the painting. The artist was Mary Ethel Hunter, who can be found on Google!

I just think it's so interesting to follow the journey of this painting over the years.

We had another quite large painting of a very miserable woman sitting at the side of a stream, flashing one of her boobs. She is known in the family a 'Titifalah'. I first remember her at Mother-in-law's house. We inherited her and she moved at least four times with us. She was at the opposite end to Captain Pearson in the big sitting room in France, and on an adjoining wall in the Bawtry house. When I moved to Tickhill she moved down to Worthing with the Captain, and is now observing all and sundry from the upstairs landing. What a well-travelled couple they are! I don't think they would have been an item in real life. He looks a bit too pleased with himself, and she looks as though life has not dealt her a good hand.

No. 2 Jnr is rather fond of Captain Pearson, but somewhat less so of Titifalah!

I'm going to sort out a few books now, then I may have a granny nap. I will most certainly not be making any scones!

Another random mix today - Take care x.

The Diary of an Incarcerated Granny. Day 62

More of the same! It's a bit relentless, isn't it?
Shopping day today, at least I've got a fresh tub of

Greek yoghurt to look forward to!

I'm surprised that lots of group events are suddenly popping up on FB, for June and July? I know that my close family members had holidays already booked for this summer, I think they have all now realised that it isn't going to happen.

It's my 'big significant' birthday in October.

No. 1, bless her, has arranged a big family weekend 'somewhere'! All will be expected to attend. I'm just hoping that by then it just might be possible?

Just looking back at all the things I have been involved with over the years. I think if you come from a background of 'doers' you tend to just follow the blueprint because that's the norm.

I think the one thing that had an enormous effect on so many of our lives was Round Table. Well over forty years on and we are all still as close as ever. Looking back it was all a bit sexist in those days! The wives of Round Table, had their own group called Ladies Circle. Both groups raised an enormous amount of money for charity. When the men reached forty, they moved into 41 Club, and us ladies decided not to move over into the affiliated Tangent Club, so we invented our own, called Upper Circle. We still meet once a month.

Over the years, we have visited Round Table in Holland, Sweden, Germany and France, for some really crazy weekends. All our children have grown up together, and still remain close. Even now (before this bloody lockdown) quite a few of us have lunch every Wednesday. My kids always refer to it as 'Aunties Lunch' as they are all the people that they have grown up with, we are all missing it so much!

James was a former President of Rotary, Chairman of Round Table, Chairman of 41 Club, a governor of a local Further

Education College, he had a finger in many pies! He was a great shooting enthusiast, game and clays, and a very good shot.

I was Chairman of Ladies Circle (they used to let me write all the bulletins!) NSPCC committee, RNLI committee, and a Magistrate for sixteen years.

My mother was a member of Rotary Ladies (I elected not to join that one!) She was secretary of the local Girl Guides Association and lots of other things, usually involving gin!

My stepfather was an amazing guy. He was awarded an OBE for his work with the prison service, Vice President of SSAFA, European Chairman of the Galvanising Association (that was a weird one, but they went to Denmark a lot!) Chairman of the local Bench, a big cheese in scouting, (he had a hat just like Baden-Powell!) What busy bees we all were!

When you look back at how many coffee mornings you have held, how many raffle tickets you have sold, how many sponsored walks, safari suppers, race nights, jumble sales, BBQ's you have helped to organise, it's all quite bizarre!

The plus side of all this, is the people that you meet along the way, that become friends, the journeys you have been on together, and the money you have managed to raise to make life better for some people.

Looking back it was a very different world then and very few wives had full-time jobs. Nowadays, most lifestyles are dependent on two salaries, childcare fees are extortionate, most families run two cars, and a long commute is the norm! It's much more of a rat race than it was then. I think I prefer things as they were! I don't think I want to change places.

As you have probably gleaned, I don't do baking. Lifeboat always had a big 'just before Christmas' coffee morning. My contribution to the cake stall were containers of my home-made chestnut stuffing. Freshly made and ready to freeze until the big day! I don't have many success stories in my life, but this turned out to be one of them. I did this on an annual basis, and it reached a stage where people were ringing and pre-ordering in case they sold out too quickly! How cool is that?

I am quite a good cook, even if I say so myself, I just don't do pastry... it makes me squirm!

No. 2 is car-hunting! She passed her test years ago, but living in London she didn't need to drive. However, if life returns to normal, No. 2 Jnr will be starting school in September, and will require transporting.

No. 2 is very fixated on what she wants, the make, the colour, the upholstery, the look of the wheels! Not much wiggle room there then, in fact none whatsoever! Yet again, I have been instructed to trawl the websites to find something that ticks all the boxes. Not as easy as you might think! Mr No. 3 works in the motor industry, so there are constant links being sent backwards and forwards, for approval. The ones you really want, are like most things... rather more than you want to pay! I think in the present climate, there are always deals to be done (but I think that about everything!) and it costs nothing to make a cheeky offer!

When you ring, they always tell you that at least three other people are interested... what a load of codswallop! They also excuse themselves to go and have a word with 'the boss', to see if there is any chance of a little bit more money off. Codswallop again, you are already speaking to the boss, there's nobody else there! Do they really think I was born yesterday? Anyway, she has drawn up a shortlist, so we'll see what happens.

If any of you have a BMW 1 series, Cabriolet diesel with automatic transmission, low mileage, in silver with a black roof, black leather upholstery, and subtle alloy wheels... will you please get in touch ASAP... we have £1,250 to spend!

It sounds as though the party at the Hobbit House might well be a goer! Plenty of scone donations and even a corned beef pie, bring it on!

That's it folks, another literary masterpiece.

I hope you are all still hanging in there. A friend of mine keeps having very strange dreams... is this a symptom of incarceration do you think? Who knows, keep safe x. Wistfully gazing downstream!

The Diary of an Incarcerated Granny. Day 63

A little bit dull this morning, my shopping delivery was delayed yesterday... so I've got Mother Hubbard syndrome!

The highlight of yesterday was *Downton Abbey* on ITV 3, starting with the very first episode and on every day at 6.30pm. I love a bit of Maggie Smith and co!

Today is 'blue bin' day. Mine is so full of ruined books that it's too heavy for me to move! My lovely neighbours always put my bins out, but I told them to leave it today. I don't want to be responsible for a double hernia!

I had to smile yesterday. No. 2 Jnr (four) was getting an ice cream out of the freezer. She took it out, held it up for all to see and said '*voila*'! Her daddy asked if she knew what that meant.

She said that if you are in a restaurant, when the 'servants' bring your lunch to the table, they always say '*voila*' when they put your plate down! Not sure where she got the servants bit from, she must be watching *Downton Abbey* as well?

The 3's are all back in harness as of today. I must admit I much preferred it when they were all safely tucked up at home!

I'm trying to think of any holidays we had, that I never got round to telling you about.

One of the many good things about James was that he was always up for a trip somewhere. I always think that even a couple of weeks before he died, if I had asked if he fancied a trek up to Everest Base Camp, he would have said, 'why not, get it booked'!

Probably a year before we moved back to England we booked a four-night trip to New York. I still to this day don't know why I booked it. He wasn't well and plans were already in place to move back to the motherland. We flew from France to London spent a couple of nights in Fulham with No. 2, then flew from Heathrow to New York. For some reason I didn't want to be there! The first night in the hotel, I woke up and had a panic attack.. never had one before or since! It really frightened me. We were on a couple of tours, which involved walking, so James had to stay on the coach most of the time. We went to Central Park, Ground Zero, Trump Tower, Times Square, all the usual haunts. We went everywhere by cab, even to Macy's, where I had to leave him in the coffee shop whilst I shopped. We had a few very nice meals out and a few quite ordinary. The coffee was rubbish, and their hot dogs were exactly the same as ours! I am however, a bit of a fan of bacon, pancakes and maple syrup! Having spent three years in a very rural part of France, I actually found it really noisy and overbearing and for some reason I felt quite unsafe. I think always at the back of my mind was what would we do if James was taken ill over there? Thinking back, I'm not even sure how we sorted out the travel insurance, maybe via our bank? I know nowadays, you can't travel to Calais without mentioning your ingrowing toenail on your insurance form!

I'm sad that my impressions of New York were clouded by anxiety. I know No. 1 and Mr No. 1 had a fabulous few days there, they only got back three days before the flights were stopped. Maybe I should give it another go one day. I think I was comparing it to Boston, which is so, so different. Never compare, never complain and never explain!

I still love Venice the most out of everywhere I've been. If only I were ensconced on the number 1 water bus on the Grand Canal, right now... I would be in heaven! Take care x.

The Diary of an Incarcerated Granny. Day 65

Yesterday was good! My neighbour from Bawtry called and brought me a geranium plant, which was so kind... I do miss her and the children!

My Lloyd Loom chairs arrived this morning... just the job.

I have discovered a breakfast cereal called Curiously Cinnamon, which I rate very highly.

No. 3 sorted me out with an app to order and deliver my meds, without hassling the doc and the chemist. Delivery due today, so let's see if it works.

It's very sunny out there, Violet-Elizabeth has been

sunbathing for well over half an hour. She has just wandered in, had a drink and scrabbled up onto her pouffe. That will be it now until five pm, when her inbuilt alarm clock will ring and she will require her dinner.

My cleaner is coming tomorrow, I think! I can't wait... I shall save her the dust, or she will be disappointed! I find it really hard to change my super-king bed, and usually end up tied in a knot inside the duvet cover!

I watched a few minutes of *Come Dine with Me* when I was having my lunch. The number of adults who don't know how to hold a knife and fork is amazing. They obviously never had the equivalent of my mother-in-law in their lives!

No. 3 has booked a few days off in July, just on the off chance we may be allowed to visit No. 2 and family by then. No. 1 and co are only an hour away, how good would that be if we could all see one another? Saying that, the photographs of the crowded beaches yesterday are horrific. Why do people still not get it?

It was great to hear about all your favourite happy places yesterday. Harrogate had quite a few mentions. Before James came back to run the family hotel, he worked for a while as an assistant manager at the Majestic in Harrogate. He was a big fan of the place. I think the area linking Harrogate, York and Knaresborough is known as the 'golden triangle' a very expensive property hotspot!

I was intrigued to learn that one of our fold, although having travelled all over the world, has never been to Yorkshire! What delights you have in store!

Someone said there's yet another bank holiday looming. Who knew? I certainly didn't. Yesterday I decided to flip through my address book and ring someone I haven't spoken to for ages. We had a great catch up and he was so pleased that I had made the call. Give it a go... we aren't exactly doing much else are we?

I have just come back inside after thirty minutes in the sun. It's really warm out there. I think the older I get, the less tolerant to high temperatures I become. My little sitting room is north-facing, so always coolish, which is a bonus sometimes. The back of the Hobbit House is south-facing, and is constantly sunny and warm, so the best of both worlds really. When I come downstairs in the morning and the sun is coming in through the French windows in the kitchen, it always makes me smile, and I know I did the right thing.

I had a statement from my letting agents this morning, I have a few rental properties, hither and thither, and so far everyone is managing to pay their rents. In the present climate it's a bit of a challenge for everyone.

Does anyone else have any rental property? I lurch between thinking it's a good investment, to wanting to sell the lot, as sometimes it drives me mad! There is always something. I think last year was the worst year on record. I put in several new kitchens and bathrooms, every electrical appliance known to man expired and along with upgrading lots of double-glazing, decorating and recarpeting, it was a pain in the arse!

I'm hoping that now everything is completed, I might have a less expensive year!

Last year we had a big family party at the Hobbit House, the weather was marvellous so we had a BBQ of sorts. No. 3 and family live in a lovely apartment with an enormous balcony overlooking a lake. Lots of room for 3 Jnr's slide and sand pit, seating and dining area, it really is fab. The downside is they aren't allowed to have a BBQ. The way round this was to buy the biggest George Foreman electric grill known to man! This is a monster, cooks loads, has a big, domed top, they brought it over for our family party and it worked a treat. I was so impressed that I bought one. It was easy to clean and very un-messy. This is definitely the way forward for those impromptu dining experiences, check it out! Mine is still in the box!

A few months ago I had lunch with some friends, and we had a bread basket with dipping oils and really sticky balsamic vinegar. The oil was smoked virgin olive oil and it was delicious. I found some on Amazon, not the cheapest, but it does make a very subtle difference. Dare I admit to a thin crust Goodfellas Pepperoni Pizza the other evening? I just have! The trick is to cook as instructed, add your own freshly grated Parmesan (not using the foot grater!) drizzle with smoked olive oil and sprinkle with chilli flakes! Tada, perfection for less than a couple of quid. It's the little things that make the difference!

Quick supper... grease an oven dish, two med tins tuna, handful of frozen peas, tin of Campbell's condensed chicken soup, mix gently. Couple of pkts of plain crisps crumbled on the top, bit of grated cheese, bung in oven till bubbling... 'Voila'!

You heard it here first!

I am still car-hunting, so my time is not my own! Unless somebody makes a decision soon, I will have gone off the boil and lost interest. Be warned, my attention span is limited. I am starting to develop an interest in Yurts, I'm not sure my garden is big enough, but I'm happy to do the research if any of you fancy one?

Till tomorrow x

The Diary of an Incarcerated Granny. Day 66

Covid 19
    I am socially isolating upstairs in my beautifully clean bedroom. I am also eating a digestive biscuit and have made a few crumbs! I shall remain up here until it's safe to return downstairs.

Just had some sad news of a very old friend who has succumbed to this dreadful disease. His wife is also in hospital with the same. How awful for them all. There can't be many people now that don't know anyone who hasn't been affected.

I'm going to tell you about our Round Table I National Conference weekend in Blackpool in 1976. I have had to ring a friend to confirm that it really happened and it wasn't just a bad dream!

Round Table was very popular in the seventies, a great way of raising money, bringing families together, and creating life-time friendships.

We all went to Blackpool, there was a fancy dress theme for the girls that was something to do with sea nymphs. I remember us going to someone's house each with a spare pair of white knickers. We then proceeded to dye all the knickers green in a bucket! These were the foundation for our costumes, which were bloody awful.

We were booked into a hotel b and b-type of place, which was pretty grim. No en-suite bathrooms, really small bedrooms with the bed pushed up against the wall and acres of brown and yellow banana leaf carpets. I remember taking my Carmen rollers, and the wall sockets were so old that my plug wouldn't fit. A dear friend was called upon to sort it, and eventually some bare wires were inserted into the socket on the wall. He came to my rescue that day, and I have loved him ever since! We were allowed to use the bar at the establishment next door, and most folk were fairly hammered before we set off! I can't remember what the men were dressed as, but our puke green seaweed costumes were less than fetching. A coach picked us up and took us to the venue, which was heaving. Hundreds of revelling Round Tablers are a sight to behold. If my memory serves me well. Ike and Tina Turner were the big act of the evening. You have to remember that this was well over forty years ago, long before Tina kicked Ike into touch and became 'simply the best' by herself! It was all a bit of a shambles, and in the middle of the performance the stage collapsed, and Ike and Tina suffered cuts and bruised egos! As they were the star performance, and it was well on into the evening, ninety-nine percent of the audience were so inebriated that I don't think anyone had even noticed that they were there in the first place. The place was awash with squashed plastic pint glasses and spilt beer the air was foggy with cigarette smoke. The evening came to an end. We had lost most of the people we had come with. Nobody could remember the name of the place we were staying... but somebody thought they might recognise it if we saw it! We couldn't find our bus anywhere, however one of our lot found an abandoned double decker, still with the keys in! It started first time and he was well chuffed. It took a lot of persuasion to remove him from the driver's cab, he was intent in taking us all back to our lodgings. Apparently the next morning, he woke in a panic, clambered over his wife and almost burst into tears with gratitude that the double decker wasn't parked outside! He still comes out in a cold sweat when he thinks about it. One couple, who shall remain nameless, were missing all night! They were found on the sea front the following morning, wearing very little, other than a couple of Viking helmets, and both carrying a shield!

Apparently they had woken up in a twin-bedded room, in an unknown hotel with another couple who were hard at it in the other bed! We still laugh about it now.

It was in Blackpool that I had my first and last oyster, makes me shudder even now! I recall us skipping down the sea front, and sitting outside Yate's Wine Lodge, waiting for them to open the doors and let us in

This was the year before we got married, so it was a harsh introduction to the wider world beyond... and I quite liked it!

One guy seemed to have acquired a policeman's helmet (a real one) and was so overcome with shame that he posted it back, First-class with a letter of apology!

Well that was Blackpool, and I don't think I have been since.

The following year we went to Great Yarmouth and I think that was probably just as eventful. We got married on a Monday, spent three nights in a lovely hotel in the Cotswolds and then went straight down to Great Yarmouth for yet another Round Table National Rally.

No grotty hotel this time..., just the biggest caravan park in the Western world. I remember James getting very drunk and we rolled him under a table and left him there. There was a pub-type thing on the caravan site and we all headed for there when we got back from wherever we went. A dentist friend of ours had brought a lady friend with him for the weekend. She was in the caravan preparing herself for a night of untold passion. He was on a definite promise so headed back after just one drink. I think we all were kicked out about three hours later, and we bumped into him outside. All the rows of caravans were identical, he of course couldn't remember which one was his and he had been walking up and down for hours! Needless to say, the romance did not last, she dumped him and she ended up marrying one of his best friends. He never forgave either of them! The day before we came home James had a crab sandwich, and got food poisoning. It was a thrilling and memorable honeymoon.

I have been given the all-clear to return downstairs. The Hobbit House is dust and fluff free. Harmony is restored, and social distancing maintained at all times. Take Care x.

The Diary of an Incarcerated Granny. Day 67

It's bit breezy in Paradise this morning, as forecast by the weather person! Years ago there used to be an old chap on the TV called Mr Froggat from Thirsk.... he was the best weather forecaster known to man. He based everything on observations of nature, and he was spot on! My faith in weather forecasters was shattered in 1987, when Michael Fish omitted to inform any of us that the worst storms in living memory were heading our way. What a cock up that was! Poor Michael, that will probably be the only thing he will ever be remembered for, maybe his gross taste in kipper ties and his dodgy haircut may get a mention, but I think that's as far as it goes. You blew it Michael! Literally!

I am very aware that I seem to use far too many exclamation marks! I think it's become a bit of a habit. Apologies.

As you must all have realised I am a bit of a bookworm. The thought of having nothing to read fills me with absolute dread. I'm always happy to reread a book if it's something I have enjoyed, hence the fact that I never get rid of any of them. The loss of so many due to the flood was really upsetting. I am on a mission to refill my shelves.

I've just re-bought Daphne du Maurier's *The Kings General* and *Frenchman's Creek*, both of my original copies were drowned.

I've been a big fan of hers since I was a teenager. I've also read her biographies, and she was a 'very' interesting character!

The Mitford family are another of my favourite topics, I wouldn't say the novels blow me away, but their life stories are fascinating.

I can hold up my hand and give good old Jilly Cooper a bit of a heads up! Frothy, upper class tales, but enjoyable nevertheless!

I am a bit of a Ruth Rendell fan, Joanna Trollope, Susan Howitch, Sarah Waters and very many others. I've read the biographies of the Churchills, the Astor family, all well worthy worth of a read!

At the moment I'm slightly into psychological thrillers, some are incredibly good, others I've sussed out by chapter two!

Hilary Mantel is my latest find, and I like the way she writes. The *Wolf Hall* ones I haven't read yet, but I'll get around to it. I find the history of the royal family (not the present lot) quite an eye opener. My all-time favourite along with *The Wind in the Willows* is *Black Diamonds*. Not a novel, but an in-depth history of the Fitzwilliam family of Wentworth Woodhouse. I shall be taking that as my book choice on *Desert Island Discs*. I think I have mentioned this several times on here. If you haven't read it, do yourself a favour. I promise to never mention it again!

Stars of stage and screen that you have fancied over the years…

When I was seventeen, I had an amazing crush on Franco Nero. I played truant for the first and only time in my life… and went to see him at the cinema in *Camelot*! I was besotted for quite a time, he was the perfect Lancelot and he had the most beautiful blue eyes. I then met a real person and transferred my affections, but Franco still holds a piece of my heart!

Looking back I don't think there were that many. What's the phrase? 'He could take the top off my egg any time.' I don't think I've uttered those words very often!

Colin Firth, as Mr Darcy was a bit of a contender at one stage, although I went off him when he sang in *Mamma Mia*. Isn't it funny how the odd little thing can put you right off? The other not remotely interesting fact concerning him, is that Colin Firth's parents bought No. 1's, husband's, granny's bungalow in Winchester a few years ago! I keep telling you I have a memory like a sponge for trivia!

I was quite a fan of Alan Rickman, he was not aesthetically pleasing, but he had something about him that I rather liked. I was quite sad when he fled the mortal coil.

What, or who would you describe as handsome?

I think that my son-in-law, the husband of No. 2 is what I think of as handsome, and he does scrub up beautifully, if you can separate him from his shorts and flip-flops! He also makes coffee exactly as I like it, which ups the brownie points in one fell swoop. No. 2 thinks he's pretty cool as well, and No. 2 Jnr married him in secret in the hall only the other week... wearing her Rapunzel dress and a sparkly crown. What a lucky person he is! James has a bit of a thing for Kim Bassinger, we worked out eventually that it was the name he liked. He wouldn't have recognised her if he had been standing next to her in a bus queue... and that would never have happened for either of them!

Poppy is being a bit odd today, she keeps trying to sit on my shoulder? Lord knows what that's all about? I am holding my iPhone in one hand, typing this with the obligatory one finger of the other hand, and she is breathing up my nose! She just loves her Mummy so much.

Occasionally she gets it wrong, and the half melon skin that had done the rounds of the garden, was not a welcome visitor in my comfy super-king!

Talking of beds, just before lockdown, I was trying to decide whether or not to buy a new mattress. A decent mattress these days is about the same price as a weekend in Paris.

I eventually decided to buy a new mattress topper to see if that made any difference. I did and it did!

Do any of you go on the Brand Alley website? I have got some really good things from them. I tend to buy my bedding from there, often up to 60% off. It would be rude not to!

That's it for today, I have an assignation with a lot of books and some empty shelves.

Keep safe all. X

The Diary of an Incarcerated Granny. Day 68

Excellent sleep with the new mattress topper. I was not desperate to get up... but I think Poppy was desperate to go for a wee! She won of course.

It's a bit of a grey day today, you never feel quite as chirpy when it's a grey day, do you?

Just had a conversation with No. 3, trying to pick her brains about what she thinks I should write about today. Everything she suggested I think I have covered in some form or another, so I'm scratching my head yet again!

The subject of books seemed to generate a good discussion, many of you are keen readers and it was very interesting to see all the different types of things you enjoy reading. I will certainly be sending for a few of your suggestions.

I have been trying to be very tidy since my cleaner came on Friday. I don't think the good lord had me down on his list as a domestic goddess. I get very irritated if things aren't put back in their proper places though. A picture that isn't straight makes me twitch!

A friend bought me a mini spirit level for Christmas... I carry it in my handbag!

I have a pair of bronze boxing hares on a beam over my fireplace. They have to line up perfectly with the decoration on the frame of the picture above them. On Friday evenings I always have a very long chat with my friend in Norfolk. This Friday, I had to pause the conversation to get up and line the bloody hares up properly. Am I worse since lockdown, I'm not sure?

Houses.

When we first got married we bought a detached cottage in the village of Brampton-en le Morthen. Did it up, put on an extension and moved when No. 2 was about a year old.

We then bought The Grange in Wickersley, a beautiful Georgian house, in need of total renovation and suffering very badly from subsidence. As luck would have it, the Coal Board were offering extremely generous grants to repair the subsidence damage. I think every ceiling had to come down, every floor came up, a huge crack in the outside wall had to be pinned and cobbled back together... they did an amazing job. We lived in a haze of scaffolding, dust, bricks, plaster pipes and hanging wires everywhere for over twelve months. There was a yew tree on the big lawn that was supposedly there at the time of the Norman Conquest. A gazebo-type building in the front corner that was a lookout for stage coaches to London, and a blocked of flight of stone steps that were supposed to lead underground to the church? The original old kitchen, still with boarded up range, stone flagged floors, had been used as a motorbike repair workshop. We slowly turned the house back to how it should have been. In the middle of this transformation we welcomed No. 3 into the fold. The house was big. My mother decided to come and live with us, and she had her own self-contained apartment with her own front door, but with access to the main house on both the ground floor and the half landing. It worked quite well, she did the odd bit of babysitting, but was never imposed upon. She also had the canny ability to detect a wine bottle being uncorked at twenty paces, therefore she spent a lot of time socialising with us and our friends!

When we bought The Grange we also inherited Mrs T. She had worked for the previous owners for years and was happy to continue. She was a star of the highest order. She knew the house well, she was thrilled to bits to see it being returned to its former glory. She loved the animals. We had two Gordon Setters, a Labrador, two cats and a Shetland pony. She was brilliant with the kids, she made buns, she had some cleaning rota that she followed, which I was never party to!

She also had a husband called Henry, he was a miner, drove a Reliant Robin and was a pretty good at handyman stuff and had a particular penchant for beetroot sandwiches. James said that miners liked something moist in their sandwiches as it was very dry down the pit? If James and I ever had a weekend away, they would move in and look after children, animals, and keep an eye on Granny!

We once had six guests staying for a Round Table International weekend. We were out and about all the time. Mrs T moved in, cooked breakfasts, made beds, baked buns for afternoon tea, tidied up everything, sorted out the animals and children, and still kept an eye on Granny!

She loved it, and we loved her!

There was always an ancient tale in Wickersley, that Old Moat rode across The Grange garden on a white pony with his head under his arm. We never saw him!

We were away once on a family holiday, when some people turned up and spoke to my mum. They had lived there as children and asked if they could just have a wander in the garden. My mother, being my mother, invited them in for a guided tour and most probably a gin and tonic! They asked her if she ever saw the ghost of the 'old gentleman' on the stairs, that seriously freaked her out, and me.

I once spent three nights there, with only No. 2 for company.

Mum was away, James was up in Scotland shooting and No. 3 hadn't quite arrived by then! I never slept a wink, I brought all three dogs into the bedroom with me.

I daren't turn off the light, every time I moved all three dogs looked at me. I thought that they had heard something, by morning I was a nervous wreck. I think I shipped in a friend for the last two nights! I don't do spooky stuff. That was Wickersley Grange in a nutshell, the people that bought it from us are still there, and have done nothing to it since the day they moved in! I think were there for nearly five years, my mother was swept off her feet and decided to remarry, and we decided to downsize a bit and use the spoils to add some new en-suite bathrooms at the hotel.

We actually moved 100 yards up the road to a much older property that became a much loved family home for a decade.

Somewhere I have some photos, but as usual I can't find the damn things. Here's one that No. 3 found! A lovely house!

Just found a couple, the wall behind the pony was a 'fruit wall' it had a row of removable grates at the bottom, they used to light a fire and the heat would warm up the stone through a cavity inside, and ripen the peaches. Clever. The other is me, on the lawn, looking a wreck, with a collection of furry friends and No. 2 as a small person.

No sign of the seal of the year! Found a note in the kitchen... I never knew she could write... she must have gone with Colin, no sign of him either!

Hope you all have a lovely Sunday, and no escaping tomorrow, just because it's a bank holiday! Keep safe.

Wickersley Grange

Angie, Aimee, Joe, Shamrock, Lucy and Drummer on the lawn at
Wickersley Grange.

The Diary of an Incarcerated Granny. Day 69

70 days tomorrow! Arghhhhhhh!

Today, I am escaping incarceration. No. 3 is shopping for me, Mr No. 3 is working from home. It was suggested that I drove over, only about six miles, and collected the shopping. It will be put straight in the boot of the car and we may chat across the car park.

It will do my car the world of good, I just hope it starts and that I can remember how to drive! I must admit to feeling a bit apprehensive...

It's a lovely day here yet again, we would all have been in a sorry state if the weather had been dreadful, wouldn't we?

I had an Indian takeaway last night from Taj Cottage in Tickhill. It was here in twenty minutes, straight from the sizzling dish.

Murgh sizzler, pulao rice and a peshwari naan. Perfection in a recyclable carrier bag!

I've had a bit of an 'eat up' this morning, ready for the restocking later. I'm fairly proud that I seem to have wasted very little over the last nine weeks. I seem to have 'gawn awf' eggs for some reason... not sure why.

I was pleased to see that there were a few fans of Alan Rickman out there. He certainly had something about him!

It's a really good job that we are all attracted by different things in people. I get on with most folk. I think that it's always possible to be civil (I will amend that to nearly!) but if they don't float your boat, then you just don't seek them out socially.

It doesn't always follow that all your friends will like one another as much as you like them. Usually around my birthday (always flexible) I have a bit of a lunch do. I contact the great and the good and if they aren't doing anything more exciting they roll up. I book a restaurant, and if I'm feeling generous I pay for it all, and If I'm not, I buy the drinks and wine and they buy their own food. Nobody seems to mind either way! Last year a friend came up from London and stayed for a couple of days. One drove up from Norfolk, just for the day and the rest were local yokels. Usually get about eighteen of us, so it's a lovely day. Well I think so!

When James died, he had been ill for so long that it was a bit of a dilemma to decide what to do regarding the funeral. It was either going to be a mega affair with people from all aspects of his life, or just us. We opted for the latter. Me, the four children and their other halves and grandchildren, nobody else. It was perfect. We then invited all our closest friends to a very nice pub/ restaurant, for what was described as James's 'leaving party'. Toby (the tall man) made a speech, we all had a smashing time and he would have loved it. When the tall man was twenty-one, James gave him a case of vintage port. Very special occasion stuff! He had got married, had two children and still not opened a bottle! I'm pleased to report that the night of the funeral he cracked open a bottle and we all raised a glass to the man himself!

Do many of you live on your own? It's a funny set up to be honest. Some people have it thrust upon them, some find themselves alone through a fractured relationship, and others can think of nothing worse than having to live a life of compromise.

Before James died the last three years were hell. I did as

much as I could, for as long as I could. I have never had a moments guilt that I didn't do everything in my power to look after him. After he died, I floundered for a while, I then pulled up my big girl pants and decided how I wanted my life to evolve. I'm fortunate in the fact that I was, and am well provided for. Financial problems mixed with despair are not happy bedfellows!

I made a list of things that really pissed me off, that I was never going to do again!

One was explain, If I don't want to go to anywhere or do anything I just say I don't fancy it. No. ten squirm-filled minutes of excuses. 'No' is a complete sentence! Try it!

Ironing, I hate it, if needs must I will get someone to do it. House cleaning falls into the ironing category. I will admit to always being a consistent loo bleacher, and a wiper of kitchen surfaces but the rest does not excite me in the slightest!

I think in the back of my mind I knew I would move after James died. I wasn't sure to where, or to what. I usually work on the principle of 'I'll know it when I see it'. That seems to stand me in good stead. Hence when the Hobbit House popped up, it was almost an instant decision.

Filling it with 'my' kind of stuff has been brilliant. No rush for anything specific, just waiting for the right thing to pop up, which it usually does.

I imagine I am slightly more selfish than I used to be. I hate being harassed. As some of my family have realised, constant chivvying will often result in a negative outcome. I try to be as independent as I can, I have no desire to be a burden or a chore to any of them.

So, basically. I have no problem being on my own. The dogs

are good company and they never ever argue!

Today's ramble is not really about anything, as you will have realised. A few disjointed thoughts, linked in a rather haphazard way.

I'm off to get my shopping now. My car is seven months old and done 543 miles, with one careful and somewhat absent lady owner...

I'm back, I remembered how to drive, I played my music at full force, and it was wonderful! Phew it's a really warm one out there today. What a lovely Bank Holiday Monday this has been so far! Never got to see No. 3 Jnr from a distance either, the transaction took place in an underground car park. No. 3 was wittering that the scampi would be thawing out, so I came straight back! Happy Bank Holiday one and all.

The Diary of an Incarcerated Granny. Day 70

I've just read an article which said Covid 19 would fade away after seventy days!

Professor Isaac Ben-Israel... I hope your prophecy was correct.

I so enjoyed my little burst of freedom yesterday, windows down, music blasting, Radley Sunglasses (which I thought I had lost!) in situ... such a cool dude!

I am having a problem with my iPhone... everything I Google lasts for about thirty seconds and then flicks back to my home page.

No. 3 says it's to do with my apps, and has suggested various things to try, none of which appear to work. Any thoughts anyone? It getting a little bit annoying now!

I have just tried to listen to a song on YouTube, and that keeps flicking back as well.

The song, if you're interested, is called 'Remember Me', by G4. It has the same effect on me as Vera Lynn and 'We'll Meet Again'! Please have a listen and tell me what you think.

After seventy days I have worked out that a lot of you drink gin. I know which books you enjoy reading, whether or not you are a slave to the ironing board, and the fact that the vast majority of you love rhubarb crumble. You all now know just about everything there is to know about me, if Boris doesn't let us out soon there will be very few tales left to tell!

Houses as you know have been big features in my life. I talked you through Wickersley Grange the other day... so the next step was Minden Cottage.

Literally 100 yards up the road from the Grange.

A very different place, lots of beams, low ceilings, open fire-places, stone floors, it was so warm and cosy, we adored it. I think if you asked the two youngest which house they would think back to as 'home' they would always choose Minden. It had a huge sitting room, dining room, hall, downstairs cloakroom, big kitchen with a scrubbed pine table that would seat ten. Upstairs were two bathrooms, one en-suite, and five bedrooms. One which opened up onto the garden which we used as a playroom. Outside it had a barn, a stable, an enormous workshop and an open cart shed and a garage. The lawn was on a higher level through a gate, and had lots of cherry trees, a big old swing, and joy of joys an above ground swimming pool!

There was a little secret passage through a door in the sitting room that led into a corner of the kitchen. To begin with we called it the back passage, after a while we rechristened it 'The Rectum'! Off the kitchen were two big rooms with stone shelving, one had a barrel gantry. James was particularly fond of that.

Meat hooks in the ceiling and a very low door. The house dated back to the early 1700s and it was a lovely family house.

After a few years we decided to have a bit of a fiddle with things. There was a stone store room which adjoined the kitchen, an outside loo and a coal store, all accessed from outside. We blocked off the kitchen side of The Rectum and James turned it into a shooting cupboard which housed all his shooting kit and a big metal gun cupboard to store all the guns. The kitchen beams were ancient and had been painted with black paint. We decided they needed sorting, so we had them sand blasted. Sand blasting outside is just about liveable with. Inside, not to be recommended! The wooden boards between the beams were the floorboards for the bedroom above. The carpet in the bedroom looked like the Sahara desert, we had to have it taken up and all the sand sucked out. The house was a real mess, but, the beams came up a treat. We then knocked through the kitchen wall into the store rooms, and made another sitting room. James called it 'The Sunday Morning Paper's room'! We had acquired a mullion and transom window from a relative up in the Lake District. Supposedly to have been removed from Littledale Hall, but not sure how true that is?

Anyway, we had that put in, we uncovered a bread oven in the wall, which we had back lit and then a new kitchen fitted! Very smart. I remember when they pulled out the old kitchen I found my carrot cake mould that had gone down the back of one of the drawers! Still have it somewhere.

James then decided he was going to build himself a car. The workshop was ideal, and after about eighteen months he had made himself an AC Cobra!

We had a lovely ten years at Minden, still with Mrs T at the helm (she came with us of course). During the time we were there we bought the cottage in France.

We always went for a month in the summer, so Mrs T and Henry would move in, sometimes she would bring her mum, and they would take care of the dogs and cats, and the garden... and the best bit was that Mrs T would take charge of the packing of the school trunks - always a bit of a nightmare!

We then noticed that The Old Hall in Brampton-en-le-Morthen had been bought from the Sitwell Estate. It was being divided into two houses. What an amazing building, Grade Two listed, the renovations were being overseen by English Heritage. Dating back to around 1540 it was a gem. Needless to say, we had to have a dip at this one! So off we went again...

Minden will always hold a special place in my heart. It was a house that hugged you!

I'm surprised that I have managed to write this, No. 2's car-hunt appears to be hotting up, she has FaceTimed me at least four times, for my opinion. She needs to sort it now, my attention span is waning and I want to move on to Yurts.

It sounds as though we may be allowed a little more freedom over the next couple of weeks. As soon as we get the go ahead I need to head south... I can't wait.

Hope you've all had a good day. I hear it's Tuesday? Take care x.

The Diary of an Incarcerated Granny. Day 71

Tired today, how can you be tired when you haven't done anything? I got up at eight-ish, sat on the sofa and dozed off until ten! Boredom is kicking in, I think.

Finally got my iPhone sorted last night, thanks for all the advice. I closed the Google app and then re-installed it and that seems to have done to the trick.

No. 2 seems to have located the car of her dreams, for which we are all truly thankful! I can now move on to my Yurt research!

We seem to be getting the odd glimmer of hope via Boris. Whatever measures he decides upon, he won't please everyone.

I still feel as though I'm viewing it all from afar. A lot of my friends are feeling very nervous about braving the big wild world again, and I think I will probably be the same.

I'm fairly sure that the percentage of people working from home will increase enormously. I think two of my sons-in-law will certainly be home-based a lot more.

When I went out for my drive the other day, I saw quite a few ice cream vans. There were two at the Mill Dam in Tickhill, parked about fifteen yards apart, and rather a lot of queues forming at both. I used to tell my lot that when you heard the jingle from the ice cream man, it meant he had sold out and was going home! Was that a little unkind?

Ooh I could just eat a '99', I love that squiggly ice cream that comes out of a machine. I wonder how much cream and good things it actually contains? Not many I bet, I still like it though.

My copy of *Wolf Hall* arrived this morning, it's a rather large tome. I hope it's as good as everyone says it is. I sent No. 2 a book called *The Mothers* the other day. About a group of women of very differing circumstances that met at NCT classes. All my girls did the NCT route and they have made some good friends because of it. I doubt there was any such thing in my day, and if there was nobody told me about it. I worked very much on the principle that ignorance is bliss. They are always quick to tell you that no two births are the same, in which case there's little to be gained by allowing your imagination to run riot. I'd be lying if I said I hadn't spent better days, but the end results were well worth the effort involved!

My father was one of nine. He was next to the youngest, and his mother died when he was two. He had no memory of her, there were five girls and four boys. The eldest daughter was sixteen when her mother died and she stepped in and brought them all up. My grandfather was a farmer and I think they had a pretty good life compared to some. I can still remember my aunt as an old lady, my father had a great affection for her, after all she had been a mother to him. I am an only one, suited me fine, what you don't have you don't miss, and I think that's quite true.

How many siblings do you have? Are you close to them?

I have a bit of a secret passion, which is Mumsnet. I'm sure you will have heard of it. Two particular 'chat' discussions are 'Am I being unreasonable?' and 'Relationships'. All life is there. Toxic relationships between couples and families are revealed and it does make it apparent that there are a lot of people out there having an awful time.

The giving and taking of advice is a tricky subject. How many of us feel duty-bound to run an idea past someone, or bare your soul wondering what to do about something personal? Most of us I think!

I always think that you know exactly how you are going to tackle a problem, before you ask the 'what would you do?' question.

Occasionally your decision comes back to bite you on the bum, and the 'I told you so' said with slightly too much relish, is hard to accept!

As we all know what's done is done. Time spent dwelling on the past is fruitless, and it really messes with your head, I know that to my cost!

Just watching Boris, a high number of deaths again today... I'm unsure if we are not moving too quickly on all of this? Those of us who are retired have the choice to do as much or as little as we personally choose. The ones that are sent back to work or will lose their jobs if they don't, are on a very different path.

No. 2, at some stage will have to return to her job in London, only two days a week, but still only viable if she travels by train.

No. 3 works in the health care sector within a private company. She can do a certain amount of work from home, but not all of it!

I am just doing as I'm told and hoping it will all go away!

They are now predicting a water shortage and a hose pipe ban, and a very hot summer! There are never any level playing fields are there? Why does everything have to be in the extreme? Someone said the other day, that they were not looking forward to the 'new normal'... I fear it will be a very different kettle of fish to the old one!

Another day of bumbling thoughts... I've only got three

houses left, so I'm rationing you!

I hope you all had a good day! X.

The Diary of an Incarcerated Granny. Day 72

Yet another lovely day in Paradise... and apparently more to come?

I weeded a bit yesterday, watered a lot, and I'm slightly hoping that Titchmarsh and Sons will put in an appearance today! They are somewhat spasmodic to say the least, so who knows?

Today I'm going to tell you about The Old Hall in Brampton-en-le Morthen.

We had lived in Brampton when we were first married. An ancient village, mostly owned by the Sitwell family. The Manor House was well known for being used as The Judges Lodgings, when Judge Jeffries was travelling the country deciding whose head was for the chop, in what was known as the Bloody Assizes!

Then there was 'The Hall', built we think around the 1540s towards the end of the reign of Henry VIII. It was a big, imposing stone house, with crowstep gables, mullion and transom windows and a tower on the West front. I know at one stage the big centre room was used as a ballroom for estate functions. Over the years it had been divided into separate dwellings. One end had been used as a sweet shop, it had been butchered and abused and when it eventually was put up for sale it was a derelict heap!

One couple saw the potential in this, and Tony and Rachael Bell bought it. Fiercely guarded by its listed building status and policed by English heritage, it was a long and difficult journey of restoration. It was decided that it would be divided into two houses. The Bells would have the half nearest the road, and the other half would be put up for sale.

This is where we came into the equation. The external work was all done. roof and windows in place, and we bought the shell. It was on three floors, lots of ancient timbers, relics of several fireplaces, and very little else. You could stand inside and look up to the rafters three floors up. We brought in a local architect and spent weeks trying to reconfigure the inside. There was no staircase, we found two sections of original oak panelling leaning up against a wall upstairs. There was a cold tap and a stone sink in a corner and that was about it. We moved into the hotel for six months that turned into eighteen months, until it was habitable. The Bells had brought a big static caravan on site, and they lived in that with their two small children.

There were lots of hoops to jump through with English Heritage, lime plaster was to be used throughout, all the timbers were to be exposed and the inglenook fireplace to be restored as much as possible. We spent weekends hunting round reclamation yards, searching for 'just the right oak beam' for over the fireplace. We found one in a farm yard in Wentworth, a foot square and eight-feet long. We lost a foot at one end, as it was rotten, but the rest was perfect. The front door we had specially made to fit into the stone archway. Solid reclaimed oak, with oak studs and beading. The staircase was custom-built and was very substantial dark stained elm and went up two floors. A real chunky monkey, I once fell downstairs and banged my head on every spindle, and knocked myself right out! Downstairs, there were stone flags in the hall, and stone windowsills throughout. Because the house was on three floors we had to use fire doors internally. We got round this by staining them dark oak and panelling them with oak coffin beading. Where there's a will there's a way!

The tower was fascinating with crow-step gables and mullioned windows. A small entrance porch on the ground floor with the big oak door, a tiny study on the first floor, and a sleeping alcove off No. 2's bedroom, which just fitted in a double mattress. (In my opinion, that was the best kids bedroom ever!)

It wasn't an enormous house by any means. A very big sitting room with the inglenook. A good entrance hall and a cloak-room and a large dining kitchen. The kitchen had an original stone fireplace that we found on the top floor and had repo-sitioned. There was a cellar, stone-flagged under the kitchen floor, reached by a trap door.

First-floor master bedroom, dressing room, en-suite. No. 3's big double bedroom with en-suite and a tiny bookshelf-clad study in the tower.

Second floor No. 2's bedroom with the sleeping nook. Guest room and shared bathroom in the eaves. Up two steps into James's office /bedroom five.

It was a charming house, and full of character..

There were several incidents a few years after we left, A lot of activity was happening up on the top floor, poltergeist-type stuff. They had to get someone in to exorcise the house!

Never felt anything when we were there, although Number

3 may say differently!

Hope you all had a good day. Stay safe X.

The Old Hall Brampton-en-le-Morthen

The Diary of an Incarcerated Granny. Day 73

Another sunny one, another day harnessed to the hose pipe! When I moved here, I debated whether or not to get a water meter. I didn't, the monthly cost is very low, so I think I probably made the right decision.!

Not often I do that!

I looked in the mirror this morning, something I try not to do too often. Not a pretty sight, my hair is a disaster, I have grown an extra chin to add to the row that were there already! No makeup has been applied for a very long time, therefore you can see the scars achieved when I fell off my bike when I was eight (two weeks in hospital!).

Generally speaking, I'm looking pretty rough! I haven't worn a bra for weeks, and I have discovered that a lot of my friends haven't either. Why would you? You are creeping about at home at the speed of a snail, everything seems to be in slow motion because you are trying really hard to fill the time by letting everything take twice as long!

This scenario probably only applies to those of us on our own... standards have reached rock bottom, and do I care? Not really, I know I have the ability to shake of the lethargy when the time is right, and I also know that I 'scrub up' quite well when the occasion demands.

If you are confined to barracks with your other half, are you still maintaining your usual exemplary standards? Are you providing a delicious dinner, encompassing the required five a day, every evening? Are you having deep and meaningful conversations as you wander hand in hand around your garden to marvel at the sunset, a glass of something chilled and fizzy in your other hand? Have you resigned yourselves to the fact that your cruise this summer isn't going to happen? Your excursion to the foothills of the Atlas Mountains is definitely on hold for at least twelve months? Have you totted up the amount you have saved by staying put this year?

Are you toying with the fact that you can probably just about afford the 'all singing all dancing' hot tub? The chance of being able to literally stew in your own juice on home turf, over the summer months is tempting... is it not?

All such possibilities can cause untold dilemmas within a household!

No. 2 has accepted that they will not be going to the South of France this summer. Therefore, a new dining room carpet and uplighters for the garden have been mentioned in lieu of.

Quite a few people have been asked to rebook their holiday for next year, thus avoiding being refunded. Do you really know what you will want to be doing sixteen months down the line? You have no idea what opportunities might have arisen in the interim. I think that is a big ask to be honest.

I am a firm believer in always trying to have something to look forward to, be it large or small, a chink of light at the end of the tunnel tends to keep you focussed.

Last year

I didn't go anywhere much, I moved house in April and then began a couple of months of building work. A few visits down south and that was about it.

A friend contacted me and said did I fancy a couple of days in Chester, and we could visit the Zoo and have a tour round the city. We had a great time, the weather was good, the zoo was fab, Chester was very interesting, we both travelled by train, stayed in a hotel and dined out every night! There is always room for a little impromptu visit somewhere, isn't there?

When you visit family, do you take stuff?

If I'm heading south by car I always seem to take enough provisions to feed us all for the duration of my stay, and then to feed my hosts for the next month!

No. 2 Jnr is a huge fan of 'truffle infused salami', only

available in Aldi. There is no Aldi in Worthing… therefore I tend to empty the shelves of every packet on display. I take lots of wine, legs of lamb, joints of pork, lots of cheeses, crackers, chocolate, steaks, and anything else I can think of. I wonder why? We usually eat out at least once, and I always insist on paying! Why do we always feel duty-bound to still provide for them, when most of them are earning a fortune?

Is it the matriarch in me, that still likes to feel a little bit in control, I wonder?

Saying that, they have no complaints and neither do I. I just wondered if any of you still do this sort of thing. It would be most interesting to find out… I suspect I'm not alone in this?

It's really warm out there, my BF who lives in the Dordogne, says it's roasting in France. They stay indoors between 11 am and 5 pm as it's just too uncomfortable to be outside. We are never really satisfied, are we? I think I said the other day that life seems to be a series of extremes. An ambient temperature throughout the day, just enough rain throughout the night, how brilliant would that be? I think *Camelot* would be the destination of choice. Everything seemed pretty perfect there. I could try my luck with Franco Nero, and take a tissue to wipe Vanessa Redgrave's runny nose!

I was once talking about the film with No. 2, and her all-abiding memory was the drip on the end of Vanessa's nose. It's weird the strange things that you remember.

Have a good day, try and work out what Boris wants you to do? I'm still at the confused end of the market! Stay safe x.

The Diary of an Incarcerated Granny. Day 74

Covid 19.

It's one pm, I'm going to write for exactly an hour, and see how much I can get done.

Another good kip on the new mattress topper, it reminds me a bit of *The Princess and the Pea* story. Although in my case it would be 'The Granny and the Gravy Bone'!

Both most uncomfortable if you are a sensitive soul, I undoubtedly am.

Sunday lunch, almost a distant pleasure these days. Even without the present circumstances.

We always had a proper Sunday lunch. Family, friends, anybody that was at a loose end were always welcome. James would go to the pub and usually manage to add to the numbers. No. 2 and 3, if they were at home for the weekend, would have been distraught if they were packed off back to school on Sunday evening having been denied 'The Sunday Lunch' experience!

I remember one Sunday, we took the girls back up to York and left a few people still sitting round the dining table. When we got back, they were all as we had left them, only far more inebriated. They had carried on drinking, helped themselves to several bottles of wine out of the cellar, and by mistake had managed to drink a very old and very costly bottle of Chateau Margaux! The man of the house was not amused. As he pointed out, they were so far gone, that they could have supped a bottle of Sarson's vinegar and been none the wiser!

We forgave them of course, we all do strange things at times

These particular friends lived down the road from us. We used to end up at their house every New Year's Eve, usually about three am when the jolly japes at the hotel were over.

I remember wearing a new Parigi dress, that was very expensive and I liked it very much.

When we arrived at our friends, the remnants of a buffet were still on the table. James was exceedingly well oiled by this time. He started flicking slices of tomato across the table, two of which landed fair and square on my highly prized Parigi frock (as my mother would say!) Said slices of tomato were covered in dressing and made a real mess. I was so bloody cross. I found a huge untouched chocolate gateau at the far end of the table. Gateau in one hand and his head in the other, I connected the two, and rubbed it well in for good measure! Probably one of the most satisfying things I have ever done! He was wearing glasses, had a beard and a moustache, and the result was phenomenal!

I think we left shortly afterwards. The following morning he had no recollection of any of it. He was given a serious wifely scolding, and made to ring up and apologise for his behaviour. I dare say I should have tendered my apologies as well, but I didn't!

We once had an 'after dinner dance party' when we lived at The Grange. This was unscripted and a spur of the moment idea.

Most people were struggling to remain vertical and wandering round the garden. One of our Gordon Setters rushed up to someone and sat straight in front of him, looking up. He was then violently sick all over the dogs head, he looked down and remarked, 'I don't remember eating that'! It took a while to live that one down, and I never forgave him... it was of course me that had to wash the bloody dog at two in the morning.

Thinking back to my Parigi dress, I never wear dresses these days, or skirts. The last time I wore a dress was at No. 3's wedding and that was nearly four years ago... I have no plans to repeat the performance.

Well, that's an hour and three minutes to be precise. Done for the day... it is day 74 after all I need a break! X

The Diary of an Incarcerated Granny. Day 75

Brick wall day today! I'm banging my head against it, if I bang hard enough I will render myself unconscious, and then I won't have to try to think of something to write.

It's my friend's birthday on Friday, she is one of 'The Aunties', and we are all so desperate to see one another! So can we, or can't we?

Can we go separately to one of our houses, sit apart in the garden, take our own lunch and just have a chat? What if one of us needs to pick someone up who is unable to drive at the moment? Can that happen?

Apparently if we need the loo, we can use one in the house, providing we swab everything down with disinfectant and wash our hands!

I don't know about you, but the number of deaths still being recorded daily are not conducive to a good night's sleep!

Half of me thinks it's all starting to be relaxed too quickly,

the other half is desperate to return to some sort of normal...
but at what cost?

What do you think? All opinions most welcome!

I had a very long chat via FaceTime this morning with No.
2 Jnr. She had obviously commandeered Mummy's phone, and
was hanging on to it! We discussed what would happen if she
ever got married (she's four). It would appear that she would
insist on still living at home with Mummy and Daddy, as they
would miss her too much if she left!

Also ('also', along with 'actually' are her favourite words!) all
her toys are in the playroom and it's very useful because you can
look through the back hall and see Mummy doing things in the
kitchen when you are playing. She will always have to live there,
because every month Daddy puts a mark on the inside of the
playroom door, so that they can all see how much she's grown.

She then decided she needed the loo, but it was no problem
because she could take the phone with her and we could keep
chatting!

A hand wash reminder was issued, and a fair amount of
splashing was detected. We then moved into the kitchen where
Mummy was making brownies and a request for 'just a few
pickley (?) crisps' was granted.

We then returned to the playroom where Chelsea (daughter
of Barbie and Ken) was just getting up! There is also a baby,
but that seems to be a little bit lost, and it might have been
thrown away by mistake, we didn't dwell on that. What she
really needs is a Barbie and Ken camper van. This would enable
them all to go to Kefalonia for a holiday, and there might even
be room for the baby, if it gets found. She's wasn't sure about
storage facilities in the camper van. Barbie has a lot of clothes

and shoes and so does Chelsea. Ken appears to be semi-naked most of the time so his luggage requirements will be minimal!

We then had to get Chelsea out of bed, and make her some cherry soup for breakfast. This involved finding some red Play-Doh and squashing it in a very small Chelsea-sized dish. We both remarked how delicious it looked and how lucky Chelsea was. I don't think Barbie is much of a homemaker, she seems quite stiff and unable to bend in any direction. I was getting quite into the swing of make believe and I asked if Ken might be up for giving Daddy a hand in the garden? She gave me a rather exasperated look and said, 'Not really Granny, it's all just pretend you know!'

That was me told!

Useful tips, do you have any?

Don't throw away your old telephone directories, cross out all the people you don't know, leaving you with a useful address book.

When you have washed and beautifully ironed your bedding, fold carefully and place in one of the pillowcases. You then have a complete set of bedding all in one place. I actually now do this!

Roasting dishes are a pain to get clean. Fill with boiling water and a dishwasher tablet and leave to soak! Works quite well.

I'm done, this will definitely win the 'don't know why she even bothered' prize today. Sorry and all that X.

The Diary of an Incarcerated Granny. Day 76

Hello everyone, I've had a very busy, interesting and enjoyable day today!

However, suddenly it's almost 5pm and I haven't even thought about today's diary.

No. 3 suggested that we rehashed my story of when I was abandoned in Italy after having my passport stolen.

I wouldn't want to repeat the incident, but I did end up being quite proud of myself. It was a case of pulling up the 'big girl pants' and getting on with it!

So here it is, these are the snippers of updates I wrote for my friends and family on my Facebook status to keep them up to date.

My Italian adventure... After the euphoria of last night's Vivaldi concert... sad to report that today took a bit of a dive! Some swine nicked my travel wallet. So, lost my passport, boarding pass for tomorrow's flight, 350 Euros, hotel entry card, return transport tickets to the airport, EHIC card, and my travel insurance documents! Then got sent on a wild goose chase to the police station, who then informed me that I needed to be somewhere else half an hour's walk away. Had to wait over an hour to be seen, with nowhere to sit down. Eventually got the paperwork that will hopefully allow me home tomorrow, only to find out that I appear to have morphed into an American citizen... If I never see any of you again you can contact me c/o Bawtryland USA. Slightly pissed off... but could be much worse in the scheme of things. Oh, and I'm cancelling Christmas, (sorry kids!) xxx

Update on Granny Ang... at large in Venice! You couldn't write this... having left the hotel at eight am, (had to purchase another ticket to the airport) arrived with paperwork from the police. Went through luggage check in, two lots of passport (using the letter from police) checks, was issued with a boarding pass, through security. hung around until time to board... and they wouldn't let me board at the gate without a passport! Was told my luggage had to come off... so waited around for that... but when it arrived it was Jacquie's case, not mine! Jobsworth said I couldn't take hers, and they would have to return it to her address in England. Was sent to the police department where they fiddled about with the letter from yesterday. Then to a ticket desk where I was told that the letter was no use, I now have to get a temporary passport (this is where it gets exciting) from The British Embassy in Milan! As luck wouldn't have it... the Embassy doesn't reopen until Monday morning. During my lengthy conversation with the Embassy. I was overheard by a lovely German guy, probably, Toby's age. He asked if he could help me, found me a hotel in Venice Mestre for three nights, and took me to get a bus ticket from the airport to the Mestre. I am now reclining in a very nice three-star hotel, five minutes from the railway station. On Monday morning I shall get the train to Milan (two and a half hours) and head for the Embassy for an eleven am appt. Hopefully, I shall then try and book a flight from Milan to Manchester, and then get the train to Meadowhall, or 'Meadowhell' as I like to call it... where I sincerely hope some bugger will pick me up! I have only the clothes I stand up in, and none of my tablets. My case found its way to Leeds Bradford, and is now back in Bawtryland... unlike me! Apparently NOBODY gets into the UK without a passport! I think I may now have a granny nap... too much excitement for one day! Sorry, there are no paragraphs! Will keep you posted xxx. I'm fine by the way!

Update on the update! Travelling early Monday morning by train to Milan. Very few direct flights available on Mondays. and the ones that are, are an arm and a leg. So, booked into an hotel at the airport, Monday night and booked a flight direct to Manchester Tuesday afternoon. At least I think that's what I've done! They say Sorrento is very pleasant, if I lose the plot. xxx

Update on the update's update! Other than the day James had his heart bypass, I think this has been one of the longest days ever experienced by the Granny! Toddled out, clutching map, to buy essentials (Tena Lady are the same in Italian!) Managed to get some meds from the chemist, so blood pressure hopefully under control. Had a walk and sat in a park for half an hour, found a supermarket and bought a few things necessary for an evening in front of an Italian TV (Dictionary?) Quite warm, had to tinker with the room heater. Have spoken to Aimee and Rachel quite a lot... and I am halfway through a very interesting book about girls' boarding schools in the sixties. The charging of laptops and phones is a bit hit and miss. The weight of the three plugs required causes the one into the wall to disconnect somewhat! However, I have cobbled together a handy device to ensure the prongs stay put (yes...Tena Lady strikes again!) So, can I just say thanks to everyone for replies and messages... they are keeping me smiling! At the end of the day, its bloody inconvenient (and rather costly!), but doesn't come close to what a lot of folk are going through. Can I request some sort of welcome home celebration? Banners on PG.? Maybe a brass band?... and of course a ride in an open top bus through Bawtryland! Bugger, no paragraphs again... a total disaster for the punctuation police. Thanks again everyone. xx

P.S. Just reading the Daily Fail on line... there will be less daffodils next Spring... due to a shortage of bulbs! I for one am gutted!

Update on all the other updates! Slept quite well, stayed in bed for ages as my top and knickers were still not dry! Washed them in shampoo last night! Were I in Delhi, I think I might have a touch of Dehli Belly! Managed to listen to *The Archers* and received a suggestion (thank you Paul Cooke) to speed up the drying of my clothes with the hairdryer. Why did I not think of that? Maybe because I was never in the Guides? I did go to Brownies, once, and they made me polish a threepenny bit with Brasso... realised in an instant that it was not for me! It's raining here now and much cooler. I have booked my train ticket for 7.30 in the morning to Milan, arrive about nine-forty-five and then hope to take a taxi to the British Embassy! My appt there is at eleven am. Train stuff all done by the lovely little chap on reception. Later he is going to print off my hotel reservation in Milan, and my flight booking details for Tuesday. Must say they couldn't have been more helpful. I shall have to give them a five star review on Trip Advisor! I am going to pop out and have something to eat later, then try to organise everything for tomorrow. Shall have an alarm call at six am... just to make sure I'm up and running for the train. Be in touch later. Replies and messages very much appreciated. Thanks xxxx.

Very little charge on this, and no plug. I have just arrived at the airport hotel... it's now five-fifteen pm and I have been on the go since six am! Have booked a shuttle to the airport at twelve noon. I fly at 2.30 local time, and hopefully rock up in Manchester at 3.30pm. Then will get a train to Meadowhell. Got my temporary passport, and that was a whole chapter in itself. Will fill you all in when I get home. Thanks for all the support! For future reference I would be more than happy to have all my passport details tattooed on my rear end. (Would have put arse but that's a bit rude!) They say it's not over until the fat lady' sings... but must admit to humming a bit!

I had better record my thoughts on the day I went to Milan for the temporary passport. Got up at six, walked to the station and caught the train from Venice Mestre at 7:30. Arrived in Milan at 9:45 and took a taxi to the British Consulate. Somewhere in my head my thoughts of the British Embassy/Consulate, was going to be a bit like a mini Chatsworth, surrounded by manicured gardens, and lots of Union Jack's fluttering in the breeze. Epic fail on that one. Substitute stately home for office on the fifth floor of a high rise office block in the centre of (a very busy) Milan. No apple-cheeked caring Brit, wearing a twin set and pearls, offering me a cup of Yorkshire tea and a scone and jam...no bloody way! Two soldiers in camouflage gear guarding the door... Much pressing of buttons and Italian voices shouting, 'Who goes there?', I was finally admitted into this inner sanctum at eleven am precisely. Quite similar to an IKEA-influenced dentist's waiting room, but with access to water. Above the water container was a note in Italian and then translated into English reminding everyone not to pour their surplus water back into the hole! Someone had not heeded these instructions, so it was a bit like being in a wet room, just after you have turned the shower off! My designated lady was Italian, but pretty hot on the English, and very helpful. She asked if I had filled in a form online and had I got my passport photographs! What form, and what photographs? I gave the English version of the 'gallic shrug' and looked bemused. Passport photographs could be obtained from the railway station she advised. 'Not on my bloody watch,' quoth the Granny. 'It has just cost me twenty Euros to get here from the station, and you want me to go back there, take photos and come back here again? In a word, not a plan I'm in favour of!' In the meantime, a few very fraught-looking folk were wandering in and out and holding their heads in their hands. Time was marching on somewhat! By this time it was one pm, and the Italian tummies were rumbling, and the staff were getting a bit twitchy... Could I just bugger off for an hour and come back at two pm.? Fine by me... got all day to waste. So I wandered off, bought a coffee and had a ciggie (apologies to my mum for smoking in the street, she would never forgive me!) At quarter to two, I decided to go back in and sit with the soldiers. Then a couple arrived who had had all their stuff stolen the same day as I had. They were called Barbara and Mr Barbara - never found out his name! They were from Blackburn and Barbara had taken things very badly and had been crying non-stop for three days! (A bit like Victoria Beckham when David told the world their marriage was hard work!) They had their cards stolen as well, but were in full possession of their luggage. Funds had been sent so they were solvent. I did get in the fact that they weren't on their own, and had plenty of spare knickers! Apparently, no emergency passport can be issued without proof of flight bookings. Barbara and Mr Barbara were unaware of this, cue more sobbing and loud wailing, 'Ohhhh Noooo', and Mr B getting a bit arsey and shouting, 'come on Barbara, calm down, hold it together, hold it together!' Mr B settled himself on the computer (for use by British Nationals only!) and started looking up flights... unbeknown to him Barbara was at the other end of the room on the phone to 'our Karen in Blackburn'... getting her to book flights home. Mr B was getting a bit excited when he found some flights and started shouting, 'I don't care how much these cost Barbara, I'm going to boooke them.' (Strong Lancs accent!) Sadly Barbara was still on meltdown and on the phone to 'our Karen' who was also booking flights from a different airport with a different travel company. Chaos! At this point I felt I had better point out that they were about to book two lots of flights, from two different airports... Uproar... that resulted in him stamping around and waving his arms about and giving Barbara a monumental rollocking, no holds barred. Barbara screeched, 'Forget it' to our Karen and threw her phone on the floor and sobbed a bit more (only louder). At this point, my designated lady came over and said she would take my photos on her phone if that was ok by me. It sure was! I handed over 100 Euros and the precious temporary passport was eventually in my clutches! Photo was a disaster, a sort of grainy impression of Noddy Holder... but apparently was fit for purpose under the circumstances... I was out of there... Mr Barbara still had smoke coming out of his ears and Barbara was still weeping and wondering if her temper tantrum had buggered her phone up! I hailed a cab, went back to the station and caught a bus to the airport. At the airport I got another cab to the hotel. Hotel was fine and I was flagging a bit by then. I am still wondering what happened with Mr and Mrs Barbara... he was never ever getting another bloody passport and going nowhere ever again after this debacle... and I reckon Barbara won't be either!

...Certainly made me chuckle.

The final chapter (thank goodness for that they all cried!) I have just had the BEST sleep ever. I woke up in my comfy super-king (with room for a pony!) to the sound of Violet-Elizabeth's extremely loud snoring! The sounds of home!

My last leg of the journey was relatively crisis free. The plane was on time and the security at UK Border Control was paramount. I had to hand in my 'emergency passport' as it was only viable for the one flight back into the motherland.

I met a lovely lady in Manchester, who was returning from a wedding in Pakistan, She was going to Meadowhall, so we sat together and attempted to put the world to rights. At Meadowhall, the lovely Fordelicious was waiting for me on the platform. We went home via Tickhill chippy, as I was starving. The Baskervilles were delighted to see me, and I them!

I'm undecided whether or not to highlight this experience, and to see if I can get answers to a few questions that are concerning me. I have been given so much conflicting advice that I really think that something must be done to iron out all the discrepancies.

Why was I told that I could hand in the police letter at the airport and it would allow me to fly home?

How was I able to get through two passport checks, security

and luggage drop? Why was I issued with a boarding card, only to be refused entry at the gate? Bearing in mind I had my driving licence, a run off of my passport details (from the hotel when we originally checked in) I still had my boarding pass that I had arrived with and other items of identification..

Having to leave your friend in a wheelchair, and being snapped at by counter staff was not pleasant. The airline had printed Jacquie's details on both suitcases (big mistake!) so when the wrong one was taken off the plane it didn't have my name on it - said suitcase appears to be on a European tour, as it is a security risk! So far it has left Venice, been to Amsterdam and returned to Venice. No one will take responsibility for it. Jacquie has spoken to Jet 2 on several occasions and has been given different information each time.

I feel that abandoning a granny in a foreign country, with the clothes she stands up in, is not an ideal situation by any means. I was lucky that I had my laptop and a debit card. What if I hadn't? What if I had no access to a phone, if I had no money... was I meant to sleep in the street?

The consulate were helpful, when I finally got there on Monday... but who would have been there for the four days I was in limbo. Answer... nobody! A very scary thought indeed. I feel I should try and take this further just to highlight what could have happened. What do you think?

Positives I have taken from this experience. When the going gets tough, the tough get going! If you are able to communicate you can find your way anywhere. British 'stiff upper lip' required... weeping in a corner (like Barbara) is not the way forward.

I have also realised just how lucky I am, to have such a wonderful family and so many friends that genuinely care about me. So much support, phone calls and messages from all over the world. I can't thank you all enough. There are some amazingly kind and loving people out there… and I'm blessed to know quite a lot of them!

Thank you. xxxxxxx

PS… I'm still wondering what happened to Barbara!

The Diary of an Incarcerated Granny. Day 77

Sunset strip day today… for those of you old enough to remember!

Apologies for the rehash yesterday, the Italy experience was rather funny looking back on it. There seems to be a coping strategy that kicks in when required!

I've had lots of chats with people re the relaxing of the rules! My findings are very mixed! A lot of people are very hesitant to launch themselves, however gently, back into the fold. Some have already headed for M&S and cleared the shelves in one fell swoop. The amount of rule bending that has been going on is laughable… and dare I say it, some of the most unlikely people are responsible for writing their own scripts. I'm talking people I know, not politicians or government advisors!

One of my sons-in-law works in the motor industry. He says that they are very, very busy. Maybe people that used public transport have decided to make their own arrangements? I have heard that caravan sales are taking off in a big way… I suppose for families, it's a way of staying relatively safe in a different bubble and in a different area. I quite like caravans, I've never owned one, but I've stayed in a few over the years. I think I would prefer a touring caravan to a static... the thought of hitching up and just setting off somewhere is quite appealing.

Boats are another thing that seem quite attractive. A friend of our used to say that you didn't need your own boat, you just needed a friend that had one! I think he applied the same criteria to swimming pools and holiday homes!

We once nearly bought a house from a dentist who was due to retire. He had bought a very flash motor home, in which to see the world and a narrow boat that was moored in Sheffield as a base in the UK. We were gazumped, so I have no idea if he ever achieved his dream.

Many, many years ago we had a friend that bought a Winnebago, an American motor home. This was the ultimate in luxury, every gadget known to man was incorporated in this mighty beast and it was the envy of all!

Sadly it kept 'going wrong' mainly electrical problems which required parts having to be shipped over from the USA. It became a bit of a white elephant. I think its final act of defiance was when it appeared to blow up somewhere heading north. It limped into a lay-by and died. As luck would have it, friends with a car were following and helped to decide its fate. It was thought that to leave it locked up in the lay-by would probably attract vandals. It was agreed that a picnic table and chairs would be brought outside, the table would be set, and the door left open. They then got in the car and drove off and left the bloody thing. It was towed away eventually, and probably sold to the lowest bidder! Still an amusing memory.

I have just had, a corned beef, vine tomato, mayonnaise and rocket and spinach leaf sandwich. It was really good. Still a bit hot to think of eating much, hardly cottage pie weather at the moment, is it? What do you eat in the evenings, especially if it's been a really hot day? Divulge all!

When we lived in France we used to buy litres of Gazpacho, they sell it there in tetra packs like we buy orange juice. Wonderful stuff!

Career, job, vocation, call it what you will - Did you ever really fulfil your ambitions?

I always wanted to work with animals. I know that if I had worked harder at school that I could have done Veterinary Medicine instead of Veterinary Nursing. Silly me! No. 2 did a degree in English. Moved to London, temped a bit for the BBC and the likes, then took a job in advertising and moved around various advertising companies for a long time. She eventually worked in recruitment, which was very lucrative until the recession suddenly kicked in. It was then decided then that it was time for a radical change of direction. She found a front of house job in London with a plc property development company to pay the bills, and then qualified as a personal trainer. Ask her now what she really wanted to do, and I still don't think she would have a clue! Although she still has the London job, two days a week! She quite likes things just as they are.

When No. 3 was about eight, she had a t-shirt, and printed on the front it said, 'When I grow up I want to be a nurse so that I can help people and see loads of willies'! She did exactly that! The week after she graduated she joined a private healthcare company. She has been with them now for nearly eighteen years, she has worked her way up through the ranks, gained many more qualifications along the way and now works in their compliance team. I can never really imagine her doing anything other than in that field.

I of course, waved goodbye to the animals, married someone in the hospitality industry, and the rest appears to be history!

Take care x.

The Diary of an Incarcerated Granny. Day 78

Raining quite heavily in Paradise this morning, and it looks as though it's been at it most of the night, judging by the puddles.

I think this socially distancing meet up in gardens, has been specifically orchestrated to coincide with a change in the weather! Smart move eh?

Just had a quick FaceTime with No. 2, the much-researched vehicle is actually being delivered on Friday... very exciting stuff.

No. 2 Jnr was displaying her somewhat tedious persona this morning! Her parting shot was, 'I don't do patience!' She's right there!

I think I have been bitten by a tsetse fly.

I keep sitting on the sofa and falling asleep! Maybe I'm compensating for all those years of insomnia?

Finished my book *The Dutch House* last night. I quite enjoyed it. I'm not sure it quite deserves whichever prize it was awarded, but that's just my opinion. I decided to re-read Daphne du

Maurier's *The King's General*. One of my replacements after the flood and a book I have read many times. I found myself remembering so many of the phrases and dialogue that she used. If you haven't read it please give it a try, I think I was probably immersed in it until about three am this morning. That's probably why I dozed off earlier, apologies to the tsetse fly!

So much cooler today, I always sympathise with No. 3 when the weather is hot. They live in an apartment, which is totally south-facing, so almost a wall of glass. They have blackout blinds in their bedroom and a very efficient aircon unit, otherwise I think it would be unbearable!

I'm contemplating writing a children's book. Years ago, I made up a bedtime story for the youngest two. They still remember it, apparently quite fondly, and keep harping on that I should try and write it all down, and see what happens. So far, I have treated myself to a three pack of A4 Cambridge Jotters and a pack of Bic biros from Amazon... and I'm ready when you are!

If there are any 'wannabe' illustrators out there... let me know. Kenneth Grahame and Ernest Shepard had a very good partnership! You may possibly need to Google them!

I do slightly visualise myself drifting down the garden to the summer house in the mornings, and sticking to a self-imposed schedule of writing and eventually turning into the next Roald Dahl. Sadly, I think David Walliams has already bagged that slot.

All pipe dreams, but you never know. Who would have thought I would still be making myself sit down and record my ramblings seventy-eight days down the line? I wonder how long it took Tolstoy to write *War and Peace*? I haven't read it, have you?

I have misplaced 'Hair Angels' again. I am so used to a bit of chat from so many of you, that I do miss you and wonder what's happened if you disappear for a day or two. This is really a joint venture you know... so please come back, all is forgiven!

I was chatting to one of my best chums the other night about our lives as magistrates and the laughs we had along the way.

I think there were eleven of us ordained in 1987. Ours were a really good bunch, a total cross-section of the community and one or two real characters. There was a lot of training involved, including a couple of residential weekends, staying in halls of residence at Sheffield University. We all got on really well, and on the overnighters we took loads of food and drink and had midnight feasts. There was one guy who was lovely, very quiet and unassuming, and it became pretty obvious that his wife wore the trousers! He wasn't allowed to stay overnight, lord knows what she thought we were going to do to him? He missed out on a lot.

It was a period of my life that I enjoyed very much. It's good to put your sensible hat on occasionally, an opportunity to wear a suit twice a week, and an introduction to many more interesting people. The magistrates courts are the first rung on the ladder for any criminal cases. Sentencing powers are limited, and more serious cases are committed to the Crown Court. The courts are very formal, and great respect is shown to everyone. I must admit it seems a bit odd to be referred to as 'Your Worship,' I soon got used to it though. I was a JP for sixteen years, and resigned when we went to live in France. Had I remained on the bench I would have been due to retire this October. If any of you are interested, it's a very worthwhile thing to invest your time in. As with all things, you never know what you can do unless you give it a try.

I'm done for today, four pm already x.

The Diary of an Incarcerated Granny. Day 79

Slightly dull, a little bit damp, and somewhat cooler. I actually don't mind it at all, and the lawn is looking better already.

I am now in charge of my own destiny on the shopping front, I have no great urge to head for the crowded aisles... in fact I think I can manage quite well for the next couple of days without going anywhere!

I think I feel a chilli con carne coming on! I haven't had any since New Year's Eve. Isn't it strange, you just suddenly get quite desperate for a particular dish. Or, you have a disappointment when you order one!

I remember years ago going out for dinner and lobster thermidor was on the menu. When they served it, there was half an inch of 'ready grated' Parmesan on the top... it was disgusting. Really put me off, I didn't have any for several years.

We were once in France over Easter and went out for lunch on Easter Sunday. I ordered lamb! You've heard of the phrase 'mutton dressed as lamb'? I could smell it when it came out of the kitchen, I don't do mutton! We were on holiday in southern Ireland, and the dish of the day was 'mutton with caper sauce'! It wasn't the dish of my day, that's for sure.

Another French 'faux pas' in my book. Quail, served with its head tucked under its arm! How could they do that?

We called one of our Gordon Setters 'Caille' pronounced 'kye', which is French for quail. You see, you're now learning a language as well!

I know that most of you know your crumble. That and gin, seems to be the one of the staples of lockdown.

Last year we went out somewhere and I ordered an 'autumn berry crumble'. It was obviously a couple of spoonfuls of frozen berries, in a ramekin with a thick layer of granola on the top... and then microwaved!

Was I being a bit picky to send it back where it came from? I didn't think it warranted the £6.50 they were charging for it. It wasn't proper crumble, was it?

You can tell I'm scratching my head today, can't you?

Perfume or aftershave? How your taste changes over the years.

For the last ten years I have staked my claim to Jo Malone's, Lime, Basil and Mandarin. I love it.

No. 2 wears Bulgari Jasmin Noir.

No. 3 has the largest perfume collection in the world.

I used to find that the smell of the duty free fragrance shop on the ferry made me feel sick.

What's your favourite?

I've just had a little interlude listening to Barbara Dickson on YouTube. I watched her recently in *The Real Marigold Hotel* on TV. She always comes over as such a 'nice' person, for a seventy-three-year-old, she certainly seems to have no interest in retiring or even slowing down a bit. I have seen her in concert lots of times, in fact, 'the tall man' did once remark that I alone had been most instrumental in providing her with a very healthy 'pension pot'! We went through a stage of the kids all saying, 'what would you like for your birthday?', 'Is Barbara on tour anywhere nearby'? Have any of you been to see her?

Once Boris calls time on this fiasco, we will check out Barbara's tour dates, and we'll hire a bus and have an Incarcerated Granny trip out to watch Barbara! Any takers?

That's two functions in the diary already...

Tea and scones at the Hobbit House, and a coach trip to see Barbara! I bet you never envisaged such excitement.

I am storming through *The King's General*, sadly I'll probably finish it tonight, then I am going to make a start on *Wolf Hall*. I've mentioned it to a few people and surprisingly got quite mixed reviews. My taste in books is very similar to my taste in anything else. I like it or I don't! Simple as that!

I have a couple of 'chapel chairs' in my dining room. They have a little shelf at the back to hold a Bible and hymn book. I'm out of religious literature, so I keep my *Bunty* annuals in mine. Why wouldn't you?

That's me done, I'm off to see the Wizard...! Take care! X.

The Diary of an Incarcerated Granny. Day 80

Wow, just had a proper downpour! Bouncing off the pavements, now fifteen minutes later the sun is out. Are we experiencing belated April showers?

I have still resisted the temptation to go shopping... one banana and three apples left, plus potatoes, peppers, tomatoes, onions. I have the makings of a feast! Loads of bits and bobs in the freezer, I have no need to go anywhere!

I finished *The Kings General* last night, I enjoyed it just as much as I did the first time!

I then started on *Wolf Hall* and managed a chapter before the eyelids started to droop. I think it will be ok. I can usually tell very early on if my boat is about to be floated. They always say when you are house-hunting that you know whether or not it's 'the one' within the first three minutes!

I seem to have had a stream of phone calls so far today, consequently I'll have done virtually nothing of a domestic nature.

I have googled Barbara's future tour dates, and she doesn't seem to be doing much around here at all. I doubt anything will be happening this year anyway, so 2021 here we come!

Friday again, how can that be? My Friday night phone call with my pal in Norfolk at ten pm is due again. What on earth we find to talk about is remarkable in itself. Neither of us will have been through the door since last week, seen nobody (she is in possession of a very grumpy husband) and generally done nowt at all! Yet we will ramble away quite happily, for two hours, reminiscing about when we went on holiday to Mevagissey when we were eighteen, on the train via Bristol with a Labrador and a terrier. We are still unsure how we ended up there, neither of us had ever been to Cornwall. We watched Alfred Hitchcock, *The Birds* (also written by Daphne du Maurier) before we set off and scared ourselves silly. We had to wait for a connection in Bristol for about three hours, in the middle of the night, everything was closed and the loos were locked. I can remember very little about where we stayed, there is a solitary photo of me eating an ice cream and looking at some fishing boats… why? There was a very creepy guy who may, or may not have been staying at the same place as us. We called him the Mevaggisey Monster, and we were convinced he was stalking us. He seemed to materialise around every corner and make us jump!

I wouldn't call the holiday an unqualified success. The following year we stayed closer to home and stayed in a small hotel in the village of Goathland, in North Yorkshire (Heartbeat Country). We spent most of our evenings in the Mallion Spout, a rather nice hotel/ pub in Goathland. We then had a ten-minute walk across the Moor to where we were staying, there were no street lights and of course we didn't have a torch! There was an old folk tale of a ghostly apparition called a Gimrack that wandered the moors at night. This frightened us to death and turned us into nervous wrecks.

Nowadays we would have been on an all-inclusive drunken week in Benidorm! How times have changed. Saying, that I doubt our mum's would have let us. We are both seventy this year, and an awful lot of water has passed under our bridges since we first met when we were seventeen and some very weird experiences encountered. I was 'the Bridesmaid', she was my 'Matron of honour'. I am Godmother to her firstborn, she would have been the same for mine… however, we never seemed to get around to the christening! We once went in The Golden Ball. (AKA The Lacquered Knacker!) in Whiston, seven nights on the trot, with a different guy every night! We married none of them. So, heading steadily towards fifty-three years, we have done pretty well I think. I admit I wasn't too keen when we first met, she had a definite air of superiority, luckily I soon worked out it was all a bit of an act! Our last adventure was the Venice debacle. She suffered an enormous guilt trip when she left me behind at the airport, and I didn't let her forget if for a very long time! We are busy wondering where it may be safe for us to go next? We thought about Iceland (not the supermarket!) I've just read the whole thing back, it barely makes any sense to me, so best of luck!

Follow the yellow brick road... x

The Diary of an Incarcerated Granny. Day 81

The number is almost laughable... eighty-one days? I'm still unsure in which direction we are heading. The death toll is not reducing significantly, over 40,000 and counting, it's still out there and I think we're starting to get careless!

It's quite pleasant in Paradise this morning, a little bit of sunshine at the moment, but I think that's probably all that we are due today.

You will be pleased to know that I'm getting on well with *Wolf Hall*. I must have dropped off, still holding the book and still wearing my specs. I woke up just before four am, sorted myself out and went straight back to sleep!

Pillows, have we shared our thoughts on pillows?

Nestling on my comfy super-king (with room for a pony!) I am the proud owner of five pillows!

No pillow is the same. They all have very different characters and all profess to be the most comfortable pillows on the planet. Well they're not.

My neck is a nightmare, it crunches and it aches, and some

mornings if it hasn't slept well, it almost reduces me to tears.

I think I have inherited my neck from my mother. She spent years on and off wearing a collar (just like the woman in the pharmacy in *Doc Martin*) and she suffered untold agonies.

Actually, they weren't untold, as she was happy to discuss her spondylitis with anyone prepared to give up several days of their lives to receive chapter and verse on the subject.

Anyway, my pillows are as follows

A Dunlopillo, foam inside, James's pillow of choice.

A feather and down pillow, little quilly bits sometimes poke through and prickle my ears.

A memory foam pillow, that is the nearest thing to a great big wad of plasticine encased in a pillow case.

A 'suffer no more with your aching neck' pillow. It has a hollow lovingly carved out of the centre which is 'head-shaped'.

A Scandinavian 100% goose down pillow, that cost an arm and a leg.

Conclusions on the pillow front... you get what you pay for!

I remember No. 2 complaining that their pillows at school were like communion wafers. I assume she meant the thickness and not the taste?

Throws... who has throws? Are they a recent (as in fifteen years) addition to our sitting rooms? I think the nearest thing in the dim and distant past was the tartan car rug. A 100% woollen blanket type thing. Woven in the outer Hebrides by women who wore gumboots and hand knitted socks. If you had a car, it went without saying you had a car rug, they went hand in hand. They were very itchy, and could never be washed or they would shrink to the size of a gentleman's handkerchief. They were almost considered to be a family heirloom and some were passed down through the generations. You look at the queen in the open carriage at Ascot, I bet some of those rugs once graced the knees of Queen Victoria! They were so handy for keeping your knees warm whilst driving, and essential for the 'let's pull into a lay-by' moment. Something scratchy on which to sit as you juggled with your thermos flask, your potted meat sandwich and your hard-boiled egg (with a twist of salt). The main and most feared enemy of the rug was of course, the moth! Consequently, wherever there was a rug there was always a faint aroma of mothballs. An evocative whiff of camphor can take you straight back to your childhood.

My mother-in-law had several very expensive fur jackets (before they were considered non-U). She refused to leave whichever one of them she was wearing, unattended in a cloak-room. Therefore the jacket was always brought into the dining room and placed on the back of her chair, the all-pervading odour was that of Chanel No19 and mothballs! Bless her.

Moving swiftly on, back to throws, polyester and acrylic were born. No self-respecting moth had the slightest interest in either of these laboratory-invented fabrics. Suddenly fleecy throws were everywhere. Reclining on the arms of your sofa, over the back of your favourite armchair, folded artistically on the bottom third of your bed. Where would we be without the throw? How much money have we saved by not turning up the heating when it turned a little bit chilly? I have gifted them to grandchildren living in freezing cold student houses and they have been eternally grateful! The throw is a thing of beauty and comfort. I have two in my sitting room now, they coordinate with everything perfectly. Only last night I watched the whole of *Inspector Morse* encased snuggly in one of mine.

You can stick them in the washing machine if you feel the need, you can give them a quick blast of Febreze to freshen them up.

The possibilities are endless. When they are past their sell by date and go a bit bobbly, you can then downgrade them to the dog's basket or bin them! Your choice.

Take care X.

The Diary of an Incarcerated Granny. Day 82

Cold, wet and indifferent... and that's just the dog! Grey mornings do have a somewhat negative affect on one. That sounds rather regal doesn't it?

I only do an hour on Sundays... day of rest and all that.

I'm debating whether or not to order Sunday lunch from The Ship in Bawtry, or wait until this evening and have a takeaway from Taj Cottage. Debating with yourself is nigh on impossible. Just chatted with a friend on the phone and she said Indian takeaway... so the decision is made.

Wasn't the 'pillow talk' interesting? There is a 'pillow culture' gathering pace out there that I knew nothing about. Have you ever really given more than a cursory nod to the existence of the pillow? I know I haven't, but I think from now on I'm going to be a bit of a fan!

Cushions are another thing, they are genetically linked to pillows, but tend to be slightly smaller and far more decorative.

Men tend to be a somewhat scathing as far as cushions are concerned, they are unable to see the cushion as an accent of design and something which can bring a room together.

You can change the look of a room purely by changing the covers on your cushions!

Hotels, beds and soft furnishings.

A whole new subject. The Kelly Hoppens of this world can wax lyrical for hours about the importance of 'dressing a bed'. I struggle with the concept. At least ten cushions of different shapes, sizes and colours. A couple of strips of contrasting fabric laid horizontally on the lower two-thirds of the bed. How marvellous it all looks fabulous in a 'Beautiful Homes' magazine, and just about ok in your spare room that never gets used. I have a bedspread with two matching 'pillow shams' that I bought from a market stall when we lived in France. That is just about as far as I'm prepared to go. When I scramble into bed, I launch the cushions through the air and couldn't care less where they land. Sometimes I put them back on, sometimes I don't. The amount of traffic through my bedroom is nil…! Sad but true.

Fancy hotels are the worst offenders. You have possibly had a long journey, unpacked, made a cuppa, raided the mini bar and are ready to put your feet up for half an hour. If you have splashed out on a suite, then you will have your own sitting room. If not, you will be reduced to languishing on a very attractive but most uncomfortable tub chair or joy of joys, the actual bed! The bed is an art form in itself, the soft furnishings are designed to coordinate with everything else in the room. This is where it all begins to fall apart. You start to peel away the layers, but where are you supposed to put them? Plump cushions are notorious for not stacking well, within fifteen seconds they have slithered onto the floor. The bedspread is obviously only there for decorative purposes, so you need to remove that as well. It's padded, very heavy, and however hard you try, it's impossible to fold into anything smaller than a two man tent at Glastonbury!

The spacious room that you were shown into an hour ago seems to be getting smaller by the minute. If you are unfortunate enough to have a 'towelling swan sculpturer' on the hotel payroll, then you may as well shoot yourself now! Why on earth, if you have a decent en-suite bathroom do you need a towel mountain, complete with swans, piled up on the end of the bloody bed? The word 'naff' springs to mind, or am I just a boring old person?

You start to realise why the rooms cost so much for an overnight stay. The number of staff involved in primping the decor doesn't come cheap. The chambermaid, shoving a trolley up and down the corridors is only the tip of the iceberg. She will be followed by the cushion-plumpers, the swan sculpture-makers, and if you have really gone to town, the petal-scatterers! Oh, and the chocolate on the pillow-placers. Nightmare!

My ideal would be a spacious room with a super-king bed and an excellent mattress. Down pillows and duvet.

White Egyptian cotton high thread count bedding. Reading lamps in the right places, a big en-suite with a bath and a good-sized separate shower. Plenty of white fluffy bath sheets and towels and bath robes. Good quality toiletries and a decent hairdryer. Fresh flowers and a well-stocked bar and hospitality tray, and a pack of Thorntons Viennese Truffles. That'll do me! The hour is up. Hurrah! Happy Sunday. I wonder what Boris's Sunday sermon will contain this week?

Stick to the rules x.

The Diary of an Incarcerated Granny. Day 83

It's cold this morning. It must have been just as cold this time last year, my FB just flagged up a year ago today, and I was lighting my new fire for the first time. I don't recall us having much of a summer last year... let's hope we haven't just had 2020's without realising it!

A friend of mine said that it was clear that I was struggling to find any new material to write about! Sadly, she was quite right.

When you resort to pillows, duvets and cushions you really are scraping the bottom of the jar.

No. 2's car has finally arrived. It's been a very long time coming. Mr No. 2 leaves no stone unturned when he is researching a big purchase. Spreadsheets have been printed off and comparisons studied. I usually take the ...ss at his attention to detail, but I must admit it actually gives you a very clear picture of the good the bad and the ugly!

When they set out on the maiden voyage, with the promise of Mummy at the wheel, No. 2 Jnr was heard to remark that maybe they should get Daddy, as she wasn't sure it was a very good idea. It was fine!

I was upset to see all the problems with the demonstrations yesterday. Watching the TV this morning, in a couple of weeks it will become evident if the lack of social distancing has produced a rise in new Covid cases.

I absolutely agree with the cause of the demonstrators, but in the present climate is it not foolhardy and irresponsible to behave in such a way?

For those of us who have tried very hard to comply with

all the advice and recommendations, I feel their actions are a slap in the face!

It looks as though Andrew's past has popped up to haunt him again. He should never have made that 'car crash' interview... and he actually thought it had gone well? The eventual outcome will be very interesting, I'm not so naive as to think that if he has the monarchy on his side, which he has, it will somehow disappear like a bad smell. What do you think?

I doubt he would volunteer to take a lie detector test, after all, this is not an episode of *Jeremy Kyle*, although it's heading very much that way!

It sounds as though the airports are in chaos, as the new rules come into force today. It's a bit late to start locking people up for a fortnight when they fly into the UK... three months too late in my opinion!

I ventured out last night to the local garage for some bread and milk. Not a soul in sight, it's a very odd feeling after so many weeks, you almost feel as though you are being stalked, and keep expecting someone to pop out round a corner and shout 'boo'! No one did.

If you could retire anywhere, and money was no object, where would you choose?

I always found it rather sad, that in our area of France there were a lot of ladies who had lost their husbands. They often lived in an isolated village, were unable to drive, had a very limited income, and had no chance of ever being able to afford to return to the UK.

My best advice to anyone contemplating the big 'move', is make damn sure you have the wherewithal to come back if things go wrong!

The older I get, the more contented I become with what I have. I live in a tiny house that I love, it's full of things that reflect my personality, I have a wonderful family and great friends... so I'm lucky. I don't need any more than that. Somewhere in the midst of your life you realise (or at least I did) that there is no 'crock of gold 'at the end of the rainbow. You have to keep pausing along the way and be thankful for the things you have. Constantly striving for bigger and better can be soul destroying and quite destructive. I'm not knocking ambition, but I've seen the hurt on children's faces when their father has missed yet another birthday, sports day and carol service, all due to the 'big job' abroad.

Sometimes it does work out well, but it's a difficult regime for anyone to undertake.

Happiness is not just another purchase away!

I read something yesterday that asked if you could spend just one hour with someone that had passed away, who would it be?

I would choose my father, he died when I was seventeen. He left the house in the morning, just as I was leaving for school, and I never saw him again. That's fifty-three years ago and the memory of that day has never left me. Someone said last week that her father died when she was in her early teens and it took her a long time to forgive God for that. I don't think I ever did forgive him! It's such a long time ago that I struggle to remember the sound of his voice, I think that is probably the hardest part, and there's a little bit of me that wonders if I would recognise it if I heard it. There are photographs of course, sadly only a fraction of the amount we would have today, but very precious nonetheless. Anyway, who would you choose to spend your hour with? It doesn't have to be a family member!

I bet there are a few Elvis fans out there?

This is a miserable ditty, if ever there was one. I blame the weather. I've been waiting all day for a call that never came... now happening in the morning. As if I had nothing better to do... fortunately I don't!

Hope you had a good day. Take Care x.

The Diary of an Incarcerated Granny. Day 84

Morning, eighty-four days in Paradise! I am becoming a recluse, a hermit, a loner, you name it, I'm evolving in a Darwin-esque way into a duck-billed platypus! Not really, but I do find them fascinating. They contradict at every twist and turn, they are mammals, but they lay eggs. They don't have stomachs, they don't have nipples, yet they secrete milk through the folds in their skin to feed their young. Google them, you may well become a fan.

I'm saddened by the fact that our zoos and wildlife parks are struggling during lockdown. As far as I'm aware there are no plans in hand for them to reopen. Having visited Chester Zoo last year, I would have thought that it was very possible to implement social distancing and the same at Yorkshire Wildlife Park? How come Alton Towers has partly opened?

The more I listen to the rules and regulations the more confused I become. Why can you travel in a taxi, albeit in the rear of the vehicle, and yet you are unable to go in the same car as a work colleague even if you observe the same precautions?

I've just watched Piers Morgan in full flight on his usual

morning rant. I'm not a fan, I find him rude and patronising, but, I can identify with the frustration of never getting an answer to a simple question. I wonder who decides who gets the short straw to represent the establishment, when the so-called 'experts' are invited to be interviewed on live TV? They must all want to run for the hills!

The response to the 'who would you spend your hour with?' was interesting and maybe a little bit predictable. There are a lot of Daddy's girls out there!

It's good to know that most of us are very satisfied with our lot! I imagine, but I don't really know, that the majority of people in this group are retired or heading that way? If this is the case, then most of us have been there, done that and got the t-shirt.

It's a huge relief when you reach the stage in life when you can happily say, 'This is me, take me as you find me!' You don't have to be anything other than yourself, you have nothing to prove and nobody to try and impress, it's quite a good feeling. Rather like the second-hand car advert 'sold as seen', warts and all!

Today's 'who would you choose?'

Dinner in a restaurant (smart or greasy spoon) and a table for six.

Who would your other five be? They can be anyone at all alive or dead, and you get to choose the restaurant.

Get your thinking caps on!

Mine would be:

1) James, my late husband, a raconteur and the teller of brilliant jokes.

2) Dame Maggie Smith.

3) King Henry VIII
4) Kristin Scott Thomas
5) David Attenborough

The Restaurant would be Chateau de Puy Robert, Montignac, France. A perfect tiny chateau, overlooking the River Vezere, twenty minutes from where we used to live. This is the one you choose, when you've had guests for a week and they want to give you dinner to say thank you!

I think No. 2 and No. 3 would agree with my choice on this restaurant.

When we still had the cottage, we were interested in buying a converted barn in the same hamlet. The owners lived in Lyon and came to stay very infrequently. We were over there for the summer and they arrived, we saw quite a lot of them, had them over for drinks and talked about the barn and they insisted on taking us all out for dinner on their last evening. No. 2 and 3 were probably aged nine and eleven, and both connoisseurs of the most expensive starter on the menu. We were feeling a bit awkward and trying to get them to share one portion between them. Our host wouldn't hear of it. They had the full Monty, and he was in receipt of a very large 'addition' at the close of the evening!

We never bought the barn, they left early the following morning and we never saw them again! I still feel a bit guilty. The foie gras was superb. This remember, was thirty years ago, people still wore fur coats, ate foie gras and watched lions and tigers performing in circuses. Times have certainly changed a lot since then. Enlightenment is a marvellous thing.

I have been making a sauce with some minced beef that I

needed to use. Years ago if you went out for lunch in a pub they would serve you with what James always called 'multi-purpose gravy'. I think I have just perfected some multi-purpose sauce. It has all sorts of stuff in it, and is really rather tasty. When I was in Italy I brought back quite a lot of spicy stuff in tubes. Italian delis are the best. Today, I have squeezed some of the contents of these tubes into my sauce and the effect is most pleasing.

James was a pie man. He loved a good pie! He was therefore unimpressed with a dollop of beef casserole in a small oval pie dish, being betrothed at the last minute to an oval of ready-made and separately baked pastry. He would always enquire how the pies were made. If it became obvious that what he referred to as a 'surrogate' crust was on offer, he would order something else!

It's now four-thirty pm, the day has whizzed by yet again. It will soon be approaching 5pm and Violet's stomach will be kicking into overdrive. If I didn't have a clock anywhere in the house I would always know when it was five o'clock! Take care x

The Diary of an Incarcerated Granny. Day 85

A bit grey again, obviously rained overnight as there are puddles.

It sounds as though schools are staying closed and zoos and wildlife parks are opening. I expect all the children will be able to visit the zoo, thus providing a significant boost to the economy?

I am getting more confused as time goes on. I am beginning to think that this is a cunning plan on behalf of the powers that be... the object of the exercise is, that if people are unable to fathom the rules and regulations, they will opt to stay at home just to be on the safe side. Clever stuff!

Lots of good dinner guests yesterday. David Attenborough was a very popular choice, along with Marilyn Monroe, and the two Dames, Smith and Dench.

Paul Newman was mentioned a couple of times as well. I was once in Castleton in Derbyshire in a pub, having lunch with my Labrador. Someone else was there but I can't remember who! Who should walk in but Paul Newman and entourage. He trod on my dog's foot! He didn't apologise, so I won't be inviting him to join me for dinner. I think he was filming in the area.

Encounters with 'famous' people. Have I touched on this already? I really can't remember.

Glynis Johns in M&S Oxford Street.

Francesca Annis and Ralph Fiennes on the next table in Bluebird, Chelsea.

Sarah Lancashire and family on the next table at breakfast at The Devonshire Arms, Bolton Abbey, the morning after No. 1's wedding.

Wayne Fontana, minus *The Mindbenders* at Manchester Airport.

Edwina Currie and husband on a bridge in Venice.

Barbara Dickson on the next table just before a concert in Scotland.

Victoria Wood in an Indian restaurant in Manchester.

I think that's about it, in fact the word 'encounters' might make you think I interacted with them. Which I didn't. None of them seemed remotely pleased to see me!

Come on, who have you spotted?

The Duke of Edinburgh is ninety-nine today. I think he's spent more time with the queen in the last twelve weeks than he has in the last seventy years!

I don't envy the 'goldfish bowl' existence of the royal family. Personally, I think they pay a high price for the privilege. Being observed through a magnifying glass is an awful way to have to live your life. The recent Markle debacle proves this point. Somehow I think they have jumped out of the frying pan into the fire... I knew early doors that the lifestyle wasn't for me. I had to turn Charles down I'm afraid, he was gutted, but he understood my reasons. The thought of being unable to eat Heinz Beanz, straight from the tin, whilst wearing my pink fluffy marshmallow dressing gown... how restrictive is that?

Thanks but no thanks!

People are starting to make holiday murmurs. One or two folk have booked log cabins and the like, just to escape for a few days.

The log cabin experience is a good one. Back in the day we used to go for a long weekend in October half term with the Round Table lot. The Forestry Commission, Keldy Castle just outside Pickering in North Yorkshire. We loved it, the kids were safe, they could spend all day running riot with their friends. Every evening we took all the little ones on 'The Midnight Walk'. The fact it was only seven-thirty totally passed them by! Little souls, they were so excited, muffled up in hats and scarves and gloves, wearing wellies and carrying torches... life was never any better than this! We followed the signs for the Paradise Walk, it probably should have taken about forty minutes, but took us much longer. Some of the daddies went on ahead and jumped out of the trees and frightened them all to death! They loved it. Many years later when they were asked to recall some of their best childhood moments, Keldy was usually at the top of the list.

I was very touched yesterday when the daughter of my BF, who also lives in France made her choice of dinner guests. She chose her brother and my four kids! They spent so many holidays and happy times together in their childhood, that to see them all together again would be wonderful. I wonder if there is a chance we could make it happen?

I'm afraid that's my lot for today. Take care x.

The Diary of an Incarcerated Granny. Day 86

Well Boris played a blinder yesterday, if you have more than one child, you have to make a choice of which one you want to 'bubble up' with! Dilemma!

Bit of news on the Incarcerated Granny front. I can't name names, so you will have to bear with me on this.

About three weeks ago, No. 3 was contacted by a TV production company who had been told about the Incarcerated Granny diary on FB. I have had several telephone chats and a Zoom meeting with them so far.

They are looking for someone to comment in a humorous way, on a new show that will begin filming over the next couple of months. The observations of an Incarcerated Granny are much sought after... apparently! We will see what happens, it might be something or nothing! Whatever the outcome, it was nice to be noticed.

I am going out today, when I eventually manage to get dressed. I am heading for Sainsbury's in Bawtry for one of their olive loaves. I am fed up with Warburtons sliced bread, magnificent though it is on the toast front! I just want some freshly baked olive bread and a big hunk of Brie. Not much to ask for in the scheme of things, is it?

I have been waiting for a parcel to be delivered. Just been in the porch and Royal Mail have pushed one of their 'no one home' cards through the letterbox. Of course I was at home, I was up and about, why the hell don't they ring the doorbell? So cross, I'll have to go to the post office tomorrow and collect it. More bedding, by the way... I must conquer the bedding obsession, my affinity with the Oxford pillowcase is becoming a little bit tiresome.

On a side note, I need cash. I have just had to give the window cleaner a cheque for a tenner. That includes the next time as well, as I am a bit lacking in the window department... I have very few!

I have just got round to putting away my boots. I love boots, I wear them a lot. I have four pairs that are the same, but all different colours. Every outfit is catered for. I have a friend in California who wears boots nearly all the time, whatever the season, she wears hats a lot as well... I like that look!

Years ago I coveted a pair of 'Lady Northampton' boots. They were very expensive and I actually bought them at the Game Fair at Chatsworth. They were blue and I loved them so much. Within a month I lost one, I think one of the dogs must have knocked it out of the back of the car as it jumped out. I always hoped that a one-legged person had found the boot and gave it a good home. I kept the other one for ages, lord knows why. I still think about it sometimes.

Losing stuff... just a few examples:

Passport, Venice, you all know about that one! It was stolen, not lost if we're being pedantic!

My mother's Parker fountain pen. Fell out of my blazer pocket when I was hanging upside down from a tree in Clumber Park. Those were the days when you wore your school blazer on Sundays! She was furious!

One of the kids took a lump of the Berlin Wall to school (a real bit, loaned by Granny) and someone stole it out of her bag. Fortunately a teacher also had a piece and ended up having to give it to her!

For No. 2's eighteenth birthday we bought her a lovely silver necklace. She was still up at school and actually sat one of her A levels on her birthday. I think we sent the necklace by post, as it was the Leavers' Ball the following weekend. She lost it! Never set eyes on it again. We were furious!

When my father died, they found a little St Christopher medallion in one of his pockets. I kept it for years and years, I think it disappeared in a house move. I was so upset!

What have you lost, that made you cross? I'll let you ponder that one... Take care x.

The Diary of an Incarcerated Granny. Day 87

Raining, raining and more raining! My parcel can remain at the post office until I can be bothered to pick it up, I'm certainly not going out in this!

Avocado on toast this morning for breakfast, very yum.

I'm a bit confused about my 'bubble'. Obvious choices have already got their bubble filled, so should I choose a friend who I can bubble up with occasionally? It's all so complicated I think I'll just have a little nap.

Titchmarsh and Sons have just appeared! The lawn is far too wet and the grass is not that long, so they are 'attending' to the borders.

I've just had a long conversation with No. 1, she's still cracking the whip as far as home-schooling is concerned. Good for her I say!

No. 2 Jnr goes back to nursery on Monday, she can't wait... I hope she isn't disappointed!

I used to love going back to school on the first day of the new school year. That and the last day of term were my favourites!

All that shopping for a new pencil case, yet another new geometry set. New rubber, pencil sharpener, crayons and cartridges for your fountain pen. No biros in those days!

When we were in France for the summer, the girls would always enjoy buying all their stuff from the supermarket, to take back to school in September. Shampoo, conditioner, shower gel, etc, just seems far more trendy if the labels are in French. Half the price as well!

We used to come back loaded up with wine, for personal

consumption. Tins of *Confit de Canard* (the very best thing ever, if cooked properly!) Big tins of whole chestnuts, ready for the stuffing at Christmas. Pomegranate syrup, for mixing with lemonade to make 'Diablo Rouge'. Rillettes, poultry and canard. Jars of '*creme de lait*' a sort of banoffi pie sauce, straight from the jar. French tinned peas, I normally wouldn't thank you for a 'tinned pea' but French ones are a bit different somehow. Tins of celery, celery wrapped in bacon and baked in a cheese sauce can be pretty special. We used to serve it at the hotel. 'Roularde Pierre a la Grand', I think James made the name up, but it was very popular.

We were never very impressed with French meat! Poultry fine, but the beef especially wasn't that good. They butcher very differently to England, and it's quite hard to recognise some cuts of meat. I like my beef on the rare side of medium, the French often serve it still taking its last breath! *Bleu*!

There are very few houses in rural France that don't have their own vegetable plot. That seems to be the domain of 'The Granny'. As you drive through the countryside you can spot the grannies, always wearing black, a big pinny, rubber ankle boots, and bent double over their rows of vegetables. French farmers wives are into preserving everything they grow. I found it surprising that other than salad stuff, few vegetables were ever served fresh. You have a peep in a French pantry and you will be amazed at the rows of Kilner jars and bottles containing everything under the sun. We once invited one of the farmers in our village for supper. I served some kidney beans, cut on the angle. She asked me what they were, the amusing thing was, that she had given them to me a couple of days before. She had never cut into one, never eaten a fresh one, and yet had dozens of jars of the ones she had preserved whole! Our French neighbours usually brewed their own '*eau de* vie' or they knew someone who did! In a couple of villages you would see a 'still' parked up at the side of the road. Very few families still held a licence to brew their own spirits, shall we say you could always get some from somewhere! We used to call it 'Rocket Fuel' it certainly made your toes curl.

We used to get ours from our farming friends at the bottom of the village. Take your own bottle, and it would be syphoned out of a carboy hidden up in the loft!

A typical downstairs room in a French farmhouse goes something like this:

A huge fireplace and maybe a stove of some description.

An enormous table covered in oilcloth,

A selection of mismatched dining chairs.

The biggest TV in the world

The biggest free-standing fridge in the world.

Maybe a battered easy chair, but that isn't compulsory!

An old, smelly, retired hunting dog, (no cats, they are strictly outdoors).

A selection of plates and jugs picturing 'our' royal family, especially Diana.

A stool for bread cutting. A loaf the size of a dustbin lid, gripped between the knees whilst sitting on the stool, and carved into slices with something resembling a machete. They were very much bordering on self-sufficient. The mother of our farming friend had never been further than a town ten miles away, in the whole of her lifetime. They were treated dreadfully during the war, and I don't think the older generation ever fully moved on from that. Very sad!

Well, I have rambled on yet again about not much. It's funny how one thing leads quite seamlessly into another!

Until tomorrow x

The Diary of an Incarcerated Granny. Day 88

I was hoping for lovely sunshine this morning, and I'm still trying to be optimistic!

The more I watch the news, the angrier I become. All lives matter... I rest my case!

Just watched HM the Q's birthday celebrations from Windsor. She is beginning to look quite frail, which is understandable. I think I expect her to go on forever.

I'm still in a quandary over my 'bubble'. I have to admit that I am quite used to being on my own. I like being answerable only to myself... and with present-day technology, I don't really miss anyone. I can see this scenario, if it continues long-term, becoming a problem. Not just for me, but for a lot of people.

It will be interesting to see what happens on Monday. Especially in places like Meadowhall, I'm unsure how they can make that work. I was speaking to someone that had ventured to M&S yesterday. They said it was a 'bun fight' and they came home!

Sainsbury's Bawtry will continue to be my salvation, they know how to do it properly there!

The rise or fall of the property sector will be a difficult one to predict. A friend of mine who is a lettings manager, says the demand for rental properties is very high. Sadly there aren't enough places out there to let.

One of the downsides of lockdown is the breakdown of relationships. Consequently a big demand out there for rental accommodation.

June/July are the busiest two months for our family birthdays and anniversaries. I think in view of the present situation, 'remote-gifting' is the easiest way of sorting it out.

Apart from the two little ones (two and four) all the others are twenties, teens, or heading that way. They really just want money, to hoard, (in Max's case!) or to put towards something special. This is where PayPal is your best friend, sorted in seconds! Moonpig are another go to in times of stress. Although they have been a bit late in delivering the last few cards I sent. Maybe I should have made the arrangements a bit sooner?

If the weather in West Sussex is up to scratch this weekend, there was some talk of paddle boarding! That stretch of the coast is perfect for water sports and No. 2 and crew are big fans. No. 2 is the fit one! She runs, and if No. 2 Jnr is around, she is put in the 'running buggy' and pushed several km as far as Sea Lane Cafe, where she is bribed with an ice cream, and then pushed all the way back home at high speed!

Pressed the button by mistake and posted too early… Then I thought, I might just call it a day!

I'm not sure why I should feel overwhelming feelings of guilt if I don't write much? Why is that?

Still plodding on with *Wolf Hall…*,

I won't be taking it to the desert island, that's for sure!

I could just eat some raspberries, and I don't have any. I have no bananas either, but I do have a melon, an avocado and some apples.

I can always go back to Sainsbury's for more supplies, I had such a lovely time there the other day!

How things have changed, Sainsbury's shopping used to be a chore. Now it's an absolute delight, an adventure, a foray back into the real world.

Today's participation!

You can choose only two items of clothing, no more, what would you choose? I would choose my boots (not sure which colour) and a fleecy dressing gown with a hood!

Think about it! Take care x.

The Diary of an Incarcerated Granny. Day 89

Very dull again today, I am going out later. I have decided to bubble up with my friend who lives on her own. She has a problem with her leg, so can't drive at the moment, so it sort of makes sense we see a bit of one another.

I'm still hoping that there will a bit more relaxation of the restrictions over the next couple of weeks. I am desperate to get down south, I haven't seen them since Christmas and I miss them!

It's Sunday, day of rest, so I don't have to write a lot.

I am feeling a little bit embarrassed, sadly my hearing is not the best on the block. My neighbour popped round yesterday and asked if I would mind turning my TV down a bit, as they couldn't hear theirs! I was mortified, I do have the TV on in the background most of the time and pay little attention to it.

I think I should maybe go and have my hearing tested? I

have quite a few friends that now wear hearing aids, they sit and whisper to one another in corners, or that's how it seems to me! I wonder if my hearing is a little bit selective, in fact I know it is! I seem able to manage to assimilate the interesting bits and totally block out the boring stuff.

I have pressed the save button again by mistake! It's difficult trying to hold the phone up and type for a long time without it slipping, that's usually when I grab it and press it.

Just had a conversation with No. 3 who says I should type it in 'notes' and then cut and paste it later! Do I look the sort of person who has the time or the inclination to 'cut and paste'? I don't even like the sound of it! I've spent the last ten years avoiding it like the plague, I'm hardly going to start now.

I think technology-wise, I'm not doing too badly. I can buy things on the internet, I can do online banking, I can even find my way round a Zoom meeting! I can send money by PayPal, I can send emails, I think I'm doing ok.

This will be my longest car journey today since before lockdown! How exciting, I'm going to incorporate a trip to the Co-op, they do good bread as well. A visit to the bank to drop off a cheque from the Inland Revenue... (it's not often that you get a tax rebate!) and the posting of a birthday card to my granddaughter Sophie, who will be fourteen on Tuesday! What a busy day ahead.

Right that's it, for once I can say, places to go, people to see! How marvellous does that sound?

Have a particularly wonderful day x.

The Diary of an Incarcerated Granny. Day 90

Yesterday was a revelation! After ten minutes it was almost as if there had been no lockdown, and things felt almost back to normal.

If this weird time in our lives has taught us anything, it must be to not take things for granted! I had a lovely time, but it was strangely a relief to get back home. Home is where you feel safe, and nothing has illustrated this more than the happenings of the last three months.

I wonder what the news will be like this evening? I did hear that the queues outside Primark were enormous, and most of the shops were discounting goods up to seventy percent.

I will be staying at home today!

I don't watch a huge amount of TV, although I do tend to have it on in the background (far too loudly!) I think the older I become, my concentration span gets less and less, and I have a habit of flitting from one thing to another. Not good!

What was it they used to say? 'Jack of all trades, master of none'!

No. 2 Jnr went back to nursery today. In her group there was her and the rest were boys. They were busy putting things in a suitcase to take on a trip to Disneyland, her suggestion of including Barbie apparently fell on stony ground! As luck would have it, another little girl turned up and I think the dynamics may well have changed rapidly, girl power and all that!

Just spoken to No. 2, Mr No. 2 has gone over to the office for a rare meeting, and No. 2 Jnr is at nursery until five p.m.

This will be one of the first days of being 'home alone' for over four years. I wonder if she'll enjoy the peace or not.

I could do lots of things today, picking up the parcel from the post office would be one of them. I have plenty of stuff to eat, and I feel quite tired. Do you think chatting for three hours non-stop might have tired me out? Feasible I suppose after three months.

I thought superstitions would be a good topic for today.

I was at my 'bubble buddy's' yesterday, and a magpie hopped across the lawn. I found myself anxiously looking around for another one. One for sorrow two for joy. Luckily another one appeared within a couple of seconds. Had it not, I would have found myself 'spitting' and saying 'Good Morning, Frank'!

My mother-in-law, would have said, 'Hello, Mr Magpie, how is your wife today?' What is it with Magpies that put you in a spin?

Another thing I would never do is put new shoes on the table. Still in the box in your shopping bag, makes no difference, seriously bad luck! I remember yelling at No. 2 as she deposited a bag containing shoes in the kitchen, 'Don't put them on the table!'.

The reply was, 'It's an island not a table so it's ok!' Phew that was a close one!

Seven years bad luck if you break a mirror. It's unlucky to cross on the stairs.

I would walk a mile rather than walk under a ladder, it freaks me out.

I would never ever, open an umbrella in the house.

If I spill salt, I throw some over my left shoulder and say 'sorry'!

Old wives tales?

Good luck omens.

See a pin, pick it up, all the day you'll have good luck.

Find a four-leaf clover, good luck.

Horseshoe with the opening at the top, good luck.

Bad luck with the opening at the bottom.

The number thirteen. We moved into a cottage that was number thirteen. Luckily the place had a name as well and we never used the number. I do remember being slightly put off at the thought of it.

Black cats?

Some say they bring luck, others say they are bad luck. Apparently they are the least popular colour, and usually the last to get chosen from rescue centres.

Friday the thirteenth!

Another one that fills me with dread, I once flew to Venice on Friday thirteenth, it wasn't an easy decision to make. For some reason it was considerably cheaper than the twelfth or the fourteenth! I think that was the deciding factor.

How many of us, mid-conversation, will look round and 'touch wood'. I do it all the time.

I have been known to say 'white rabbit' on the first day of the month. These have to be the first words you have spoken on that day!

Bad luck happens in threes. How often have you been relieved when a third dodgy thing has happened in an awful day. You almost feel that everything will now be plain sailing.

Superstition is a strange thing, you don't really believe it, or do you? However, you still go along with all the little rituals, just to be on the safe side! Tell me which ones you pay homage to, or do you think it's all a load of bull?

I would say the female of the species are far more likely to involve themselves in superstition. I think the chaps pretend it's a load of codswallop, but they still salute a single magpie when they think nobody is looking!

Watches… Do you wear one? I have an inbuilt 'worry gene' that always needs to know the time. I always wear a watch, the faff of having to look on your phone is not for me. I have quite a lot of watches, some very good ones and some very ordinary ones.

When James was in a nursing home and then hospital for several years, he, like me always needed to know the time. I bought him a Timex watch, big numbered face, cheap as chips, with a leather strap. It had a tiny button that when pressed would illuminate the screen, so you could see the time in the dark. After he died I actually wore it myself for ages. I found it the other day when looking for something else (the story of my life!) The watch is still going, but one of the clips holding the strap is broken, I think I'll get it sorted. I probably have more affection for that watch, than all the others put together. It does exactly what it says on the tin!

Do you still have a toy from your childhood? I still have my teddy bear which I had for my fifth birthday. He only has one eye and resides in my spare room. They say the Prince of Wales still has his teddy, so I'm in good company.

Take Care x.

The Diary of an Incarcerated Granny. Day 91

Happy Birthday Sophie Lister, fourteen today!

I loved being fourteen, I was still obsessed with horses. Boys were still a bit of a mystery... you can thank an all-girls schools for that!

I saw a photo the other day of me and my friends all dressed up for a wedding. I had a pale grey suit, with a white lace collar, navy shoes and handbag, and a Marks and Sparks blue and white gingham bra! (You couldn't see the bra on the photo!) I remember feeling so grown up. We were all a little bit in love with the groom, and kept pushing our way back in the 'hearty congratulations' queue, so that we could kiss him again!

I saw him only the other day, he is fast approaching eighty and still a lovely guy... but I am no longer in love!

First love - It's true you never forget your first love. In most cases the fact that they were your first love indicates that you moved on and had future relationships. I have friends who have been with their other halves since they were fifteen, and that is well worth a mention!

I was eighteen he was twenty-three, I fell hook line and sinker, I discovered six months down the line that he was engaged to someone in Scotland.

He broke my heart, and it was a very long time before I dipped my toe back in the water!

I still wonder what might have been.

TV adverts.

Some of these really annoy me, it can be the way a word is pronounced, or a stupid look and I find they set my teeth on edge. There is an ad for guide dogs for the blind. Lovely guy and dog, the dog is called 'Quince' and I don't like the way he says the name! I just don't, and I feel really bad about it!

Another one is a toothpaste ad, she is sweating away in a work out class and says 'I know how to keep my body healthy, but how do I keep my mouth healthy? ' The tone of her voice makes me want to slap her! Sorry!

I know the old advertising mantra is, there is no such thing as a bad ad! You notice it even if it's for the wrong reasons, and that has to be true.

There was once an advert for Dulux paint, which had a catchy song and I loved that one. 'May the windowsills of Winchester shine', 'May the doors of Wales dry hard as nails', etc

Do you remember that?

Another one that made my toes curl, was Cillit Bang and Barry Scott!

Who on earth came up with the name Cillit Bang? What qualifications did Barry Scott have to wax lyrical over the cleaning prowess of some squirty stuff in a plastic bottle?

I never bought any, the name was enough to put me off!

Isn't it odd how some little things really get on your nerves. Manners, or the lack of them is a big thing with me.

It's quite an easy thing to get someone 'on board' by being polite and pleasant. It's also easy to alienate someone by being rude and arrogant. It should be obvious which course of action to take, but some people still don't get it!

I feel I'm a fairly good judge of character, and I can usually spot a liar. We are all economical with the truth sometimes, often to spare someone's feelings.

I think it will be interesting how the Duke of York handles

the intrusive questioning that is surely to come! I'm pretty sure he will not be sparing anyone's feelings, other than his own! Can anyone see him ever being back on the payroll as a 'working' member of the royal family? I don't think I can.

I haven't had any Chinese food since way before lockdown. For some reason I tend to go to restaurants rather than have a takeaway, my 'bubble chum' is coming to stay at the weekend. I think it will be a 'China Rose' takeaway to celebrate. I shall spend a lot of thinking time deciding what to order..

When we are down in Worthing we always go to Thai Street Food. During lockdown Yamin has provided free breakfasts for families short of money. She has managed to get people to offer a hour of their time to help with a delivery service to customers that are unable to get out. She has been generous with her time and her food, and has kept her little business up and running all the time. She has a huge following in the town. She works so hard with only a few helpers in her tiny kitchen and produces amazing food. Her number 1 fan is undoubtably No. 2 Jnr, who, as mentioned earlier, started going to Thai Street Food when she was still in Mummy's tummy! Yamin always makes a big fuss of her, and she just loves going there to eat. It's a real make-do kind of place, Formica tables, boxes of tissues instead of napkins... but the food speaks for itself.

It's a bit dull and clammy today. It's a 'not quite sure what to have for supper' kind of day. I am guilty of leaving the decision later and later, and then having a bowl of cereal instead! Then I think, I can have whatever I want, I have only myself to keep happy. I don't have to conform to 'meat and two veg' if I don't feel like it. One of the joys of living alone.

Take care x

The Diary of an Incarcerated Granny. Day 92

Out on a mission today, so I thought I had better do thirty minutes on here before I go.

Very dull again, I think I read somewhere that storms are forecast. When we lived at Maraval in France, storm watching was a popular pastime. We lived on a hill, with a river valley running down below. The storms were spectacular!

I still haven't picked up my parcel from the post office. Our post office is inside the SPAR and can get very busy, not sure I want to be queuing in such a confined space! I have lived in the Doncaster area for nearly thirteen years. I have been into town three times, twice searching for late night chemists, and once to register James's death. Other than being dropped off and picked up at the railway station, I'm afraid that's it, How exciting am I? Not very!

I have been to Meadowhell four times, three of them to the cinema. I fear I am a poor example of a 'granny on the go' with lots of time on her hands. I do lunch a lot though!

I was thinking last night that maybe the lockdown has affected me more than I care to admit. When you get up in the morning and the first thing you think is, 'Do I have to go and do anything today'? ...and the huge feeling of relief when you realise that you don't.... That's got to be an odd reaction, hasn't it? Maybe it's because I'm on my own, I found that talking face-to-face for three hours the other day totally wore me out. I came home and fell asleep!

I feel fine, I'm quite happy, but I think I'm slowly turning into a duck-billed platypus!

I have decided that my car doesn't make me smile. The last one did, and I should have kept it. Had discussions with my cousin and a friend only yesterday, both looking to change their cars, my advice... find one that makes you smile. If you think about it, other than buying a house, a car purchase is probably one of the most expensive things you will ever fork out for! You're selling yourself short if it doesn't make you pleased to see it!

My last car was a Renault Captur, ivory, with a black roof. Nothing special money wise, but boy was it good to look at! The latest is a new VW T-Cross, it's blue and that's about it.

No. 2 has just got her little BMW soft top, it's ten years old, so fairly long in the tooth... but I know she looks at it sitting on the drive, under No. 2 Jnr's bedroom window and smiles. She told me!

No. 3 has a Toyota C-HR, it has a very interesting shape, and you think 'wow, look at that'. If it doesn't make you smile then at least it should make you say 'wow'!

Today I'm taking my 'bubble chum' out to look at some things, and then, we may have fish and chips sitting in the car... that doesn't make me smile!

Just walked back in. All the places we went to were still closed, despite the fact they said they were open when I Googled them.

The fish and chips were good though and then we went and did a bit of food shopping, so not a wasted day. My petrol light lit up on the way home, so a detour had to be made to fill up when I got back to Tickhill. I then realised that No. 1's birthday card is still in my bag and I forgot to post it. Too many things happening at once today and very hot and sticky as well.

Something has gone wrong with my emails, and they aren't showing up on my iPhone. I sent an email last night and all was working then, as the person has just phoned me. I shall have to speak to No. 3 who knows how to put things right. I'm terrified that I will press something and everything will disappear never to be seen again!

Time now for the 'dogs dinner' it must be five pm as Violet is awake and looking peckish. Take care x

The Diary of an Incarcerated Granny. Day 93

It's raining and Vera Lynn has died... not the most cheerful start to a Thursday morning. I still have to venture to the post office, followed by a trip to replenish the stock of gravy bones. Violet-Elizabeth and Poppy have been rationed over the last few weeks, as I have been breaking them in half! Talk about desperate times, calling for desperate measures!

Avocado on toast again for breakfast, and very nice it was too.

I do wonder what qualifications are required to be allowed to decide if an avocado is 'Ripe and Ready to Eat'? Inspecting avocados as a full-time job, I have to say, has never ever crossed my mind. Sadly it has come to my notice that the 'people' in charge of such monumental decisions don't have a bloody clue! An avocado is a thing of beauty and should be treated as such. Unripe it's awful, overripe it's black, mushy and disgusting. It becomes apparent that timewise, there is only a tiny window of total perfection that must be recognised and acted upon!

You will have probably worked out that my latest batch of ripe and ready to eat avocados were neither ripe, nor ready to eat!

No. 2's wedding anniversary on Sunday. I can't believe that it's six years already, that seems to have gone really quickly!

They were married in Lewes at a lovely hotel called The Shelleys. A friend drove us down the day before and we all stayed overnight with the bride to be. The drive down was atrocious, and ended up taking just over eight hours. At one stage we were sent via Luton as there was a an accident on the motorway. James was wheelchair-bound at that stage, and the logistics of trying to get him up the stairs to our room was not one I would want to repeat! We decided to stay downstairs as long as possible after we had dinner, and just make the one journey upstairs at bedtime. The Shelleys was a very old building, no lift and certainly no bedrooms on the ground floor. We somehow managed to get him as far as the half landing and then his legs totally gave way and we couldn't move him any further. As a family we are blessed with several strapping, tall, strong, chaps, that are able to pick up a wheelchair, including the contents, and carry it up or down stairs as if it were as light as a feather! Unfortunately, none of them were arriving until the following morning. What a performance that was! Eventually we had to send for the hotel manager's boyfriend, who 'phoned a friend' who came to help and between us we managed to haul him up the stairs. Many tears of frustration were shed that night.

By the following lunchtime, all our troops had arrived, James was smartly attired in his morning suit, decanted into the wheelchair and carried downstairs by his son and son-in-law!

Easy peasy! The traumas of the previous evening were forgotten.

We had an amazing day, the weather was glorious, the bride was beautiful, the groom very handsome, and a marvellous time was had by all!

So on Sunday, Father's Day and the wedding anniversary both falling on the same day... is that what is known as a 'double whammy'? There is now an adorable four-year-old daughter to add to the mix. Either way, it will be expensive!

Lots of feedback on the car front. I have given this a lot of thought, and I am going to look into changing my car if at all possible. I really do need to have something that makes me smile! I shall have to take advice, as six months into a four-year lease is probably not the best of timing!

I quite fancy a Mini Cabriolet, it doesn't have to be a new one, I don't do long journeys nowadays and The Hobbit House has no off-road parking, so it would have to live on the road outside my front door.

At least I will now happily spend the next few days trawling the internet, and looking on Auto Trader and similar. When I have a bee in my bonnet I can be rather focused!

It must have rained a lot in Sheffield, just had a call from my letting agents to say that the drains are overflowing outside one of my properties. Brilliant, more expense. I think as I've said before, if you aren't playing the landlord already, don't bother, it's a pain in the neck!

Hope you are all full of the joys today. Take care x.

The Diary of an Incarcerated Granny. Day 94

I have been out and about with my bubble chum... and we got a lot of things done. Then guess what? We went on her suggestion to McDonalds... on the odd occasion in your life 'only a Big Mac will do'! This was one of those occasions! She hasn't been for twenty years, and is quite happy to wait another twenty before she goes again. Bearing in mind she will be about 153 by then, we are in no rush!

There was certainly a lot more action happening in the big wide world today. The roads were busy, the car parks were busy, it just seems as though the pubs and restaurants are the only things waiting to get going. I'm not sure how the two metre rule will really make this possible. Boris seems to be adamant that he isn't going to reduce the distance, I think it's a watch this space scenario!

I am looking at the possibility of changing the car. I have spoken to the finance company and the settlement figure is pretty high. My son-in-law with Moroccan sunset hair is crunching the figures for me.

I had an email from the VW garage in Wickersley yesterday. They reopened with a big fanfare a couple of weeks ago. Yesterday's message was to inform all their customers that they were closing down for good as of today! Such a shame, there has been a garage and showroom there for as long as I can remember, including Listerdale Motors which belonged to one of our clan.

Passing by earlier all the transporters were outside loading up the cars from the showroom, probably a sign of things to come.

My cleaner has just arrived, she's been stuck in traffic on the M1 for ages... so it seems the roads are going back to normal.

People are making big plans for next week, as the weather is supposed to be fantastic. Lots of BBQ's and coffee and cake meet ups and general lurking about! Fingers crossed

Michael Fish wasn't in charge of the forecast!

I have just 'done' Sainsbury's, quite painless and they did have most of what I wanted. We are celebrating our little bit of freedom with a China Rose takeaway tomorrow evening, and either Sunday lunch from The Ship or a Taj Cottage on Sunday evening.

I arrived home with an audible sigh of relief, and then realised that I haven't even started the diary... arghhhhhhhh!

Violet-Elizabeth is now tripping the light fantastic around the sitting room, dinner is thirty minutes late and *Downton Abbey* is on in fifteen minutes. I had better get my skates on, hadn't I! Quick heads up re the 'thirty seconds of fame'.

This coming Sunday morning, ITV, 8.30 am!

Hope you all had a good day x .

The Diary of an Incarcerated Granny. Day 95

Ah, the first morning with a house guest for ages! As an ex-hotelier-type person, I provide my guests with a hospitality tray!

There is method in the madness, it saves tottering up the staircase of doom carrying a cup of tea first thing in the morning.

Isn't it fab to chat? I went in and sat on the bed, Poppy came too, and suddenly an hour has passed. We then negotiated the stairs of doom and took up residence in the sitting room. Still in dressing gowns and with unbrushed hair... we decided we might have a coffee and take our tablets! What a pair of old dears we are.

Bit more discussion about nothing in particular and we suddenly realise it's eleven-fifteen am. The subject of breakfast rears its ugly head. Should we have it now, or we won't be hungry enough later when we have a takeaway?

Showers put on hold until after breakfast. We waffle our way through toast and thick cut marmalade (with a hint of ginger) a bowl each of cherries, blueberries, strawberries, grapes and bananas and a glass of orange juice. It's now heading for midday. The bubble chum has headed for the shower, and am scratching my head for some content for today's diary.

I can't say I'm looking forward to the little TV slot tomorrow. No. 2 said, 'You will hate how you look and you will hate how you sound!'...And she's probably right!

What was it Robert Burns said...
'*O wad some power the giftie gie us,*
To see ourselves as others see us.'
Scary stuff indeed.

Our local strawberry farm is opening today. Pick your own, and ready picked. Also bags of fresh peas in the pod! Have you ever got as far as cooking fresh peas, I haven't?

You can give Poppy a handful of pea pods and she will manage to open them all and extract every single pea, clever girl.

James always used to say that in every house, somewhere, is

a lost and forgotten pea, most probably all dried up, where it rolled under the fridge just after the war! If you have a look, I bet you'll find one!

I'm wondering whether to have crispy duck with pancakes and hoisin sauce. My favourite, it always was an 'in-between' course, but now I sometimes have it as my main course. Did you know that the cucumber and spring onion that accompanies this gastronomic delight, is actually cucumber and leek! I never knew that and I've been eating it for years. Apparently according to No. 3, there is a YouTube video instructing you on how to chop the cucumber and leeks for perfect results.

We have the TV on at the moment, *Racing from Ascot*, I think you need to be a hardened 'student of the turf' to get much enjoyment out of this type of programme. One guy doing the commentating, dressed up like Willy Wonka and the odd jockey wearing a mask?

I am trying to visualise the queen in her sitting room at Windsor, glued to the box! I think she's had a couple of winners already this week. I bet she's not still idling in her dressing gown and slippers, and still with her rollers in... Is she?

She will have been woken at eight am, with a cup of Earl Grey and a Tunnocks Caramel Wafer. Her bubbly bath will have been lovingly prepared and she will then have popped on her jodhpurs and headscarf and done a quick circuit of Windsor Great park on her Fell pony. Socially distancing from her 'bowler-hatted groom', before heading indoors and breakfasting with Philip. I imagine to get into the Ascot mood, she will don a bright ensemble, plus a matching or maybe contrasting hat?. She will ensure she has put her binoculars round her neck, and will have got someone to print off the race card for her. Pencil in hand, she is now ready for the off! There may well be a Zoom call involving the Tindalls and the princess royal, they of course will be dressed accordingly. Anne will be wearing a lime green suit, last aired in 1973, when she went to Kidderminster to open a bandstand. I love the way she recycled her outfits. Meanwhile Philip will still be in his pyjamas and Norfolk jacket, reading *The Telegraph* and trying to do the crossword. He really wants to be back at Wood Farm on the Sandringham Estate, minding his own business and nipping out for a carriage drive with Penny Romsey. Being royal is not all it's made out to be, you can't always do exactly as you please

I think the Queen is an example to every one of us. I actually can't imagine her not being at the helm and I do wonder what differences the next generation will introduce.

It's suddenly well into the afternoon, my bubble mate is sitting outside in the sunshine, and probably nodding off... as one does!

I hope you all have a good day, and a good Father's Day tomorrow if you are able to meet up with any. x

The Diary of an Incarcerated Granny. Day 96

Good morning, it was really rather rubbish wasn't it? Thanks for looking if you did, and wise move for the ones that had a lie-in!

Enough said!

Had a takeaway from the China Rose last night, it was ok!

This is turning into a pretty average sort of weekend.

It's Father's Day, so I hope some of you are managing to celebrate. When I think of James on Father's Day, I always imagine him sitting on his cloud and quaffing a large glass of Chateau Margaux and eating a very rare roast beef sandwich. Cheers sweetheart! X

Also a wedding anniversary today for No. 2 and Mr No. 2! Six years and counting.

I'm sitting here trying to motivate myself to do something. The washing needs hanging out, I need a shower, we still haven't decided on breakfast or what to eat later... and I am somewhat rooted to the spot. I didn't sleep well and I could quite easily go back to bed now and snore away the day!

Orange juice, toast and marmite, another box ticked. It's now twelve-twenty and we are getting nowhere fast.

My bubble chum is now perusing the menu for Taj Cottage, I always have the same from there, so I'm sorted. I think a baked potato, beans and grated cheese will be on the menu tomorrow.

Looking a bit dull out there again, do I hang out the washing or put it indoors on the rack?

Too many decisions for a Sunday.

I only realised yesterday that the church bells in Tickhill ring at set hours during the day, yesterday they were playing, 'There's no place like home'. How cool is that?

Another mind blowing fact involving Marmite!

Did you know that there is a small flat area on the side of the Marmite jar? When you are getting towards the end, you put the jar on its side and the remaining Marmite will collect there so you can easily scrape it out! Who knew?

I was still thinking about the changing the car, however, I

spoke to my son-in-law this morning who has been doing the sums and I think I need to accept the fact that unless I want to lose approx. £3,000 to get out of the lease early, I probably am better sticking with what I have! Sad but true. Maybe the love will grow over time... and one day it might make me smile?

£300 maybe, £3000, no way!

Maybe I should go back to researching yurts?

Now, my next question, has anybody ever rented a motor home? Do they come with an automatic gearbox, and are they suitable for a couple of old dears that want to become carefree, windswept, and interesting?

My bubble chum went to the same high school as me. We were talking about our school hymn this morning and she can't remember it! Granted she had left before I started, but I thought school songs were for life and not just for Christmas! I have looked for it on YouTube and found it but with a different tune? Is there anyone on here that went to Rotherham High School for Girls and can remember 'O brother man'? That includes you RC, in fact you should be able to play it for me!

It's Sunday, and I only do an hour on Sundays!

Thanks for watching the TV debut, I think it ranks about the same as the Prince Andrew debacle!

Happy Father's Day to all the daddies in my family, you are all very special! X.

James and I

Aimee and Chris (No. 2)

Pip and Niall (No. 1)

Rachel and Dave (No. 3)

Toby and Catherine (The Tall Man)

The Diary of an Incarcerated Granny. Day 97

It's Monday apparently, I must admit I am slowly starting to remember which day it is.

I have just taken my bubble chum home, called at the farm shop, and picked up the parcels from the post office.

I received some beautiful flowers this morning from Cactus TV, thanking me for taking part in the programme. A very nice gesture!

Not wishing to be a wasteful sort, I've finished off the crispy duck and pancakes from Saturday for my lunch, and very good it was too!

No. 2 and family eat a lot of Chinese/Thai-type food. She buys all her sauces and spices from the Chinese supermarkets. Lots of interesting things that really add distinctive flavours to the food, totally authentic and a fraction of the price! Give it a try!

We watched *An Audience with Billy Connolly* on the box last night. A very old programme, in fact most of the celebrity audience are with us no longer! It was very funny.

Billy Connolly makes me smile, he always has. He has a twinkle in his eye. I once saw him live in Sheffield and I was a bit put out by the use of the 'F' word in every sentence. He didn't need to do that to enhance his performance. I am no prude, and I can swear quite nicely when extremely cross, but I feel if you don't reserve it for especially annoying occasions you lose the impact.

Watching the news this morning, it was rather frightening to hear that Germany seems to be heading for a second wave of the virus. It's still out there and it's still an unknown quantity. I'm not sure we have taken enough notice of the countries that were ahead of us to begin with. Surely their experiences and codes of practice should be taken into account?

The few days of rain certainly got the lawn back into shape. Down by the riverbank the weeds are suddenly two-feet high and growing through the gravel. I shall have to have a designated 'weed pull day', before long.

Somewhere in my sitting room there is a very big spider. My bubble chum spotted it last night, she said it was the size of a donkey!

I don't do spiders unless they are really tiny, I am sitting here, and I think I can feel it looking at me. My mother used to have

324

a Siamese cat called Lishka, that was trained in the art of spider extermination. She was an absolute pro. If you yelled 'spider' she would come whizzing into the room ready for action.

Somebody once told me that spiders walk over you during the night when you are sleeping. I don't like the idea of that at all... it's little wonder I am a poor sleeper!

Cockroaches, we used to have them in the biology lab at school. Locusts as well. They turn my stomach, I could not be knowingly anywhere near one. Creepy crawlies are out as far as I'm concerned!

Now furry things, no worries, you can load me up with mice and rats and not a whimper.

My call up papers for . better not be in the post!

I have just woken up. An almost two hour granny-nap! I haven't had one since Thursday, all this entertaining and being the life and soul of the party must have worn me out. I shall enquire if my bubble chum will be returning overnight this weekend, if she is, I'll not change her bed and I won't wash the 'visitors' dressing gown.

The 'visitors' dressing gown is a thing of beauty, and much admired by all who are fortunate enough to be allowed to wear it.

My BF came over from France and fell in love with the original one. She kept spilling stuff down it, and waxing lyrical as to how marvellous it was, that it was eventually decided that she would keep it and buy me another one! It was from Dunelm and very pretty.

I think the weather is about to hot up. The changes in temperature are confusing to say the least... and I for one am easily confused these days.

Not much content today, I'm afraid, I think it will be much easier just doing a Sunday edition. That will keep us all in touch with each other, and that's really what it's all about at the end of the day.

Fingers crossed for a little bit more freedom, but keep an eye on those that came before us in all this! I still think there are lessons to be learned.

Keep safe. x

The Diary of an Incarcerated Granny. Day 98

Lovely day, unpacked all my new bedding which is exactly what I wanted. If you have never looked on the Brand Alley website, then do!

My all singing and dancing toaster has expired! It went out with a bang, all the electricity to the downstairs wall sockets went off and there was no toast! Of course I know where the fuse box is, and where to turn the water off, I'm a fully paid up member of the 'live on your own and sort stuff' brigade!

For some reason my track record with toasters is not good, this was the third in about four years. I don't feel that my consumption on the toast front is excessive.

The sad thing is, that the toaster matches the kettle and was specifically chosen to coordinate with the wallpaper in the kitchen.

The kitchen had just been redone when I moved in and the wallpaper grew on me!

I am a F&B emulsion sort of person, so this was very much

outside the box for me.

Anyway, do I buy another matching kettle and toaster, and take the present kettle down to use in the summer house? Or do I replace the original toaster? Or do I never eat toast again for the rest of my life? Too much to think about on a sunny Tuesday morning in June!

I need a new front gate, and a new side gate, I need all the paving changing and re-levelling outside the kitchen. Common sense dictates that I keep my virtually brand new VW T-Cross, and spend the money it would cost me to get out of the lease elsewhere!

Oooh, some friends popped in for a socially distanced coffee... so nice to see them!

Spoke to the 'tall man' last night. We both decided that most people have really taken the social distancing on board. Therefore if the rules are relaxed, common sense will still dictate that people will still be quite guarded and keep their distance. Of course there will always be the 'idiots' that break the rules, but there always are.

Just had a hummus and beetroot sandwich, one of my favourites. Give it a whirl!

Whoops dropped the phone and pressed 'post' by mistake! I keep doing that, don't I?

Spider talk was interesting, seems you either like spiders and are scared of mice or vice versa.

We had a friend in France who had a holiday cottage, he only came out for a few weeks every year, and never let it when he wasn't there.

Consequently, it was riddled with mice. They would run across the mantelpiece and up and down the kitchen cupboards, it always made for a very interesting evening! He had bought some humane mouse traps, this involved catching them unharmed and releasing them into the garden. They would then come straight back into the house as he always left the doors wide open...

He once came dashing into our cottage one summer evening. He had been sitting under his little overhanging porch contemplating his navel and watching the sunset. Suddenly, an adder dropped down off the porch roof and went straight into his house. He was terrified, he commandeered a very ancient villager, James and a couple of others to go and check the house. Such a funny sight, a posse of slightly inebriated chaps, wearing wellingtons and carrying stout sticks marched up the lane to rid the building of the squatter!

They searched the house from top to bottom, and there was no sign of the intruder. It was suggested that he left both front and back doors open, and slept in the car. Which he did for the next week, just to be on the safe side! Adders are very common in rural France and there are warning signs everywhere. There is an emergency number to ring if you get bitten, and a helicopter will come and get you. When we lived at Maraval we had adders in our wood pile! You just had to be a bit careful, they won't get you if you don't frighten them.

Apparently adders have live births. They don't do eggs and hatching and all that malarkey. They produce lots of teeny-weeny wriggly baby adders that whizz of into the undergrowth and make their own arrangements! Perfect parenting!

That's today's wildlife chapter over and done with. When we all become unincarcerated you will be able to command a fat fee, for your services as a lecturer, recounting all the interesting facts I have provided you with over the last hundred days!

It's a warm one, my tomatoes need some TLC, and I can't think of owt else to write!

Take care, keep your distance, and we may be ok. X

The Diary of an Incarcerated Granny. Day 99

Gosh, it's like crossing off the days on the calendar to the end of term! I break up tomorrow.

Picked up my 'bubble chum' this morning. Socially distanced coffee and home-made scones planned with friends.

Visit to the docs, then a bit of shopping, then 'car park' fish and chips. A real proper all-singing all-dancing day out!

I thought it would take me longer to adjust, but I don't really think it has. The writing is always going to be on the wall, but we need to be sensible and aware and be alert... I think as I've no doubt said before, 'your country needs lerts'!

I'm hoping to head south at the end of next week. There is a little lady down there that I haven't seen for six months, and I can't wait! Six months is quite a long time when you are only four. She is starting school in September and I don't know where the time has gone. I shall have to be popping to Aldi to buy up all the truffle infused salami! That's what any half decent granny would do... isn't it?

I have debated long and hard, with myself of course, and decided to buy a new four-slot toaster, dark blue to match the kettle. Hang the expense I say!

It's quite important that the slots on your toaster are deep enough and wide enough to accommodate crumpets, bagels, scotch pancakes and the odd croissant. Times have moved on since yesterday's stale slice of Mother's Pride made an appearance in the two-slot toaster. I can actually remember toasting bread with a toasting fork in front of the fire when I was a little girl.

Toast is a very evocative smell, as is frying bacon, and the inside of our tent at Pony Club camp!

Having spent a fortune on a not very memorable Chinese takeaway last weekend, bubble chum and I will be dining at home this Saturday evening.

Rumour has it, that she has a fine pair of Barnsley chops from Lawns Farm in her freezer and is prepared to bring them along!

In return I will prepare the hospitality tray with care, and include a couple of tasty Digestive biscuits for good measure. I won't have to change the bed, or launder the visitors dressing gown for another few days. Life is sweet!

Do you take a drink up to bed with you? I never do. Every night I always drink half a pint of cold water in the kitchen, before I attempt to conquer the summit of the staircase of doom!

I read somewhere that it stops you having a heart attack?

I remember when I was heavily pregnant with No. 2 and she was pressing on a nerve in my back, I was barely able to move and I was in agony. I had to take really strong pain killers throughout the night. Solpadeine, they were huge and beastly and tasted foul.

I woke up at four pm to take the pain relief and discovered that the father-to-be had woken up and drunk all the bloody water out of the glass on my bedside table. I think that was one of the first indicators that he was going to be trouble! I don't think I ever took a drink upstairs after that night! Once bitten and all that.

Now what you don't know, is that it's twelve-fifteen am in the morning and I'm trying to gain a bit of ground on post number 99.

I've lots to do tomorrow and this will help me out enormously if I'm half way there.

Just got home, at three-thirty. I'm actually quite tired. We passed on the fish and chips, far too hot, plus the fact we had pigged-out on scones, clotted cream and jam! We really weren't very hungry.

I was quite civilised this morning, tidied up everywhere, put the dishwasher on, put some washing in, took the rubbish out. I even sprayed the sofa with Febreze, I'm always worried that I might be 'nose blind' and the house might smell of dog and I may not have noticed. The smell of dog is not very marvellous, and the smell of wet gun-dog is even worse! When you have two hairy Gordon Setters and a Labrador sharing your living space you need to be fairly on the ball. Not only do they pong a bit generally but they do tend to fart rather a lot as well.

Saying that, now the dog tally is just two Shih-Tzu, I must commend Violet-Elizabeth for her ability to vacate a room within ten seconds of releasing one of her specialities. She may be small, but her wind is fierce! I'm sure the Bard will not mind that I have modified one of his quotes!

We are really hitting rock bottom, when you get to Day 99 and one of the main topics is farting dogs. Just tomorrow to go, then you'll all be footloose and fancy-free again. I will of course be checking up on you on a weekly basis. I feel a granny nap coming on, all this rushing around is quite exhausting.

I really wanted to be in Sussex tomorrow, as No. 2 Jnr has her 'uniform day' for her new school and I wanted to see her in her new stuff, normally I would have gone down at the weekend.

Had to laugh earlier on, my bubble chum and I were heading for the little Co-op that sells the fab bread. She looked at me and said, 'It doesn't feel like Wednesday, does it?'

I said 'I'm not sure really, does it feel more like Tuesday?' We ended up not having a clue what today 'felt like'! Is this a direct result of lockdown fever? I think it might be!

Tune in for the 100th day of the Diary tomorrow. Keep safe x.

FINALLY GOT IT FINISHED. Today at 14.45.

The Diary of The Slightly Less Incarcerated Granny. Day 100

We made it folks, I never thought for a moment that it would last for so long!

We aren't out of the woods yet, but neither are we stuck indoors sanitising everything a dozen times a day.

What can I say? It's been a pleasure to have had such a lovely group of people following the diary. How we managed to get up to 850 people in the group I will never know. You all shared and asked your friends to share, and suddenly there you all were! So thank you all so much. I think there is very little of my life that you aren't aware of. I tried, probably not very successfully, to not name names. Numbering the kids and grandchildren was a bit of a chore, but it did give them a slight degree of anonymity. The hotel was sussed out pretty quickly, but as there are quite a lot of Rotherhamites on here, I suppose that was inevitable.

It would be sad if so many fabulous people suddenly lost touch with one another. The general opinion was to just do a bit of a diary page once a week and see how we go from there.

I'm lurking today, washing cushion covers and sofa throws. According to my youngest daughter there is a storm heading our way, and a chance of flash flooding. In which case I need to go down to the summer house, move any books that are on the bottom shelves of the bookcases and stack all the furniture! I think I'll take my chance, and if I end up with an 'I told you so', then whoops!

They seem to have put some sort of electronic device down by the Mill Dam, so that if the water levels begins to rise, then the sluice gates open automatically.

Let's hope it works, there was so much flood damage last year. There are a couple of bungalows opposite the Mill that still seem to be unoccupied after all this time.

I am hoping that Titchmarsh and Sons will be here tomorrow, they only come every two weeks and last time it was so wet they didn't do the lawn. It's now about six-inches high, maybe I should get a goat? Or make hay?

I'm not a fan of goats, as pets, or in a sandwich! They have such expressionless eyes. You are never sure whether they are overjoyed or seriously pissed off. I find this to be quite disconcerting. I have quite a few friends who are, or have been, enthusiastic goat keepers. They are converts and I accept that. Did you know that per capita, world-wide, goats meat is the most widely eaten meat?

I think I might miss you! Most evenings have been spent seeing who has replied to the questions and replying to people's anecdotes. Quite a few of you have a bit of chat happening between yourselves, and all in all it's been something that has kept things going, certainly through the first six-to-eight weeks when the news was dire and you couldn't help but be depressed.

I suppose I really should thank No. 3 for setting up the group. I would certainly not have given it a thought, as far as I was concerned it was something to do every day, and post on my FB page to cheer up my pals. So thanks Rach, you did a grand job. I might buy you a Thai Street Food, next time we go to Worthing!

I'm off now, I've never been one for long goodbyes and this isn't a BAFTA speech, and neither will it ever be, not after last Sunday's experience!

Normal service will be resumed on a weekly basis on the fourth July... Independence Day.

Thank you all so much for your input, your kind words and most of all your humour.

Always remember 'if you can find some humour in a difficult situation... then you've won!'

Cheers all x!